Navies and the American Revolution
1775–1783

Navies and the American Revolution 1775–1783

Edited by Robert Gardiner

CHATHAM PUBLISHING

LONDON

In association with
The National Maritime Museum

First published in Great Britain in 1996 by
Chatham Publishing,
1 & 2 Faulkner's Alley,
Cowcross St,
London EC1M 6DD

Chatham Publishing is an imprint of
Gerald Duckworth & Co Ltd

British Library Cataloguing in Publication Data
A catalogue record for this book is available from
the British Library

ISBN 1 86176 017 5

Designed and typeset by Tony Hart, Isle of Wight
Printed and bound in Great Britain by
Butler & Tanner Ltd, Frome

Contributors

Nicholas Tracy
Introduction 1763-1775
Part I: The War at Sea and in the Dockyards 1775-1777
Part II: America and the West Indies 1778-1783
Part III: European Waters 1778-1783
Part IV: East Indies 1778-1783
Postscript

Robert Gardiner
Boston and Bunker Hill, June 1775
The Campaign against Canada, May 1775-May 1776
A marine artist's sketchbook
The Battle of Valcour Island, 11 October 1776
Lake warfare vessels
The first naval moves
Parker and Clinton at Charleston, June 1776
Assault on New York: first phase, June-August 1776
Colonial warfare vessels
Assault on New York: second phase,
    September-November 1776
Rhode Island: a textbook amphibious operation
The Continental Navy
Guerre de course
A forgotten incident in the trade war
Occupation of Philadelphia
The road to Saratoga
The French Navy
D'Estaing in America: the French view
Ships of the battlefleet
Penobscot fiasco, August 1779
Siege of Savannah, October 1779
Capture of Charleston, 1780
West Indies 1780
Struggle for the Chesapeake, 1781
Yorktown – the world turned upside down
Aftermath of battle
'The Other Armada'
The Spanish Navy
Gibraltar besieged
The war on trade
John Paul Jones's cruise
Single-ship actions
Spanish successes
The Dutch Navy
Dogger Bank, August 1781
Gibraltar: the second relief and after, 1781-1782
Lord Howe takes over the Channel Fleet, 1782
The carronade: a British secret weapon
The grand assault on Gibraltar, September 1782
Howe's relief of Gibraltar, October 1782

David Lyon
West Indies 1778 – St Lucia
West Indies 1779 – Grenada
Florida and Central America 1779-1780
West Indies 1781 – St Eustatius
St Kitts, 1782
Battle of the Saintes, April 1782
The Battle of Ushant 1778
The Moonlight Battle, 1780
Suffren and Hughes
Battles in the eastern seas

Roger Morriss
Colonial seafaring
The Royal Dockyards
George III and his navy
Gunpowder – the sinews of war
Supplying the British Army in America
Copper sheathing – the saviour of the Royal Navy
Naval administration

Julian Mannering
Notes on artists

CONTENTS

Thematic pages in italic

INTRODUCTION 1763-1775	9
Colonial seafaring	12
PART I: THE WAR AT SEA AND IN THE DOCKYARDS 1775-1777	15
The Royal Dockyards	21
Boston and Bunker Hill, June 1775	24
The Campaign against Canada, May 1775-May 1776	28
A marine artist's sketchbook	30
The battle of Valcour Island, 11 October 1776	32
Lake warfare vessels	34
The first naval moves, fall 1775–spring 1776	37
George III and his navy	39
Parker and Clinton at Charleston, June 1776	42
Gunpowder—the sinews of war	46
Assault on New York: first phase, June-August 1776	49
Colonial warfare vessels	54
Assault on New York: second phase, September-November 1776	57
Rhode Island: a textbook amphibious operation	62
The Continental Navy	64
Guerre de course	66
A forgotten incident in the trade war	70
The occupation of Philadelphia, summer 1777	72
The road to Saratoga, May–October 1777	75
PART II: AMERICA AND THE WEST INDIES 1778-1783	77
The French Navy	82
D'Estaing in America: the French view	84
West Indies 1778—St Lucia	88
Ships of the battlefleet	92
West Indies 1779—Grenada	95
Florida and Central America 1779-1781	98
Penobscot fiasco, August 1779	100
Supplying the British army in America	102
Siege of Savannah, October 1779	104
Capture of Charleston, 1780	107
West Indies, 1780	108
West Indies 1781—St Eustatius	111
Struggle for the Chesapeake, 1781	114
Yorktown—the world turned upside down	119
Copper sheathing—the saviour of the Royal Navy	122
St Kitts, 1782	124
Battle of the Saintes, April 1782	126
Aftermath of battle	129
PART III: EUROPEAN WATERS 1778-1783	133
The battle of Ushant 1778	137
Naval administration	140
'The Other Armada'	142
The Spanish Navy	144
Gibraltar besieged, summer 1779	146
The war on trade	149
John Paul Jones's cruise, 1779	152
The Moonlight Battle, 1780	155
Single-ship actions	157
Spanish successes	160
The Dutch Navy	162
Dogger Bank, August 1781	164
Gibraltar: the second relief and after, 1781-1782	167
Lord Howe takes over the Channel Fleet, 1782	170
The carronade: a British secret weapon	172
The grand assault on Gibraltar, September 1782	174
Howe's relief of Gibraltar, October 1782	178
PART IV: EAST INDIES 1778-1783	180
Suffren and Hughes	181
Battles in the Eastern Seas	183
POSTSCRIPT	186
SOURCES	187
NOTES ON ARTISTS	188
INDEX	191

PREFACE

WE LIVE in an age of mass, and instantaneous, communication. In recent wars, even scenes from the battle-fronts have been beamed via satellite and television direct to the sitting rooms of the world. Politicians and military men understand its potency and often seek to restrict media access in the name of maintaining public morale in the face of all-too-immediate images of death and carnage. This contrasts with the wars of earlier centuries, where the written word was the chief medium of information, and often written after the event by those who were not present—covering the story, in P J O'Rourke's phrase, 'from Mahogany Ridge'. In these circumstances, war was easily glorified, and far from seeking to censor the writers, the military usually encouraged surprisingly detailed accounts of their exploits.

But even in the eighteenth century, the written medium was not the only source of information. A sophisticated print-selling industry evolved, producing relatively cheap, and sometimes tasteless images of a nature that even modern tabloids would eschew, purporting to depict recent events of public interest. However, among them were also to be found fine engravings based on the works of well known artists, including remarkably detailed maps and charts of land and sea engagements, which often stand up in point of accuracy to modern research.

The industry in Britain was given a considerable boost by the outbreak of hostilities in the North American Colonies. This was unfamiliar, even exotic, territory to most Britons, and as the civil unrest escalated into open warfare a demand quickly grew up for illustrations of the topography in general and the exact locations of the fighting in particular. Furthermore, the time-lag between event and publication was astonishingly short—often a couple of months to transport original information across the Atlantic by sailing ship, compose a picture, engrave or etch a plate, publish and put it on sale. In Britain, publication was controlled by Act of Parliament, so the release date is usually printed in the bottom margin, as a proof of the timescale involved.

In this fashion the public was provided with an image of the great happenings of the time, and the 'Chatham Pictorial Histories' are intended to recreate this impression in the naval sphere, which for an island nation like Britain was a paramount concern right down to recent decades. Of course, besides the public prints, there were also more formal representations like the oil paintings commissioned by those involved, but by their very nature they are celebratory and, although often the result of the most meticulous research by the artist, they lack immediacy. They are also now quite well known, and another of our concerns has been to seek out the less familiar, and in some cases the never previously published, so while we do use some finished paintings, we have preferred the artist's own sketchbooks where available; they reveal not only the lengths the painters went to get details correct, but often cover occurrences that are not otherwise represented, or where the art world has lost track of the finished work.

In the search for original and, if possible, eyewitness depictions, we have also dipped into some of the logs, journals and contemporary manuscripts. Naval officers, in particular, were encouraged to observe closely, and part of the training process involved making sketches of everything from coastal features to life on board. To a lesser extent, this was true of army officers, who were often fine mapmakers—especially those in the technical branches like the engineers and the artillery (today most people in Britain are unaware of why the best official mapping of the country is called the Ordnance Survey).

However, the series was inspired by the Prints and Drawings Collection of the National Maritime Museum at Greenwich, on the outskirts of London. Reckoned to comprise 66,000 images, it is a surprisingly under-used resource, despite the fact that an ongoing copying programme has made three-quarters of it available on microfilm. While this forms the core of the series, we have also had recourse to the Admiralty Collection of ship draughts—itself running to about 100,000 plans—as well as some reference to the charts collection in the Navigation Department and logs and personal journals kept by the Manuscripts Department.

It is amazing how many incidents, even the minor and obscure, can be illustrated from this collection, and the coverage is by no means confined to British publications. However, there is an in-built bias in the collection, for reasons pithily summed up by the art historian E H H Archibald:

One of the problems in this subject area was that people only commissioned pictures of their victories and the public only bought prints of them if their country had won. As the French nearly always lost there were no commissions. By the same token, the painting of naval battles in England and the subsequent sale of prints flourished exceedingly.

He goes on, however, to point out that the French performance in the American War of Independence was better than usual, so there were some official works commissioned by the Ministry of the Marine after the war. For different reasons—there was simply no developed trade in prints in the thirteen colonies—the American side of the story is not well represented graphically at Greenwich. For this volume, therefore, we have gone to archives in the United States which have strong collections from this period, emphasising the original and first-hand wherever possible, as for the rest of the book. Much of the warfare from the naval point of view was what the British called 'littoral' (what would today be termed 'amphibious'), so there are many pictures of American towns and geographical features, and a fair sprinkling of maps and battle plans—but since the theme of the book is the naval contribution, some of the famous land campaigns are not represented.

The series is intended first and foremost to illustrate the great events of maritime history, and we have made little attempt to pass artistic judgement on any of the images, which were chosen for content rather than style. The pictures are grouped, as far as practical, to show how events were presented at the time. Since this is not primarily a work of art history, for the technical credits we have relied on the Maritime Museum's extant indexing, the product of a massive and long-running documentation programme by many hands with some inevitable inconsistencies, depending on the state of knowledge at the time each item was catalogued. We have reproduced what information there is, only correcting obviously wrong attributions and dates, and quoting the negative number or unique reference number of each illustration for anyone wishing to obtain copies of these from the museum or archive concerned.

Acknowledgements

Researching and assembling the illustrations for this volume has been an arduous but enjoyable task, and the acknowledgement of help and support is a pleasant and fitting conclusion. The project would have been impossible without the co-operation of those at the National Maritime Museum's publications division, initially David Spence and latterly Pieter van der Merwe, who negotiated and set up a workable arrangement. I received generous and friendly advice from Clive Powell on logs and journals and from Brian Thynne on charts, while the staff of the library were endlessly patient with demands for myriads of photocopies and frequent requests to put right snarl-ups in the microfilm readers. Karen Peart organised the crucially important visit to the out-station where the original prints and drawings are stored, and Nick Booth was a tower of strength in hauling out and reshelving more than sixty boxes that I needed to investigate.

However, none of this would have resulted in a book —certainly not in 1996 at any rate—without the efforts of Chris Gray, Head of Picture Research, to whom fell the task of organising and executing our huge and complicated orders for photography in the unreasonable timescale demanded by the publication schedule. He, and David Taylor of the same division, coped with crises great and small and by extraordinary effort drove a large bureaucratic machine at a speed it was never designed to reach. We owe no greater debt to anyone involved in the project.

Beyond Greenwich, we received the fast and efficient collaboration of a number of American libraries and museums, notably the Library of Congress, the New York Public Library and the Peabody Essex Museum of Salem, Massachusetts. At Annapolis, Sigrid Trumpy, Curator of the Beverley R Robinson Collection, cheerfully gave up time to explain the workings of this fine depository of prints, while Mary Beth Straight Kiss of the Naval Institute picture library supplied both photographs and background information. However, my greatest personal debt is to Major Grant Walker and his wife Annick for their hospitality and good company during my visit to Annapolis.

Robert Gardiner
London, September 1996

INTRODUCTION 1763-1775

THE CAUSE of the American Revolution was essentially the economic growth of the Thirteen Colonies to the point where the most powerful commercial leaders in the Colonies felt that their interests were not served by the management of imperial trade in London. With the conquest of Canada from the French, British army units stationed in the Colonies came to be seen less as a needed defence than as a curb on American expansion into the territories reserved by treaty for the native peoples. Those who had most to gain by overthrow of imperial government were able to make use of the irritants of eighteenth-century aristocratic life which independent farmers and townspeople in the Colonies came to find intolerable. A campaign of disobedience brought civil government to a standstill. The irritants were increased intolerably when, as a result of the riots known as the Boston Tea Party in December 1773, the port of Boston was closed to trade and a British army under General Thomas Gage quartered there. Although Gage believed that only an army of 25,000 could reduce New England to obedience, on 19 April 1775 he struck the first blow of the war when he sent a force to seize a cache of arms at Concord, and two rebel leaders at Lexington.

It is questionable whether London should ever have attempted to manage American political problems by force. American geography gave the revolutionaries important advantages. There was over a thousand miles of American coastline, with hundreds of harbours through which the revolutionary forces could be supplied with arms from European friends. There were no great cities the capture of which would have a decisive effect on the American economy in general, and the vast hinterland made it possible for the revolutionary army to avoid decisive contact with the professional armies Britain employed. The unprecedented scale of the military effort which Britain would have to sustain across the width of the Atlantic Ocean was to be a major factor in the eventual survival of the Republic. The shortage of marine transport was never entirely overcome. When the news reached Europe in July 1775 that General Gage had attempted a frontal assault on the rebel forces posted on Bunker Hill overlooking Boston, Louis XVI's Foreign Minister, the Duc de Vergennes, wrote: 'It will be vain for the English to multiply their forces there…no longer can they bring that vast continent back to dependence by force of arms.'[1]

However, the British did not agree that the tactical problem was insurmountable. The military potential of the colonists had been demonstrated as recently as the campaign to take control of New France and Acadia in the Seven Years War, and British officers were not inclined to overrate it. In London, the key to the outcome of the Revolution was believed to lie in Europe. In November 1775 the Earl of Rochford, retiring Secretary of State for the Southern Department, urged his successor Viscount Weymouth to seek a treaty of guarantee amongst the European colonial powers which would 'make the Americans despair of that foreign aid which their Congress has hung out to them'. He was confident 'it would Conquer America sooner than 20,000 soldiers'.[2] Obtaining such a guarantee from France would have been the ultimate achievement of the system of naval deterrence which had underpinned British foreign policy since the Seven Years War.

It had been recognised soon after the Peace of Paris in 1763 that France was bound to seek revenge for her defeat at the hands of Britain. 'It is not easy to imagine,' noted the instructions given to the Duke of Richmond when he was dispatched as ambassador to France in 1765,

that, after so great Disgraces both by Sea and Land, and after the Cession of so vast a Territory to Our Crown in Consequence of their late unsuccessful War, the Court of France, as well as That of Spain, should not have Thoughts of putting Themselves in a Condition to recover in Time their lost Possessions, and retrieve the Reputation of their Arms.[3]

To confront this anticipated danger, British foreign policy was based on a structure of deterrence, employing the potential which existed in the battlefleet. In September 1764 it was estimated that it would cost £2,003,785 to put in condition a fleet of the best 121 ships which had survived the war. In 1768 a commissioner of the Treasury, Charles Jenkinson, when preparing notes for the defence of the navy's 'extra' estimate, wrote: 'The two great ends of security and oeconomy may seem at first view to combat each other but it is our duty to reconcile them. Security must have the first place.' Nevertheless, unless the debt which had been incurred by the Navy Board during the war were pared down it would be evident to all that Britain could not afford to risk another war. It is ironic that one of the means experimented with to pay for defending the empire was the Stamp Tax, which proved to be a catalyst for colonial revolt.

British intelligence was aware of French plans to concentrate on naval reconstruction, and London had to reckon with the probability that Spain would support France: 'We shall,' Jenkinson noted, 'begin the next war with two Enemies at a time'. Spain had no interest in supporting colonial revolt, but Spain had been drawn into the Seven Years War out of concern for the disproportionate naval and maritime power Britain was acquiring, and her losses

---

1. To the Duc de Guines, 20 and 27 August 1775, H Doniol, *Histoire de la participation de la France à l'établissement des Etats-Unis* (1886-92), pp171-2.

2. To (Weymouth), 28 November 1775, Thynne MS 'Official Correspondence'.

3. State Papers 94/268 f37v.

during the war had only heightened that concern. British intelligence agents, especially the consuls at Rotterdam and Turin, kept London informed of the progress of French and Spanish naval reconstruction so that foreign policy could be determined by strategic assessments, and crisis management by immediate tactical assessments of the ability of the Bourbon courts to send fleets to sea.[4]

In the belief that only clear indications of British determination would keep the Bourbon monarchs honest, squadrons had been dispatched to demonstrate, and if necessary to take direct action, when in 1764 the British Government of George Grenville responded to French and Spanish encroachments in the West Indies, at Turks Island and Honduras, in Newfoundland waters at St Pierre, and in the River Gambia. Less successful efforts were made by Grenville's successors to resolve,

without the use of force, problems with Spain over the Manila Ransom, and with France over the demilitarisation of the port of Dunkirk, and in 1768 over the French annexation of Corsica. Lord North came to head the British Government in January 1770. Recognising the dangerous consequences of the lost prestige, he reacted strongly when France appeared to be working to establish a defence relationship with the Ottoman Porte which could establish French control of the eastern Mediterranean, and when Spain seized a British post in the Falkland Islands. Timing his reaction for the autumn when British trade was returning home with full crews who could be pressed into the navy, North ordered an emergency mobilisation.

In three separate steps, fifty-five ships of the line were brought forward for service. These included the squadron of 'guardships', nomi-

nally twenty in number, which were kept partly manned and with some of their stores on board, so that they could be mobilised quickly in emergency. Actually, some of that number were always on service, or laid up, but this permitted quiet modifications of the state of readiness without having to announce an increase in the number of guardships. By 4 January 1771 the guardships could be fully manned should their recruiting parties be called in. The remainder were still 7000 men short of complement, but the muster-books show that at the beginning of 1771 the first forty ships ordered were 61.5 per cent manned, so that it would have been possible to fully man twenty-four ships.[5] This number is consistent with the experience of the Seven Years War, during the first year of which it had only been possible to raise 25,824 men, enough to man thirty-nine ships of the line. After seven years of war the navy had been able to muster 84,770.[6] The evident capacity of the Royal Navy to go to war in 1771 ensured that it would not have to.

Deterrence is never comfortable. In 1772 Edmund Burke described the situation as 'an armed peace. We have peace and no peace, war and no war. We are in a state to which the ingenuity of our ministry has yet found no apt name.'[7] In 1773 it was again necessary to order a naval mobilisation to forestall a French naval deployment to the Baltic to control Swedish politics. The outcome for Britain was not entirely satisfactory because the hope of forming an alliance with Russia had to be sacrificed, but the inevitable was accepted. In any case, London did not feel any great concern for British security because of the evident capacity of the navy.

The Boston Tea Party focused attention on the revolt in America, but the style of British foreign policy was not immediately affected. In early 1774 the North Administration was warned of a possible Swedish-Bourbon manoeuvre to oblige Turkey to accept French mediation. Although King George III thought 'The Conduct of our Colonies make Peace very desirable,' it is probable that the British response would have been up to form had the Bourbons made the expected move.[8] A measure of the confidence felt by the North administration can be gained by the decision which was made to reduce the strength of the fleet by 4000 men in December 1774, although 2000 of

The Royal Navy was ill-equipped to function as a revenue enforcement service, which in American waters was a role increasingly thrust upon it in the years leading up to the outbreak of fighting. To attempt to deal with the widespread evasion of unpopular trade legislation and duties, the navy purchased a number of American-built schooners from 1764, like the Chaleur *shown here. Their zealous application of customs regulations made these vessels the focus of colonial wrath, and one, the* Gaspee, *was boarded and burnt by an irate mob at Rhode Island in 1772—one violent step on the road from civil disobedience to outright war.*
NMM neg 4518

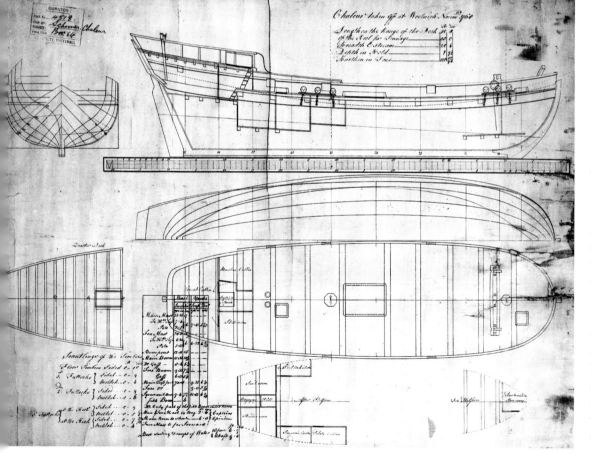

these were restored to the naval strength in February 1775 probably because of the need for crews in American waters.[9] London's continued self-confidence was further demonstrated when there was a brief war scare in April 1775.

The receipt of news in London of Bunker Hill, however, produced a profound change in the security policy of the British Government, in part because of the technical demands of the military campaign on the far side of the Atlantic, but primarily because the confidence of the North Administration was undermined. Attention was focused on events in America, distracting attention from the all-important task of isolating the colonial revolt from European intervention. Work in the dockyards of Britain, France and Spain, and the diplomatic manoeuvring of the governments of those countries, was as important to the naval history of 1775 and 1776 as the action on the coast of America. In the long run it was the weakness of British action in home waters that was critical. The hope in London, that the line could be held in Europe by sustaining the image of deterrence without its underlying muscle, while putting down the rebels, was too transparent in Paris. When Spain entered the war in 1779 Britain found herself in a more difficult a situation than she had had to face in her previous conflicts.

What proved to be an insurmountable problem for British diplomacy was that her victory in the Seven Years War had been so decisive that it eliminated the incentive for her old allies to confront Bourbon aggression. It was recognised as a central requirement of British strategic planning that an alliance with a continental military power or powers was needed in order to give Britain greater influence in European affairs, and in particular to ensure that the French could not concentrate their efforts upon building naval forces. The Duke of Newcastle had warned in 1749 that 'France will outdo us at sea, when they have nothing to fear by land.'[10] This thought was very much in the mind of the First Lord of the Admiralty, the Earl of Sandwich, when after the Spanish declaration of war in 1779 he lamented to King George III that this was the first time that Britain had been forced to engage 'in a war with the House of Bourbon thoroughly united, their naval forces unbroken, and having no other war or object to draw off their attention

One of the earliest examples of American printmaking is this representation of British troops being landed in Boston in September 1768, engraved and published by Paul Revere. The political tenor of its publication is apparent in the tone of the caption, which notes how the ships 'Anchored round the Town, their Cannon loaded, a spring on their Cables, as for a regular Siege' before the troops were landed and 'Marched with insolent Parade, Drums beating, Fifes playing, and Colours flying' into the town.
Stokes Collection. Prints Collection, Miriam and Ira D Wallach Division of Art, Prints and Photography, New York Public Library.

and resources'.[11] The Swedish crisis had put an end to the hope of a Russian alliance; Frederick II of Prussia still had not forgiven Britain for what he considered to have been Britain's betrayal in 1762 when the Anglo-Bourbon peace was negotiated before Prussian ambitions were satisfied; and an Austrian princess was Queen of France.

Superior strategic direction by the Admiralty, and by the Secretary of State for the Colonies, Lord Germain, might have managed the complexities of American tactical operations and European deterrence, but there was no one in the administration in London who proved to have outstanding ability. Sandwich had been an unusually effective peacetime administrator, but he had no genius for strategy, and unfortunately he attracted bitter political opposition. He was held to have betrayed his old friends when he reached high office, and they were out to discredit him at all costs. Their sympathy with the American cause had some reality to it, but more policy. Their parliamentary attacks spread to the fleet, and were

to prove highly destructive to discipline and morale. The Royal Navy that fought the Americans, French, Spaniards, and ultimately the Dutch, was a fleet divided against itself.

4. British Library Add MS 38366 ff359-366.

5. State Papers 42/47 (Admiralty to Rochford, 25 December, and Rochford to Admiralty, 21 and 26 December, and to Secretary at War, 26 December), War Office Papers 1/680; and State Papers 42/48 ('State of the Guardships etc 31 December' in Stephens to Sutton, 4 January 1771).

6. Public Record Office 30/8/79 f279.

7. 2 December 1772, The Speeches of the Rt Hon Edmund Burke (London, 1816), I p138.

8. To North, 3 April 1774, The Hon Sir J W Fortescue, ed, The Correspondence of King George the Third, 6 vols (London 1927), nos 1436-8.

9. Luke Hansard, Parliamentary History (London 1763-78), Vol 18 Col 305; J Almon, printer, The Parliamentary Register (London 1775), Vol 1 pp13, 51 (Lord John Cavendish and Lord Sandwich); and Admiralty Papers 7/567 f95.

10. To Hardwick, 10 September 1749, British Library Add MS 35, 410, ff153-4.

11. Fortescue, No 2776.

This shews the Schooner Baltick coming out of St Eustatia ye 16 of Nov 1765

1

2

Colonial seafaring

IN 1776 the North American colonies that proclaimed their independence were all maritime provinces. They consisted of Massachusetts (including present-day Maine), New Hampshire, Rhode Island, Connecticut, New York, New Jersey, Pennsylvania with Delaware, Maryland, Virginia, North and South Carolina, and Georgia. Excluding the 200,000 slaves—more than half concentrated in the coastal region of Virginia—these thirteen colonies contained more than one and a half million Americans. In places settlement

had long spread more than 200 miles from the coast. Nevertheless, the great bulk of the colonists remained close to the coast, many in seaport towns, working in trades that fed a growing merchant shipping industry.

In New England, Massachusetts and Rhode Island surplus capital and labour were almost all channelled into fishing, shipbuilding, shipping and seaborne trade. Boston, was the commercial metropolis of colonial America; it imported molasses from the West Indies to be distilled into rum, much of which was re-shipped by sea. New Hampshire' chief wealth lay in its forests, sources of masts and ship-timber. In Pennsylvania an iron industry existed, with a shipbuilding industry centred on Philadelphia. North Carolina produced tar, pitch, resin and turpentine, valuable to the Royal Navy and shipbuilding across the Atlantic. Other crops like rice from South Carolina and tobacco from Maryland and Virginia were also shipped in great quantities across the Atlantic.

However, the mercantilist system imposed on her colonies by the government in London placed restrictions on the trade in which American colonists could indulge. The Trade and Navigation Acts from 1660 barred foreign ships from American ports, intending to give British and colonial shipping a monopoly of trade to and from British colonies. To exact import and export duties, Britain was also made an *entrepôt* for colonial trade: certain colonial goods including molasses, rum and naval stores had to be sent first to Britain before they could be exported to foreign markets. Similarly, colonial imports had come from Britain.

Some of these restrictions benefited the colonies. American shipbuilding flourished, especially in the north which possessed virtually inexhaustible supplies of timber and almost all other materials. The skills necessary to build ocean-going ships were developed early: a 300-ton ship was launched at Salem in 1641. Between 1674 and 1714 New England (mainly Boston) built 2300 vessels, of which 240 were sold abroad. In this period New England built twice as many vessels as all the other colonies put together. Shipbuilding had its slumps as well as its booms. During the 1730s Boston was building more than 40 ships a year; in 1741 it built as many as 164 ships; but in 1749, with the end of war with Spain, only 15. Even so, by 1770 New England was building about 15,000 tons of shipping a year; the middle colonies nearly 3000; and the southern colonies nearly 2500 tons a year.

Under the impetus of this industry, colonial merchant fleets grew. In 1708 Rhode Island citizens owned only 29 vessels; by 1739 they possessed over 100; and by 1750 more than 300 vessels over 50 tons. But a large proportion of the ships built were sold to British purchasers.

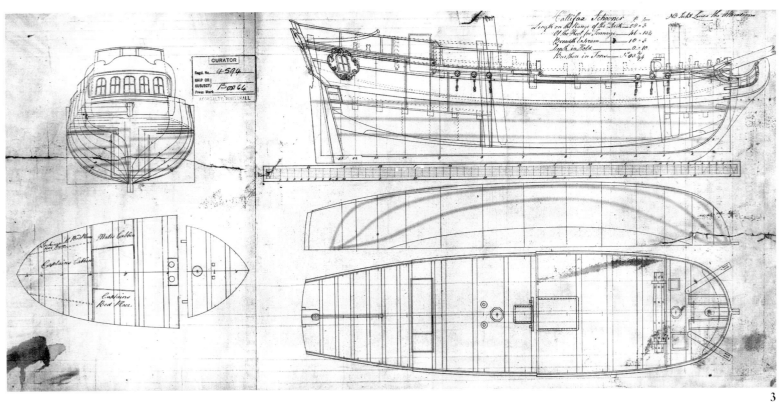

By 1775 of 7694 ships engaged in the Atlantic trade 2342 were American- or West Indian-built. Indeed, it has been estimated that invisible earnings from shipbuilding were second only to the American income from tobacco: in 1768 ships from the southern colonies brought in £94,000; from the middle colonies, £165,000; and from New England, over £296,000.

Fishing also absorbed many vessels. By 1770 New England as a whole had almost 1000 vessels engaged in the cod and mackerel fisheries. At the same time Nantucket claimed a whaling fleet of 125 vessels. Needless to say, most of these ships were American-owned and -manned. In 1775 one in six Bostonian males were part-owners in merchant ships. Almost as many were actively engaged. Tax rolls for Philadelphia in 1774 reveal that 9 per cent of the population were mariners, with another 5 per cent involved in building and fitting ships. Similar proportions were true for Boston, New York, Charleston, Norfolk and Baltimore. The nascent United States of America had probably close to 40,000 seamen available for seafaring on the verge of the American Revolution.

However, although British trade restrictions encouraged some parts of the colonial economy, they did not suit others. New Englanders obtained a large part of their molasses from the French West Indies where it was cheaper than in the British islands and where they could pay for it with timber and consumable provisions (1). Had they been forced to pay the heavy duties imposed on the import of foreign sugar into British colonies, they would have been promptly ruined, for their purchases of British and European goods depended on the sugar they refined from the cheap molasses.

Naturally, the Royal Navy and customs service policed the trading regulations. To avoid these revenue and naval brigs and cutters, the Americans gradually developed their skills at building their own fast sailing sloops and schooners and the British revenue vessels attracted great American hostility. The *Gaspee*, attacked

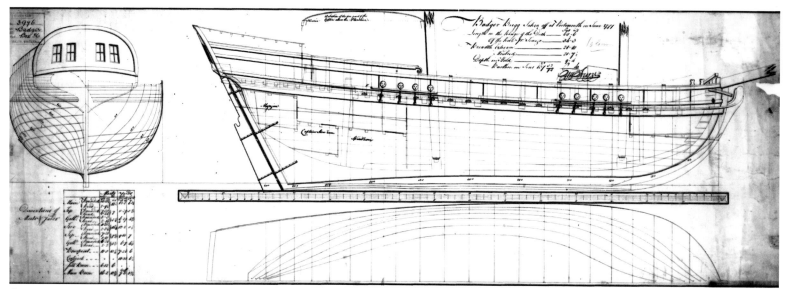

5

and burned when aground off Providence, Rhode Island, in June 1772 was one of theses hated British revenue schooners (2, 3). When war came, the American response was to turn many of their own fast trading vessels to war purposes; after all, following an order-in-council of April 1776 authorising the destruction or seizure of all American ships and property on the high seas, American peacetime trades were devastated by British warships and privateers. The Americans retaliated by themselves equipping their vessels as privateers (4-6), turning to war account the resources which had brought them to resent British rule.

---

1. 'This shews the Schooner Baltick Coming out of St Eustatia, ye 16th Novr 1765', anonymous watercolour. This 45-ton vessel, built at Newbury, Massachusetts in 1763, may be the earliest named and identified American merchant ship.
Peabody Essex Museum, Salem, MA neg 11749

2. 'Marble Head Scooner Built at New York in July 1767', draught taken off after purchase by the Royal Navy as the *Sir Edward Hawke* for revenue

protection duties. This was typical of the small fast vessels built in New England, which the Navy found necessary to counter like with like. Admiralty Collection.
NMM neg 4520

3. One of the more detailed draughts of American schooners purchased by the Navy is the *Halifax*, an 83-ton vessel some 58ft long. Admiralty Collection.
NMM neg 4594

4. An American brig from a portfolio of ship drawings by Edward Gwyn of about 1775. Although America is often thought of as the home of the schooner, most of the more common seagoing rigs were also to be found in large numbers under American ownership.
NMM ref PAG3867

5. Conditions of the war placed a premium on fast sailing, and some sharp hull forms were developed. The ex-American *Badger* captured in 1777 shows a steep drag aft (drawing far more water aft than forward) and a curved or rockered keel rabbet. Admiralty Collection.
NMM neg 3976

6. By the end of the war purpose-built privateers were at sea, and these were naturally designed for fast sailing. An example of an extreme hull form is the *Rattlesnake*, captured by the British in 1781 and renamed *Cormorant*. Admiralty Collection.
NMM neg 6185

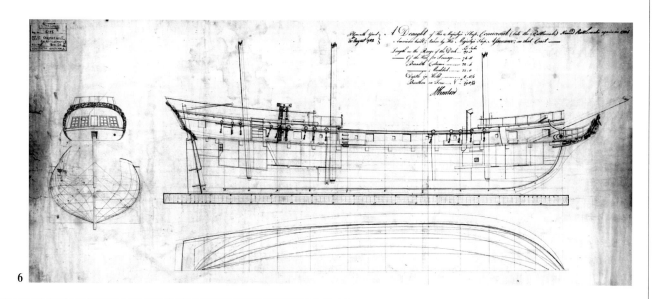

6

Part I

THE WAR AT SEA AND IN THE DOCKYARDS, 1775—1777

THE TASK of the Royal Navy's North American Squadron, in holding the line for constitutional government following the clash between the American rebels and British soldiers at Lexington, was an operational as well as a political impossibility. At the beginning of 1775 this small force, under the command of Vice-Admiral Samuel Graves flying his flag in HMS *Preston*, comprised thirty frigates, sloops, schooners and brigs. During the year it was to be reinforced by three 64-gun guardships, *Somerset*, *Asia* and *Boyne,* which had been authorised by Cabinet on 3 October 1774, and by twenty-four other smaller ships sent out as they were available. The guardships were required in home waters to deter French intervention in support of the rebels, however, and in August 1775 they were recalled, being replaced by 44- and 50-gun ships. The fifty-one ships and 7555 men on the station at the year's end were inadequate to provide seaward protection for towns held for the Crown and to watch the coastline from Newfoundland to Florida. In order to man this number the Privy Council had agreed on 16 June to authorise impressment for North American service. On 27 September it also agreed to increase the navy estimates to 26,000 men from 18,000, at a cost of £1,352,000; and on 27 October it agreed to further increase the fleet to 28,000 men which it was subsequently estimated would cost £1,456,000.[12]

The attempt to intimidate the rebels by sending an army to Boston had backfired. The army at Boston was too small to be able to control the heights around the town, let alone to threaten offensive action. Graves had to station ten of his squadron at Boston because of the size of the harbour, and because of the ease with which rebel privateers could intercept store ships making for Boston past the smaller harbours of Massachusetts Bay. The only efficient means of intercepting the rebel commerce raiders before they could capture the supply ships was to attack their bases. On 17 October the town of Falmouth was destroyed by bombardment from the sea, but this was regarded as a barbarous act, and in fact Graves did not have enough resources to systematically reduce all the rebel ports.

No less important than the defence of Boston was the defence of Nova Scotia where, at Halifax, was the only dockyard in British North America. The invasion of Canada in 1775, by small forces under Richard Montgomery and Benedict Arnold which were defeated on the glacis of the fortress of Quebec, suggested the vulnerability of Halifax. Graves deployed five of his ships to its defence, and to the defence of the smaller Nova Scotia towns which the rebels might have used as advance bases.

Graves's command was so large that the few ships in his squadron were too dispersed for him to retain effective control over them. Often their captains had to act on their own initiative. In January 1776 firing broke out between the British ships in the Delaware and rebels in the town of Norfolk, Virginia, which ended with the village being destroyed by gunfire. In May 1776 loyalists had to be evacuated from Tucker's Mill Point. At Savannah, attempts to purchase supplies for the Boston garrison having failed, eighteen merchant ships loaded with rice were seized.

These defensive requirements impeded the navy in its vital role of isolating the theatre of war. The Delaware was used by the rebels to receive the arms shipments from France and from the French and Danish islands in the West Indies, but there were too few naval resources available for its many mouths to be effectively blocked. The efforts to deny munitions to the rebels had to be extended to the West Indies, where there were separate commands in the Leeward Islands and at Jamaica. The legal and diplomatic difficulties of stopping American ships 'naturalised' by false French papers and flying the French flag were immense. Efforts were also made to arrest American munition ships outbound from the Netherlands, in the English Channel. On 22 December 1775, to reinforce the legal position of the naval and revenue officers, Parliament passed the Capture Act proclaiming the Thirteen Colonies to be in a state of rebellion, and prohibiting trade with them. Letters of Marque were issued to merchant ships so that they could be armed, and naval escort was ordered for Ordnance department store ships, and for the Newfoundland fishermen.

The consistency, or otherwise, of London's response to challenges by France was the best evidence in Paris of the confidence of British leaders that they could protect British interests. Challenges by France there were in plenty. Apart from opening French ports to American gun-runners and privateers, work began to be undertaken in the reconstruction of Dunkirk as a port from which British commerce could be raided, and the French East India Company began to fortify Chandernagor, both in defiance of the Peace of Paris. Most important were the movement of battalions of French infantry which were to garrison French islands in the West Indies, and the fitting of a French naval squadron for training manoeuvres.

In the mood produced by Bunker Hill, Rochford's response was to advise the British Ambassador at Versailles, Lord Stormont, to make no formal complaint about French supplies being sent to the rebels. He even sought French mediation between Spain and Portugal to settle their quarrel over Paraguay. London did not trust the intentions of the Portuguese minister, the Marquis de Pombal, but Portugal was Britain's oldest ally and before Bunker Hill it was inconceivable that Rochford would have made any sort of common cause with France against her. In February 1776, following the receipt of the news that American forces were besieging Montreal and Quebec, Stormont

---

12. PC 2/119 pp9, 124, 166 and 193; Almon III p83 and Hansard Vol 18 Col 841.

unwittingly summed up London's new capacity for wishful thinking:

> France does, and must see our difficulties with that Secret pleasure, with which it is natural to behold a Rival's distress, [but]…I do not think it likely that the present French ministry will take a bold and open part against us.[13]

In May 1776 the French Royal Council decided that France should assist the Americans with funds for the purchase of munitions, and that the fleet should be put in a state of repair. The

French Minister of Finance, M Turgot, resigned in protest.

In December 1775 Graves had been replaced in command of the North American station by Rear-Admiral Molyneux Shuldham, who immediately pressed on the Admiralty the need for reinforcements for his overworked and undermanned squadron. So inadequate were the naval resources that when in the winter of 1776 an American squadron was assembled it was easily able to get out of Delaware Bay. Commodore Esek Hopkins, with eight ships, drove off the sloop stationed at Providence in the Bahamas, seized the munitions in the

town, and on his way back captured two small British warships, the schooner *Hawke* and brig *Bolton*. A third, the 20-gun HMS *Glasgow*, was only just able to fight herself clear.

News of the incursion into Canada had reached London in December 1775. The decision was made to send immediate reinforcements in the form of a regiment of infantry, which was shipped out in three small warships, two transports and three victuallers. This force arrived at Quebec on 6 May 1776 and relieved the besieged garrison. It was followed by two much more substantial troop convoys which eventually brought the army at Quebec up to 11,000 men.

The relief of Canada was to be the preliminary to an incursion into New England from the north. This plan effectively divided Britain's military effort because it was decided that the largest part of the forces in America should be concentrated at New York, as a part of a general plan to defeat the rebellion by taking decisive action during the 1776 campaigning season. Boston had at best been a useless post for the British army because it was too easily kept on the defensive. The movement to New York was precipitated when, on the night of 4–5 March 1776, the rebels seized and fortified Dorchester Heights above Boston. From there American gunners could fire into the town and also command the approaches to the harbour. General Howe, who had been left in command when Gage was recalled after Bunker Hill, decided to move his force. By threatening to burn the town, he obtained a truce to make possible an easy withdrawal.

A small British squadron had wintered at New York and had sustained fairly amicable relations with the citizens, but when the rebel army entered the town in the spring of 1776, the squadron commander, Captain Hyde Parker, withdrew rather than use his guns against soldiers sheltering in the town. He thought the collateral damage which inevitably would have been inflicted on the citizens was unacceptable. Howe packed the army into as many ships as could be manned, but these were inadequate to enable him to retake New York directly; the ships were so crowded that it was impossible to load them tactically for a contested landing. The army had to be trans-

'A New and correct Map of the United States layd down from the Latest Observations and Best authorities . . .' by Abel Buell, published New Haven, 1784. This, the first map of the newly independent United States as in 1783, shows both the length of the coastline and the depth of the hinterland, geographical factors that worked so strongly in favour of the revolution and against the limited forces available to the British.
Stokes Collection. Prints Collection, Miriam and Ira D Wallach Division of Art, Prints and Photography, New York Public Library.

ported to Halifax, where it had to wait until 7 June when enough shipping had been assembled for it to be re-embarked. It then began its move to New York, seizing Staten Island. Meanwhile, it had been decided in London to send two troop convoys to New York, to bring Howe's army up to a strength of 25,000 men.

It had also been decided in October 1775 that five regiments (later increased to six) should be sent to the Carolinas to support a rising of the loyalists. Administrative limitations delayed the departure, and it was May 1776 before they arrived off Cape Fear. By then the loyalists had staged their rising, and been defeated on 27 February 1776 at the battle of Moore's Bridge.

General Clinton and Admiral Peter Parker, the expedition commanders, decided against all strategic sense to seize Charleston. But the army and navy did not co-operate effectively, and the attempt of the squadron to silence the guns of a battery on Sullivan's Island guarding the harbour failed dismally. The walls of the fort were made of palmetto logs backed by 16 feet of earth, and the naval guns made little impression. *Actaeon*, a 28-gun frigate, went aground under fire and had to be burnt by her crew. There was then no option but to re-embark the army and join Howe's forces at New York.

The whole strategic plan had been too ambitious for Britain's naval resources. By the summer of 1776 the Navy Board had chartered 416 transports, and the Treasury, which was responsible for supplying the army in the field, had chartered another 76 transports. The administrative and technical difficulties were so great that the operation suffered protracted delays. It was not until late in the summer of 1776 that Howe's army was up to strength and he was able to commence operations to capture New York, and defeat the Continental Army under General Washington which was occupying Brooklyn Heights on Long Island.

Even that late in the season, decisive action at New York might have been able to defeat the Revolution. The American Congress had only agreed to the Declaration of Independence a few months before, and the defeat of Washington's army could have had profound psychological consequences. However, General Howe was at best ambivalent about the use of force against the rebels. The naval command was soon to be put in the hands of his brother,

Admiral Lord Howe, who was one of Britain's foremost sailors. As Admiral Howe had close connections in Massachusetts he was more interested in his role as peace commissioner than he was in carrying out his orders to conduct a reign of terror at sea against the rebels.

General Clinton urged on General Howe the advantage of making an amphibious movement up the Hudson River to occupy the Bronx. Operations could then be carried out at leisure to force the surrender of Washington's forces which were highly vulnerable to operations in their rear. Howe, however, preferred a more methodical movement, first to Long Island, and then to Manhattan and the Bronx. He may have been influenced by concern that any reverse suffered by the British could serve to turn Washington's rabble into an army, and certainly he had to allow for the impossibility of replacing any casualties.

Technically, the amphibious operation was executed with great skill. A feint was made up the Hudson while the landing force went ashore at Gravesend. The rebels were driven into the untenable works at Brooklyn. General Howe, however, held his men back from assaulting the position until a regular siege could be mounted, and Washington was able to withdraw across the East River in heavy weather. Admiral Howe, probably because of his concern for the American batteries on Brooklyn Heights, had failed to position his ships to destroy the army on the water.

Howe then crossed to Manhattan himself, making his landing at Kipps Bay, and drove Washington out of New York, thereby giving him a chance to fight another day. Again an amphibious movement carried the British army to the Bronx, landing at Throgs Neck and, when it proved to be impossible to get off the peninsula, crossing to Pells Point and moving inland towards White Plains. Washington had time to withdraw his men, except for those he unwisely left in Fort Washington who were ultimately captured by the British. At White Plains the Continental Army stopped the British with an indecisive defensive action, and then withdrew into secure positions to the north.

The American batteries on the Hudson had been run on 9 October by three frigates which entered the Tappen Zee and blocked American

communications. At the same time as Howe moved into the Bronx, British forces also occupied the Jersey shore. Clinton wanted to take a detachment into the Delaware to cut Washington's line of retreat inland, but Howe preferred to send him, with 7000 men, to occupy Newport, Rhode Island. This strategically irrelevant movement is hard to explain; by wasting scarce British resources the defeat of the rebels during the 1776 campaign was made impossible.

Had Washington not been able to refuse action and withdraw into the hinterland, that might well have been the outcome. As it was, the commitment of the bulk of Admiral Howe's squadron to operations at New York and in Canada, at the expense of the efforts to stop the flow of munitions into rebel harbours, was to make the task for British forces in 1777 all the more difficult. At the end of 1776 the Royal Navy force in North American waters numbered seventy-four ships, only twenty of which were not committed to support of the army. In a country with little in the way of roads, the navy had to provide most of the transport. The problem of manning all the light craft needed to move and supply the army along the river systems reduced many of the warships to the point where they were unfit for active service. The main reason why the 50-gun ships were especially valued was because of their larger complements of men than the frigates.

The relative failure of the New York campaign made the weakness of British action in European waters critical. At the beginning of January 1776 Weymouth had alerted the consul at Turin to watch for naval mobilisation at Toulon, and at the end of February solid intelligence was available of the preparation of a *flotte d'evolution* to be commanded by no less a personality than the Duc de Chartres, a cousin of the King. By then Stormont had his own intelligence of the armament which he thought would number sixteen ships taken from the Atlantic as well as the Mediterranean dockyards. It was discovered that the Brest division under Admiral du Chaffault was to meet the Toulon division at Cadiz where the Spanish Admiral, Don Gaston Miguel, was preparing his forces. The Duc de Chartres sailed on 3 May 1776, and it was discovered that the remaining ships of the line at Toulon were being put in a condition to enable them to be fitted out on short notice.

The Portuguese minister Pombal urged upon London the wisdom of launching preventive war against the Bourbon powers before they gained enough strength to openly court war. That course of action was very far from London's intentions, but a report that the Spanish Government was itself urging France to precipitate hostilities had to be taken seriously. Madrid was concerned that Britain would seek to compensate her losses in North America by making conquests in the Indies, and France was concerned to ensure that Britain would not be able as she had in 1755 to sweep French shipping from the sea prior to a formal declaration of war. The reason for the resignation of M Turgot was unknown in London, but intelligence of preparations at French dockyards continued to flow in.

On 20 June Sandwich had a 'Precis of Advices and Intelligence' drawn up, at the end of which it was noted 'that France and Spain have, or will soon have a larger number of Ships in Commission in Europe than we have, and that they may have double the number unless we immediately take proper measures to keep pace with them in our Equipments'. He warned Cabinet that, although there were nineteen guardships which might be ready 'with the aid of a press' for sea in a fortnight, and one other ordered fitted as a guardship, 'all our Frigates (that do not want considerable repair) including Ships of 50 guns, and two of 64, are in America, or appropriated for the American Service.' There were about 15,000 seamen in the American service and 8000 at home with 7000 on other stations.[14] It was another month, however, before Sandwich could persuade the Cabinet to authorise fitting nine additional ships of the line as guardships with the three which were already being brought forward to replace those sent to America.

In August 1776 Vergennes finally obtained authorisation from the King's council to make deliberate preparations for preventative war. The pace of work at French dockyards gave some indication. All the same, it was not until 25 October that *Thetis* was ordered to cruise in company with a sloop and a cutter off Brest, ready to send a warning if the French sailed. Three days later the Cabinet agreed to a general impressment of seamen, which was carried out that night. The next day the Admiralty instructed the Navy Board to prepare twenty-seven guardships for four months' service with full complements. The men in the dockyards were ordered to be employed as many shifts extra as was necessary, and the ships building at merchant yards were to be finished without waiting for seasoning.

In the King's speech at the opening of Parliament on 31 October 1776, the opportunity was taken to restate the importance of deterrence.

> An early and timely preparation on our part would have the effect of *substantial economy* it would probably be the last expense; for, by incurring it in time, it might, perhaps, prevent a much greater.[15]

The Commons was asked to increase naval

'The Seat of War in New England by an American Volunteer, with the Marches of the Several Corps Sent by the Colonies, Towards Boston, with the Attack on Bunkers-Hill', published by R Sayer and J Bennett, London, 2 September 1775. Massachusetts was a centre of resistance to ministerial authority and it was perhaps inevitable that fighting should first break out in and around Boston. Thanks to detailed and accurate maps like this, often published with amazing speed in London, the British public could follow the course of the conflict surprisingly closely.
NMM neg 272.

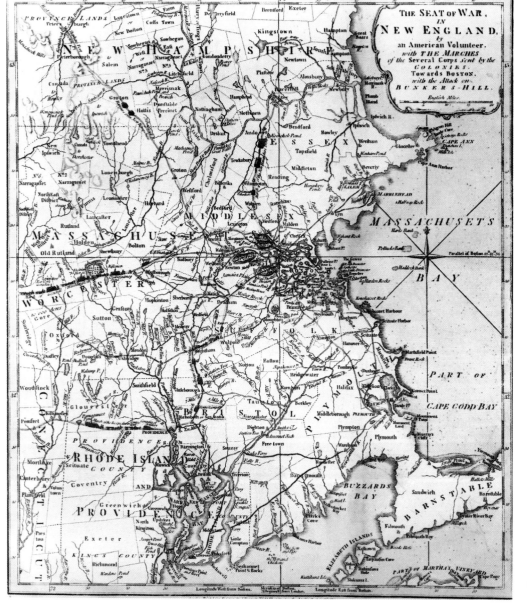

manning to 45,000 men, and London began to take a firmer line in its representations. French preparations to send a squadron with embarked soldiers to the West Indies was the most alarming consideration in London, and after two weeks of the most strenuous representations Stormont was at last able to report that Vergennes had agreed to review with Louis XVI the orders to du Chaffault. It soon became evident that General Howe's occupation of New York, news of which had reached France, had impressed the French court with the need for caution. On Christmas Day Stormont was finally able to report that M de Maurepas, Louis XVI's chief minister, had stated definitely that du Chaffault's squadron would not be sailing.

The muster books show that on 24 February 1777 twenty-nine ships were fitting in British ports and ready for taking on men, including five of 90 guns, with a nominal complement for the whole of 17,910. These were short by 2588 seamen and 1997 marines, but with 249 supernumaries slightly reducing the deficiency this amounted to a general increase in readiness in the capital ships in port to 75 per cent manned. A total of 22,542 men were available in British ports or depots, and the overall worldwide total was somewhere between 46,231 and 46,503 men.[16]

Part of this fleet was actively employed at sea in home waters in an attempt to intercept American munition ships, as well as to deter France from more direct intervention on behalf of the rebels. From late December 1776 the Admiralty began to supplement the regular frigate patrols with Third Rate ships of the line cruising in the Channel approaches, off Capes Finisterre and Ortegal, down into Biscay, and convoying the Iberian trade. The list book for June, by which time the guardships were all fitting for active service, showed six Second Rate and thirty-one Third Rate ships in British waters, of which no fewer than thirteen were at sea on patrol. Even in the middle of the following winter the capital ship patrols continued with ten Third Rates at sea in January 1778.[17]

The effect was escalatory. In March 1777 du Chaffault sent out his first ship of the line patrol, which encountered one British ship of the line. Later that month the *Robuste* encountered the *Exeter* on patrol and Captain La Motte-Picquet used strong language which Vergennes later was obliged to excuse. La Motte-Picquet was reprimanded for exceeding his instructions, and for the time Vergennes felt constrained to tolerate the British inspection of French merchantmen once clear of the French coast. In April the 80-gun *Foudroyant* was sighted on patrol, and du Chaffault responded by ordering his ships to patrol in groups. He was given instructions to maintain two 74s and a 64 on station.

An idea which Maurepas had first suggested in December 1776, that there should be a mutual reduction of armaments, served to reinforce Lord North's reluctance to authorise bringing more ships forward for service, but there was no slackening of French preparations. Twenty thousand stands of arms, and a large quantity of cannon, powder and ball, had been put onboard du Chaffault's squadron. It was expected that they were intended for the West Indies. The agent reported that there was no talk of more troops, but battalions expected in Brest to repair the fortifications could easily be intended for overseas service. North was eventually persuaded to authorise fitting out five more ships to replace those being sent out to join Howe, and this led to a renewal of the French overture, but not to any slackening of their preparations for war. Stormont warned Maurepas in early April that 'if a French Fleet does appear in those Seas an English Fleet must and will follow instantly,' and that he 'thought it better, if he had such an Intention, to give up all Idea of this Desarmament We had been Planning'.[18] The French tried to lay the blame on Spain for the break-down of negotiations, but London speculated 'that the French Ministers may think such a measure may cast too much despondency on the American Rebels.'[19]

14. 'From Lord Sandwich 1776', 'Remarks on the State of His Maj.s Fleet 20 June 1776', 'Precis of Advices and Intelligence 20 June 1776', and Cabinet minutes 20 June 1776, in Thynne MS 'Admiralty Affairs'; and Cabinet minutes 20 June 1776, G R Barns and J H Owen (eds), *The Private Papers of John, Earl of Sandwich*, Navy Record Society (London 1932), I p212; and Fortescue Nos 1894-6.

15. Hansard Vol 18 Col 1384; and Almon VIII pp1-31.

16. Admiralty Papers 8/53.

17. Admiralty Papers 8/53-4 and 2/102 (Admiralty Orders).

18. 10 April, State Papers 78/302 f49.

19. Hardy to Weymouth, 11 April and Weymouth to Stormont, 9 May 1777, State Papers 94/203 No 12 and f191.

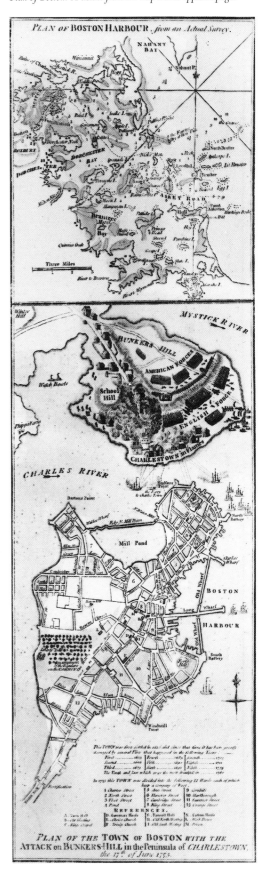

Plan of Boston. A detail from the map on the opposite page.

In April 1777 King Joseph of Portugal died, and Pombal was disgraced. That, and a Spanish victory over Portugese forces in South America, put an end to any immediate interest in Madrid for arming for a war with Britain. The French Government decided to use transports to carry their soldiers to the West Indies, because it was clear that a naval movement would oblige London to respond.

The strain on the Royal Navy's resources had become immense. The logistic requirements of Howe's army had been made much more demanding by Washington's winter campaign which forced the abandonment of New Jersey. The army had to be supported on rations transported across the Atlantic. The increased activity of American privateers, often sheltering in French ports between cruises, made necessary the development by the end of 1777 of provisions to convoy virtually all British trade. In order to extend the blockade as widely as possible, especially off the New England states, Howe had to deploy his frigates singly, risking their destruction. On 7 June the 28-gun frigate HMS *Fox* was captured on the Grand Banks by the *Boston* and *Hancock* under Captain John Manley, but in turn he was taken prisoner and the *Hancock* captured by a light British squadron comprised of HM Ships *Flora*, and *Rainbow*, with HM Brig *Victor*, which also managed to recapture *Fox*. Thirteen frigates of the Continental Navy were either captured, destroyed or bottled up in port, and scores of American merchantmen were seized, but that was not enough to stop the flow of ordnance and powder to the Continental Army.

Land operations in 1777 were disastrous for the British and their loyalist allies, largely because they were pursued in defiance of strategic logic. The movement of the northern army under General Burgoyne from Canada to the upper Hudson was not co-ordinated with Howe's own plan for an amphibious movement to the Chesapeake to capture Philadelphia. That seaborne operation consumed so much of Admiral Howe's naval resources that the blockade of the coast, and efforts to intercept munitions ships, had to be severely curtailed. Admiral Howe requested that he be sent ten ships of the line with reinforced crews to support army movements ashore, but the need to provide against French belligerency made it impossible to send him

more than five. By the beginning of 1778 Lord Howe's squadron of eighty-eight ships was committed almost entirely to supporting the army strung out in isolated posts along the coast.

It took a month to carry the army to Elk River on the Chesapeake, and another two months for the squadron to clear the barriers which the rebels had built to block the Delaware River. Before the job could be completed, Fort Mifflin and Fort Mercer had to be taken by combined operations. The Hessian soldiers mounting the assault were beaten off with heavy loss; *Merlin* and *Augusta* went aground, and the latter caught fire. *Merlin* had to be destroyed before the flames exploded *Augusta*'s magazine. On the second attempt, on 10 November, overwhelming British gunfire silenced Fort Mifflin, and the garrison escaped across the river. The Americans then abandoned their defence of the Delaware, but three months of the 1777 campaigning season had been wasted by the nearly immobile army. On 31 October, the army on the Delaware learnt the news that Burgoyne's army had surrendered at Saratoga after running battles with New England militia.

In September 1777 the Cabinet had at last agreed to bring forward more ships for the fleet, and it was decided that ships had to be retained in home waters, but only six ships were authorised. On both sides of the Channel the leaders were waiting the outcome of the 1777 campaign in America. News of the surrender at Saratoga, which was received in London at the beginning of December, put an end to the period of equipoise. Vergennes' prediction was wrong, that the defeat in America would lead the British to choose a European war as a means of recouping their losses. North's Cabinet was incapable of such a plan, and King George would not permit North to resign so that Chatham could be brought in. It was the French who set the pace towards war. Vergennes' belligerence was made urgent by his concern that Saratoga would lead to a compromise peace which would preserve for Britain the exclusive navigation to America upon which the strength of the British navy was believed to depend. In response to the avalanche of intelligence from French dockyards, the Admiralty sent orders between 27 and 31 December to the Navy Board to prepare

for sea a total of ten additional ships of the line. An eleventh followed on 5 January 1778.

It was known that orders had been sent to Brest to hold in readiness three ships and a frigate, victualled for four months. It was believed they would be used to convoy gun-runners out of European waters. On 31 December North advised King George that Sandwich intended to bring up in Cabinet the next day the question of the orders under which Commodore Hood was watching the Biscay ports of France. Two days later secret orders were issued instructing Hood to intercept any convoy bound for America and to seize ships found with warlike stores 'notwithstanding any remonstrance from the convoy [*ie* the escort] to the contrary'. He was to instruct his captains to treat the French with 'civility', but 'For the more effectual performing this Service, you are not to allow your Ships to be less than two in Company.'[20] As Camden remarked in the Lords on 2 February, 'the ports of L'Orient and Nantz are blocked up by a British naval force ...to intercept succours going to America, and to put a stop to that very commerce which the French King, in his public edicts, pretends to prohibit.'[21]

Had such orders been issued when first Versailles opened French ports to American gun-runners and privateers, it is not improbable that the drift of the French ministry into war could have been arrested. Now, however, it was too late. Attention was focused on the hope of concluding peace in America before the storm broke in Europe, but Benjamin Franklin succeeded in obtaining a French signature on a Treaty of Friendship, and Vergennes made certain of a British reaction by instructing the French ambassador, M de Noailles, to formally advise Weymouth. The weakness of London's handling of the requirements of deterrence between 1775 and the summer of 1777 has to be added to the strategic mistake of the Saratoga and Philadelphia campaigns, and to the tactical defeat which was to be suffered at the battle of the Chesapeake, in creating the military conditions which led to the successful establishment of the United States of America.

20. 2 January 1778, Admiralty Papers 2/1334.

21. Almon Vol X p174.

The Royal Dockyards

IT WAS from the Royal Dockyards at Deptford, Woolwich, Chatham, Sheerness, Portsmouth and Plymouth that the fleet was fitted out and maintained throughout the American War of Independence. The importance of these main shore bases lay in their provision of docking facilities. Timber-built ships required regular docking for hull cleaning and repairs, and the only dry-docks available to the British navy lay in these six main yards. Small vessels could be careened for some hull work; but frigates and ships of the line had to return to the English yards whenever they became crank, leaky or battle-damaged. Not only did these yards possess docks, but they also stored all the materials demanded by wooden fighting ships—the timber, masts, hemp, tar, pitch, iron, copper and canvas—and manufactured almost everything they required in the way of equipment. There were smitheries at each and ropewalks at four, at Woolwich, Chatham, Portsmouth and Plymouth.

Inevitably, owing to differences in their age and geographical situation, the value to the Royal Navy of each of the yards differed. Because it was close to London, and at the centre of the Thames shipbuilding industry and commercial trade in naval stores, Deptford was still important in 1776 (1). But, founded in 1513, it was small and specialised in new building, and the distribution of stores to the other five yards and the fleet overseas. Woolwich, equally old, was confined in space and limited principally to refitting frigates (2). Its main problem, as for Deptford, was the silting of the Thames, and the long distance ships had to haul up the river, often against the prevailing westerly winds. With only one single and one double dock each, neither yard bore much of the refitting and repair burden of the fleet.

Founded in the reign of Elizabeth I, Chatham too had similar problems (3). However, the yard was more spacious, possessed four docks and provided large repairs for ships of the line that were reduced in draught at the mouth of the River Medway, and hauled up its long, winding reaches. Sheerness, paced out by Pepys in 1665, was still by 1776 makeshift in character, hulks holding its foreshore from being washed away (4). At the mouth of the Medway and close to the Nore anchorage in the mouth of the Thames, it was a useful resource for small ships requiring rapid attention. However, it had only two small docks and most ships of the line depended on the facilities at Portsmouth and Plymouth.

Portsmouth yard, established by Henry VIII, had one double and four single docks by 1776 (5). Serving the fleet anchorage at Spithead, during the American War the yard was at the height of its importance. Even so, located on Portsmouth harbour, which possessed a narrow entrance across a shallow bar, large ships had to unload guns and equipment before being brought into harbour for docking. Nevertheless it was still able to dock more ships than Plymouth yard with one double and only three single docks. Plymouth yard, built in the

3

Shipwright, who managed all the principal departments of artificers in the yard: the shipwrights, caulkers, house carpenters, smiths and labourers. Most of the administrative work connected with these operations was performed by the clerks of the Clerk of the Cheque, responsible for the time-keeping and payment of the artificers; the Storekeeper, who managed all the different storehouses; and the Clerk of the Survey, who surveyed quantities of stores delivered and work performed.

Refitting involved inspecting and making good caulking, sheathing, fittings, rigging, cables and replenishing stores and provisions. Refitting a 74-gun ship on average took only three weeks in dock, but there were always other delays. Stripping and unloading them ready for docking took about five weeks, and preparing them for sea again about another six. In all, ships of the line thus took four months to be refitted. Frigates took less time, about two months.

Repairs of course took much longer in dock, depending on the amount of work to be done. All wooden ships suffered from dry-rot, while ships constructed on a right-angular system of framing tended to 'work' or distort in the action of the waves. Ships of the line thus tended to require some degree of repair every three to four years. When ships were surveyed at the dockyards, their defects were classified according to whether they needed a small, medium or large repair. On average, a small repair took ten weeks, a medium one ten months, and a large one sixteen months. Those coming in from the sea and deemed in need of a large repair were usually relegated to the Ordinary, the backlog of ships laid up as hulks waiting for repair. This ensured that the ships

1690s to confront Brest across the mouth of the English Channel, was well positioned to receive ships returning from across the Atlantic (6). But its anchorage in Hamaoze and Plymouth Sound was less secure against southerly gales, which could also bottle up a fleet, so that watering and shelter for the Channel Fleet was usually found in Torbay.

One of the problems common to all the main dockyards was the need to reduce the draught of ships to float them in and out of docks that were little deeper than low tide level. Most ships had to be hauled in and out on the highest spring or neap tides, threatening damage to their keels and sheathing. Co-ordination of undocking of one ship with the docking of another was essential to gain the greatest use of each dock; and when ships were docked work had to proceed with the greatest intensity. This was achieved by close co-operation between the Master Attendant, responsible for the safety and movements of ships in harbour, and the Master

4

brought forward were those in need of least work and took the shortest time to complete and return to sea. In consequence, ships of the line waiting for repair accordingly had to wait from six months to a year before receiving attention.

The average time in an English dockyard for the 74s in the Royal Navy that served all five years of the European war, between March 1778 and March 1783, was one year three months. Owing to the urgency of refitting and repair work during the American War, little new building work was performed in the Royal Dockyards. For new ships, the Admiralty mainly depended on contract builders or on prizes purchased into the Navy.

Nevertheless the Admiralty did try to hasten the performance of work in the Royal yards by the introduction of piecework for shipwrights. Before the war several trades in the yards did some form of piecework. However in 1775 when Lord Sandwich, the First Lord of the Admiralty, attempted to introduce piecework for shipwrights he was answered by a series of strikes, especially at the western yards. At the beginning of a war, when hostilities were brewing, the shipwrights had greater bargaining power than the Admiralty and Navy Boards. In consequence, Sandwich was only able to introduce piecework for shipwrights at the smaller eastern yards which were closer and therefore more familiar with the commercial pressures of the Thames merchant yards. Hence from 1775 shipwrights at Deptford, Woolwich and Chatham worked by the piece, while those at Chatham and Portsmouth resisted it until 1783, with those at Plymouth holding out against it until 1788.

In 1783, at the end of the war, the Admiralty unsuccessfully attempted to abolish the yard artificers' 'chips' in return for a cash payment. The practice of artificers taking chips as a daily perquisite had grown up because they were paid quarterly and usually two or three quarters in arrears. A daily perquisite of, for example, offcut timber was therefore a valuable source of immediate cash and delayed their entry into debt. The problem was that the shipwrights had a reputation for cutting up whole timber to obtain their perquisite, which some then used to cover embezzlement. Lord Sandwich was more successful in preserving timber by the introduction of sheds that permitted wood to season before being used in ship repairs or new construction.

However, the reduction of waste by such improvements made only a small reduction in the immense cost of maintaining the Royal Navy's fleet of over 600 warships, including over 170 ships of the line, by the end of the American War. The cost in materials was added to by the practice of clerks at the dockyards, as well as in all other departments of the Navy, receiving fees from contractors at every delivery of stores or other transaction.

5

In 1784 a Royal Commission of inquiry into the amount of unofficial emoluments received in departments of government showed that dockyard clerks obtained 60 per cent of their income from fees from contractors. Inevitably, such fees were an incentive not only to hasten clerical work but to overlook discrepancies between the demands of a contract and the actual delivery. Furthermore it is clear contractors did not allow these payments to reduce their profit: their cost was added to the total price of undertaking contracts.

Practices in the dockyards nevertheless conformed to standards elsewhere in the government of eighteenth-century England. Indeed the problems of the yards enhance, rather than detract from, their achievements. Under great pressures—in repairing and refitting the Channel fleet in 1778 and 1779, and the North Sea squadron in 1781, for example—the yards made extraordinary contributions to the war against the European powers. What is remarkable is that not only were fleets maintained in home waters, but a fleet off North America too. Employing over 10,000 working men of all trades, together the six main dockyards formed the greatest industrial complex in Britain, and probably the world. In them the commercial and military power of the country were united to create and maintain the greatest single naval force the European powers had yet seen.

1-6. An anonymous series of black and watercolour pen and ink illustrations of the Royal Dockyards, dating from about 1770.

1. Deptford Dockyard. *NMM neg 6803*

2. Woolwich Dockyard. *NMM ref PAH3219*

3. Chatham Dockyard. *NMM ref PAH3217*

4. Sheerness Dockyard. *NMM ref PAH3218*

5. Portsmouth Dockyard. *NMM neg 2534*

6. Plymouth Dockyard. *NMM neg A445*

6

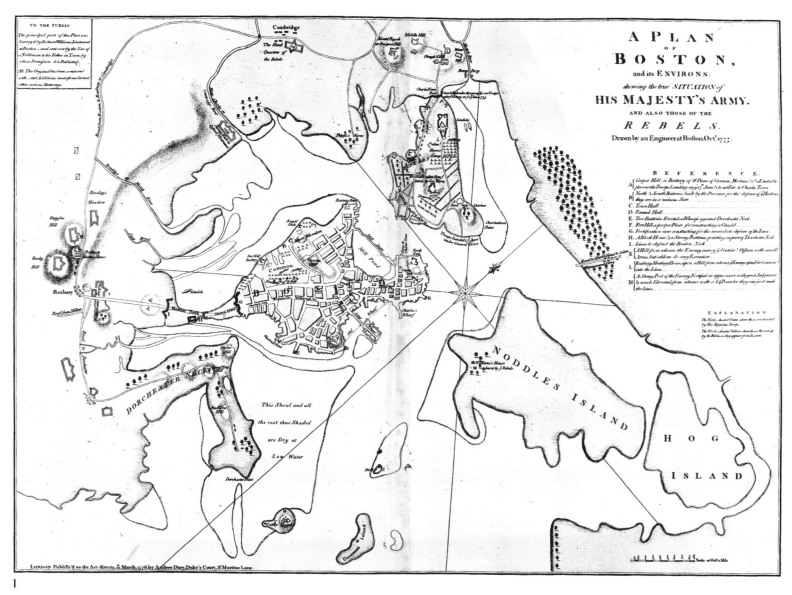

1

Boston and Bunker Hill, June 1775

ACTUAL FIGHTING in the colonies was sparked by an order from Lord Dartmouth, the Secretary of State for the Colonies, to General Gage instructing him to take firm action against the dissidents flouting royal authority. Receiving his orders on 14 April 1775, Gage decided on a military sortie to round up stockpiles of military supplies and to arrest the perceived ringleaders, but despite great efforts at secrecy, Paul Revere's famous ride warned the surrounding countryside that the British were coming. As a result the advance to Lexington and Concord ended in a bloody skirmish and an ignominious retreat for the regulars. America was outraged: Congress mobilised 13,600 troops, and the neighbouring Colonies formed militias to march on Boston. Suddenly, the British army in the town was under siege (1). Gage received reinforcements in May, including three Major Generals, William Howe,

Henry Clinton and John Burgoyne, allowing him to contemplate a more active role.

Although a fine harbour (2), Boston was a difficult place to defend since it was surrounded by high ground on two sides, and in June Gage decided to occupy one of them, Dorchester Heights to the southeast. Once again the rebels were ahead of them, and Boston was awakened on the morning of 17 June by the sound of heavy gunfire from the *Lively:* colonial forces had taken the heights above Charlestown on the opposite, northern, side of the harbour. They were supposed to occupy Bunker Hill—which lent its name to the ensuing battle— but in fact they fortified the lower Breed's Hill, which was nearer Boston. This threat needed an instant response, and on 17 June Howe was sent across the harbour with 1100 men to retake the promontory.

The Royal Navy's command of the waters made the

2

landings easy, but advancing uphill proved both slower and more bloody than anticipated. Howe was reinforced and batteries on the Boston waterfront and warships in the harbour were ordered to bombard Charlestown with hot shot and set the houses on fire. A sketch by a British officer on the spot (3) shows the *Glasgow* and *Lively*, 20s, in action, while far right reinforcements are ferried across to the burning town. Also lending fire support were the 64-gun *Somerset* and the sloop *Falcon*, 14 guns.

Burgoyne, in command of a Boston gun battery, described the scene:

And now ensued one of the greatest scenes of war that can be conceived; if we look to the height, Howe's corps ascending the hill in the face of intrenchments, and in very disadvantageous ground, was much engaged; to the left the enemy pouring in fresh troops by thousands, over the land; and in the arm of the sea our ships and floating batteries cannonading before them; straight before us a large and noble town in one great blaze—the church-steeples, being timber, were great pyramids of fire above the rest ...the hills round the country covered with spectators; the enemy all in anxious suspense; the roar of canons, mortars, and musketry; the crash of churches, ships upon the stocks, and whole streets falling together, to fill the ear ... and the reflection that, perhaps, a defeat was a final loss to the British empire in America ...

3

It was not the final loss, but it was perhaps the first. Although the Americans were eventually driven out, the British casualties were enormous—226 dead and 828 wounded—and the so-called Battle of Bunker Hill made an enormous impression in Britain. Many maps and depictions were published, the best of the former being by William Faden from an original by Howe's ADC, Lieutenant Page; this modified version (4) was used in Stedman's *History*, but still confuses the two hills. The prints were also less than precise: this illustration (5) from a contemporary history shows Breed's Hill as a cliff face,

so exaggerating the strength of the American positions.

Most American casualties were inflicted by *Glasgow* and the armed transport *Symmetry* during the retreat across Charlestown Neck, but the death of 'the famous Doctor Warren, the greatest incendiary in America' as Lord Rawdon called him, at the height of the struggle gave the rebellion its first major martyr. John Trumbull, arguably the greatest painter of the American Revolution, produced a dramatic, if stagey depiction of the battle, which was so popular in America that it was the model for numerous published engravings (6).

4

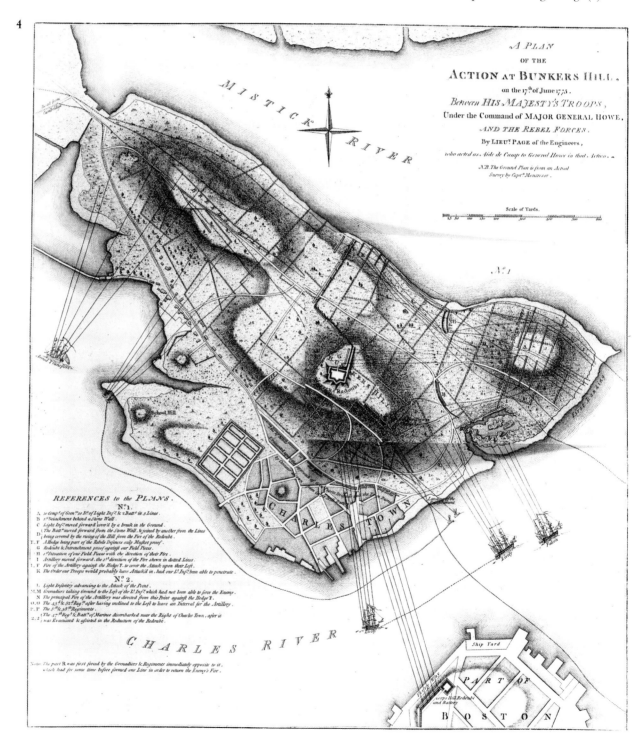

BOSTON

CHARLES TOWN

5

1. 'A Plan of Boston and its Environs Shewing the True Situation of His Majesty's Army and also Those of the Rebels. Drawn by an Engineer at Boston, Octr 1775. Engrav'd by Jno Lodge from the Late Mr Jefferys', London, 12 March 1776.
NMM neg 2175

2. 'A view of Boston', published by J F W Des Barres, London, 19 May 1775. From *The Atlantic Neptune*.
NMM neg 1023

3. Bunker Hill, with Charlestown on fire, 'Taken by a British officer from Beacon Hill, Boston'. The original was given to Lord Rawdon, a British officer present at the time, and acquired by an American collector from one of his descendants.
Emmet Collection, Prints Collection, Miriam and Ira D Wallach Division of Arts, Prints and Photography, New York Public Library.

4. 'A Plan of the Action at Bunker's Hill, on the 17th of June 1775, between His Majesty's troops under the Command of Major General Howe, and the Rebel Forces. By Lieut. Page of the Engineers, who Acted as Aide de Camp to General Howe in That Action. N.B.: the Ground Plan is from an Actual Survey by Captn. Montresor', published by William Faden, London 1775. This later state is from Stedman's *American War.*
NMM neg 273

5. 'View of the Attack on Bunker's Hill, with the Burning of Charlestown, June 17, 1775', engraving by John Lodge from a drawing by Millar. Engraved for Edward Barnard's *New, Complete and Authentic History of England* (London 1983).
NMM ref PAD5325

6. Battle of Bunker Hill, coloured lithograph engraved and published by T W Strong, after the famous painting by John Trumbull done in 1786. The main protagonists are identified in the sketch below.
NMM ref PAF4630

BATTLE AT BUNKER'S HILL.
"THE PATH TO LIBERTY IS BLOODY." *Franklin*
Fought, June 17, 1775.

6

1

The campaign against Canada, May 1775-May 1776

THE GEOGRAPHY of northern New England was dominated by Lake Champlain, from which the Hudson flowed south to New York and the Richelieu river north to meet the St Lawrence at Sorel, making up the main north-south route through otherwise almost impassable territory. One of the first American offensive actions was to send forces under Benedict Arnold and Ethan Allen to seize the strategically vital but lightly garrisoned Fort Ticonderoga, and the British post at Crown Point on the lake in May 1775.

2

After much debate the Continental Congress decided on an invasion of Canada to encourage the population to join the rebellion. In September a force under Richard Montgomery, who had seen action in Canada during the Seven Years War, was dispatched north from Champlain to take Montreal and then pressed on to Quebec, the key to Canada. While Montgomery was besieging St John's on the Richelieu, Ethan Allen launched a premature attack on Montreal, was defeated and captured. St John's eventually capitulated after fifty-six days on 2 November, and ten days later Montreal (1) surrendered on terms, Sir Guy Carleton the Governor of Canada having withdrawn his forces.

However, there was another prong to the American assault. In September a force of nearly 1100 men led by the erratic genius of Benedict Arnold advanced from the Maine coast up the Kennebec and down the Chaudiere rivers through the wildest country. It was an epic struggle, with men dying from disease, exhaustion and even starvation, but on 9 November the survivors—fewer than 700—reached the St Lawrence at Point Levis (2) for their first sight of Quebec. A probing attack proved that the place was too strong for direct attack and Arnold awaited the arrival of Montgomery before they settled to a regular siege.

Quebec (3), seen here from across the St Lawrence, was a natural fortress and almost impregnable from the river side, on a natural promontory with its north flank protected by the Charles river. When capturing it in 1759, Wolfe had attacked from the Heights of Abraham (behind the citadel, to the left) and it was here that Montgomery and Arnold settled down to await the right moment (4). The St Lawrence was the city's link with the outside world, but it froze in winter, so the Americans knew they had nearly six months before relief could arrive. A grand assault was launched on New Year's Eve under the cover of a snowstorm, but it was beaten off with heavy casualties, Montgomery himself being killed and Arnold wounded. Thereafter, the besiegers endured the fiercest winter weather, but despite disease and desertions kept up a blockade into the spring of 1776.

Seapower had allowed Wolfe to take Quebec—using charts prepared by the great navigator James Cook (5)—and in 1776 the city looked to the Royal Navy for its salvation. It came on 6 May, when the frigate *Surprise* dropped anchor, heralding the arrival of reinforcements in the sloop *Martin* and the 50-gun *Isis*, which had forced its way through over 100 miles of ice into the river. Faced with Carleton's counter-attack, the Americans retreated down Lake Champlain, abandoning their artillery and baggage, but the British advance halted at St John's: there were no roads south and Arnold had improvised a lake flotilla, so until this could be countered, troop boats could not be risked on the lake.

3

1. 'An East View of Montreal, in Canada', published by Carington Bowles, London, c1770.
NMM ref PAD7573

2. 'A View of the City of Quebec, the Capital of Canada, taken from the Rock on Point Levis, by William Peachy, Oct 23rd 1784', published by Robert Pollard, 1 November 1786.
NMM ref PAH2888

3. View of Quebec, by J F W Des Barres, c1777, from *The Atlantic Neptune*.
NMM neg A5070

4. 'Genl. Arnold's plan of Quebec with the Americans Besieging it Winter 1776', sketch by Justin Winsor in *A Narrative and Critical History of America* after an original by E Antill. American positions are marked AAA,BBB, CCC, and a dotted line from Wolfe's Cove (L) along the river front denotes the American attack at point K where Montgomery was killed.
Chatham Collection

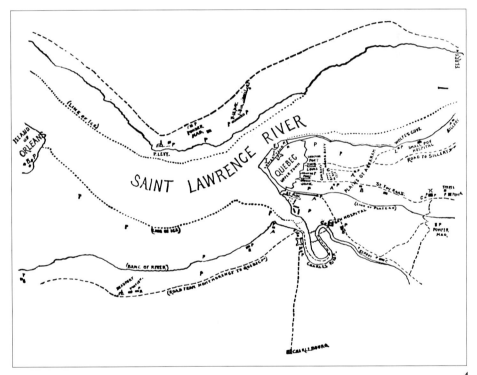

4

5. James Cook's chart of the St Lawrence to Quebec, 'by order of Vice-Admiral Charles Saunders 1759', as used in Wolfe's campaign of 1759. Published by Thomas Jeffrys.
NMM neg A123

5

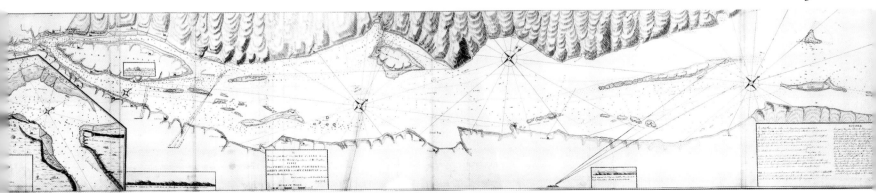

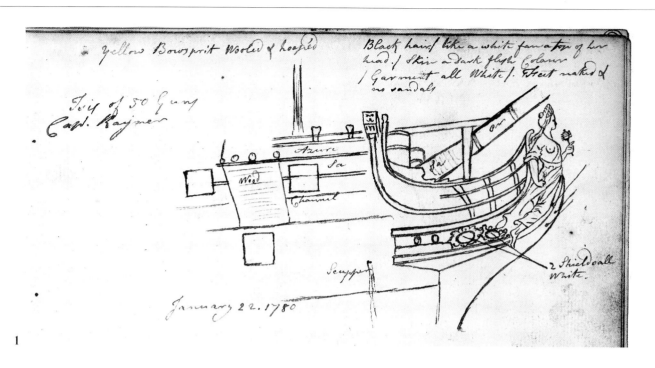

1

A marine artist's sketchbook

WHILE PAINTING cannot claim the literal veracity of the camera, nevertheless many of the professional artists of the eighteenth century took considerable pains to make their works accurate. This was particularly true of marine painters, whose patrons were often naval or merchant marine officers, practical seamen all who may not have known much about art but certainly knew the proper appearance of a ship in a seaway and expected it to be reflected on canvas. Not surprisingly, many of the most highly regarded artists in this field had firsthand experience of ships and some, like Nicholas Pocock, had even commanded their own vessels.

One such was Thomas Luny (1759-1837), who served in the Royal Navy during the Napoleonic Wars until invalided out about 1810 with rheumatoid arthritis. He

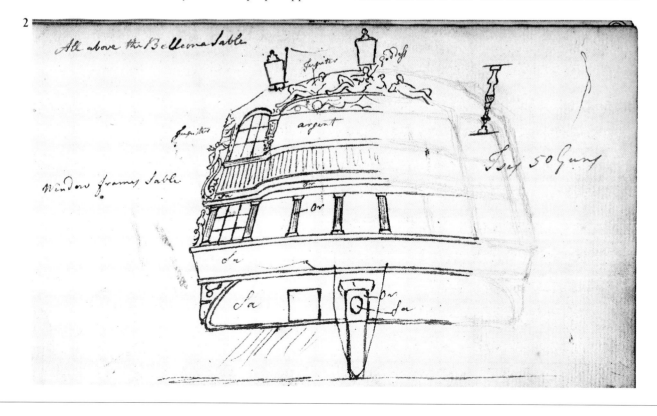

2

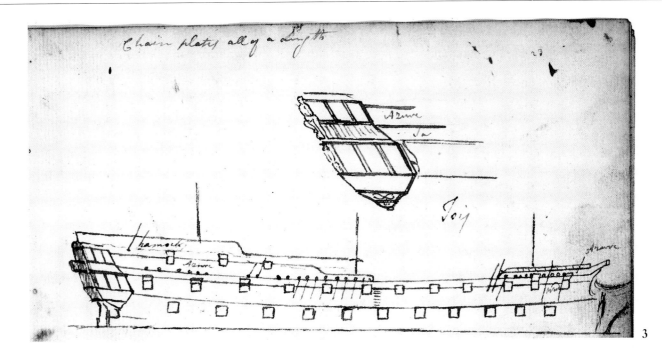

3

continued to paint, however, often at the rate of a picture a day, and his life's output has been calculated at nearly 3000 works. Yet despite this speed, his sketchbooks—admittedly from his early years—reveal astounding attention to technical detail. The accompanying sketches are devoted to the decorative work and colouring of the 50-gun ship *Isis*, the saviour of Quebec, although the final painting for which it was a study has not been identified.

Colours are given in the traditional heraldic convention—argent (silver, effectively white), or (gold, yellow), gules (red), azure (blue), sable (black), vert (green), purpure (purple)—but some features are noted in detail. The figurehead (1), for example, is fully described: 'Black hair/like a white fan on top of her head/Skin a Dark flesh Colour/Garment all White/Feet naked & no sandals',

while the trailboards have '2 Shields all White'. On the stern (2) the taffrail figures are identified as a 'goddess' in the centre, with 'Jupiter' to port, but there is the further annotation 'All above the Bellona Sable' so the central figure may be the goddess of war. Besides the drawings, the sketchbooks contain extensive notes, with precise dimensions for aspects that are not visually obvious, like the height of the hammock netting above the quarter-deck, and the masts and spars.

Before the pressure of work in the shipyards during American War ruled it out, the Admiralty had insisted on 'as fitted' plans being produced as each ship completed. These usually included some depiction of the carved work, and one such draught exists for *Isis*, reproduced here (4) for comparison with Luny's sketches.

1-3. Thomas Luny Sketchbook, 75 leaves of brown pen and ink sketches, *c*1780. Sketches of *Isis*, 50 guns, Captain Rayner, dated 22 January 1780

1. Bow. *NMM PAE9619*

2. Stern. *NMM PAE9618*

3. Broadside. *NMM PAE9617*

4. As fitted sheer plan, *Isis*, 50 guns. *NMM neg 1481*

4

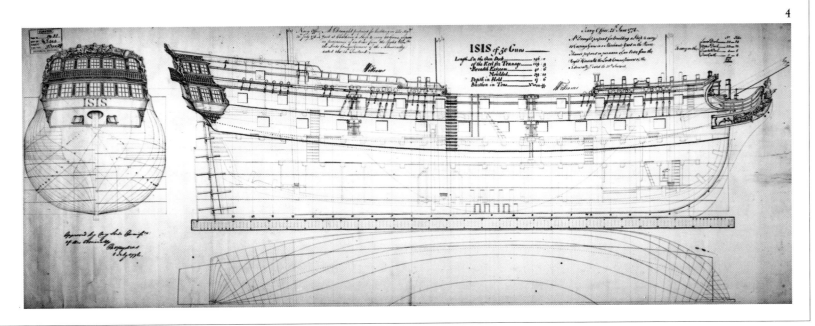

1

The battle of Valcour Island, 11 October 1776

WITH THE failure of the American invasion of Canada in 1775, Benedict Arnold (1) began a brilliant campaign of delay against the British counter-attack under Sir Guy Carleton and General Burgoyne. The keystone to the defence of New England was Lake Champlain, and the American-held forts at Crown Point and Ticonderoga, which formed choke-points on the main north-south route. A successful British joining-up of their forces in Canada and New York would have separated the northern states—regard-ed as the seat of the rebellion—from their southern allies, but this was frustrated by Arnold's command of the lake.

Displaying great energy and ingenuity, he had impro-vised a force of armed vessels—three schooners, four gal-leys and eight gondolas (or gundalows). For most of 1776 this force dominated Champlain, but the British were actively assembling a fleet using the considerable exper-tise and manpower of the Royal Navy's squadron in the St Lawrence. Two schooners and a ship were taken apart,

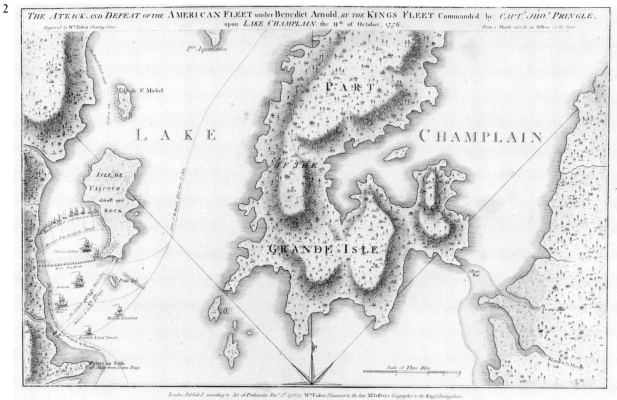

2

1. A portrait of General Arnold 'peint par Wilkenson à Boston. Se vend a Londres chez Thom Hart' c1780.
British Museum Department of Prints and Drawings 1902-10-11-7068

2. 'The Attack and Defeat of the American Fleet under Benedict Arnold, by the King's Fleet Commanded by Capt. Thos. Pringle, upon Lake Champlain, the 11th October 1776. From a Sketch taken by an Officer on the Spot.' Engraved and published by William Faden, 3 December 1776.
Beverley R Robinson Collection, Annapolis

shipped overland through atrocious conditions and reassembled at St Johns, at the head of lake navigation; to these were added a powerful radeau (or prame), a large gondola, and twenty rowing gunboats. This squadron was far more powerful than anything Arnold could field, but it was not until 4 October that the British flagship, the *Inflexible*, could sail to begin offensive operations.

Arnold retreated to Valcour Island, halfway up the lake, and anchored in a half-moon formation that he described as 'in such a form that few vessels can attack us at the same time, and those will be exposed to the fire of the whole fleet.' (2) The British did not spot the colonial squadron until they were past the island, forcing them to engage from leeward and too far apart for mutual support, but once the attack was launched fighting was intense. The American *Royal Savage* was soon beaten out of the line, captured and then burnt, but the British *Carleton* (3) was roughly handled, and had it not been for the bravery of a Midshipman—one Edward Pellew, later to become one of the Royal Navy's most famous frigate captains—the schooner would have been lost. At nightfall the British anchored, intending to deliver the *coup de grace* at daybreak, but during the night Arnold's remaining ships slipped through their lines, and a three-day chase ensued, the Americans losing two gundalows in the process. On the 13th *Inflexible* and the two schooners finally caught up with the Americans and despite a gallant defence by *Washington* and *Congress* (4) the force was routed, Arnold eventually burning the *Congress* and four gundalows, their crews escaping overland to Crown Point. Only two galleys (one incomplete), two schooners, a gundalow and a sloop survived, and this last, the *Lee*, was taken the following day to add to the *Washington* and the gundalow *Jersey* which were already British prizes. The American flotilla prior to the action is depicted in crude caricature in a contemporary illustration (5).

The tactical victory had gone to Britain, but the strategic victory was decidedly Arnold's since the season was too far advanced for British forces to capture Crown Point and Ticonderoga, setting the scene for the disastrous campaign of 1777 which ended at Saratoga. By the standards of fleet engagements, Valcour Island was little more than a skirmish, but its consequences were immense: it was, in Admiral Mahan's famous phrase, 'a strife of pygmies for the prize of a continent'.

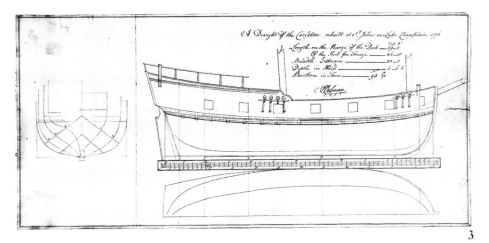

3

4

5

3. The lines plan of the *Carleton*, 1776; described as a brig, but actually rigged as a schooner. Admiralty Collection.
NMM neg 5118

4. 'A Description of the Engagement on Lake Champlain,' published by Sayer and Bennett, London, 23 December 1776. The caption identifies the main vessels: the British ships (right to left) are 1. *Inflexible* ship, 2. *Carleton* schooner, 3. *Maria* schooner; far left 4 is the *Congress* galley 'run a Shore, with other Vessels blowing up'; between *Maria* and *Carleton*, 5 is *Washington* galley striking; far right, 6 is a gunboat coming up.
Naval Institute Press

5. 'God Bless Our Arms: New England Vessels at Valcure Bay – Commander B. Arnold - 11 Octobre [sic] 1776'.
Naval Institute Press

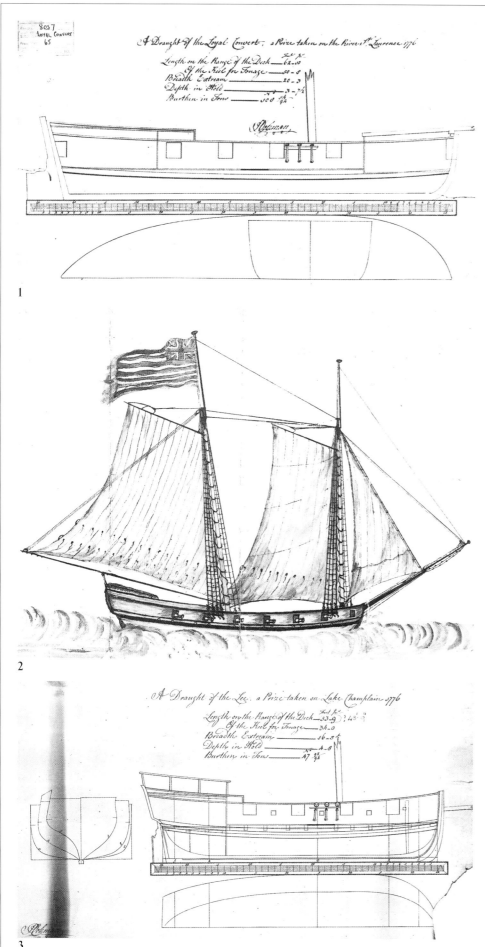

1

2

3

Lake warfare vessels

CONSIDERING THE speed with which they were assembled, and the *ad hoc* nature of their composition, a surprising amount is known about the fleets that fought on Lake Champlain in 1775-77. The bureaucratically efficient Royal Navy made (and preserved) draughts not only of their own vessels but also of the captured American types as well. Furthermore, there are a number of crude but believable contemporary sketches, while the gundalow *Philadelphia* was raised in 1935 and is now preserved in the Smithsonian Institution, Washington DC.

The Colonial advance into Canada was supported by a number of large flat-bottomed, double-ended boats known as gundalows (gundaloes or gondolas) ranging in size from 50ft to 64ft, with 16ft to 20ft breadth. Some were decked with six to ten small guns, but some were little more than open boats with perhaps a single bow gun. They were built locally, below the rapids at Chambly and in the St Lawrence, and the usual propulsion was a single square sail with sometimes a topsail. These were mostly destroyed during the British advance in June 1776, but the *Convert* was captured, rechristened *Loyal Convert* and her lines taken off (1). She was dismantled and re-erected above the falls at St John's, when she had a gaff mizzen added. She was measured at 62ft 10in by 20ft 3in by 3ft 7½in, for 109 tons, and carried two 12pdrs and six 6pdrs in British service.

The American squadron

When St John's was abandoned in June, the American fleet comprised three vessels: *Enterprise*, a large sloop armed with twelve 4pdrs and ten swivel guns; *Liberty*, a schooner or ketch armed with two 4pdrs, four 2pdrs and eight swivels; and the *Royal Savage*, a British schooner captured by the frontiersman Jacobus Wynkoop in 1775, and armed with four 6pdrs, eight 4pdrs and ten swivels. A contemporary sketch of this vessel (2) may be the earliest known representation of the Colonial 'jack and stripes' ensign. With characteristic energy Arnold had a schooner built at Ticonderoga (*Revenge* armed with four 4pdrs, four 2pdrs and ten swivels), and a new shipyard at Skenesboro (Whitehall, New York) was set up from almost nothing. It set out to build a small cutter based on frames carried away from St John's, four large galleys and nine gundalows.

The cutter became the *Lee*, which was eventually captured by the British and its lines taken off (3). It measured 43ft 9in by 16ft 3½in by 4ft 8in for 48 tons, and was armed with one 9pdr in the bow, one 12pdr firing astern and four 4pdrs on the broadside. The galleys were named *Washington*, *Congress*, *Trumbull* and *Gates* (although the last was never completed). Again, *Washington* was captured and measured (4): dimensions were 72ft 4in by 19ft 7in by 6ft 2in, 123 tons, and armament two 18pdrs in the bow, two 12pdrs and two 2pdrs in the stern, and six 6pdrs on the broadside. The other galleys seem to have been very similar if not identical. Arnold decided to concentrate on the galleys and eventually only eight gundalows were completed: *Philadelphia*, *New York*, *Jersey*, *Connecticut*, *Providence*, *New Haven*, *Spitfire*, and *Boston*. The wreck of the *Philadelphia* was raised in 1935 and proved to measure 53ft 4in by 15ft 6in by 3ft 10in, and like the other gundalows carried one bow gun, a 12pdr, and two 9pdrs. Weathercloths normally protected the crews, but there were not enough at Valcour, so evergreen boughs were used instead.

The service appearance of these ships, and their British opponents, is depicted in a pair of contemporary drawings by a British naval officer, Lt C Randle (5), which also lists their armament (compared with American sources it occasionally exaggerates the calibres though not the numbers of guns). While the hull shapes are not very detailed, the rigs are clear, in particular the lateens of the galleys standing out.

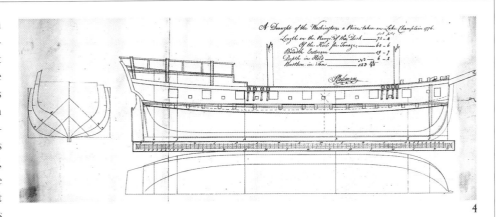

4

The British squadron

Shipbuilding facilities on the St Lawrence were comparatively good, and the British had the advantage of a well-manned squadron of the Royal Navy to call upon for expertise. However, to reach the head of navigation on Lake Champlain, at St John's, there were twelve miles of rapids at Chambly to be negotiated. A ship and two schooners were available, plus the captured *Loyal Convert*, but they were below the falls. At first the British planned to construct a road and transport the hulls complete, but the ground proved too boggy, so the ships were dis-

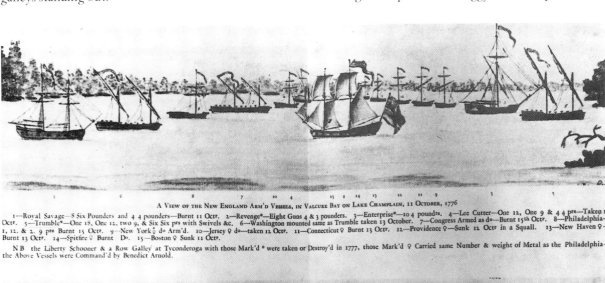

A VIEW OF THE NEW ENGLAND ARM'D VESSELS, IN VALCURE BAY ON LAKE CHAMPLAIN, 11 OCTOBER, 1776

1—Royal Savage—8 Six Pounders and 4 4 pounders—Burnt 11 Octr. 2—Revenge*—Eight Guns 4 & 3 pounders. 3—Enterprise*—10 4 pounds. 4—Lee Cutter—One 12, One 9 & 4 4 prs—Taken 1 Octr. 5—Trumble*—One 18, One 12, two 9, & Six Six prs with Swivels &c. 6—Washington mounted same as Trumble taken 13 October. 7—Congress Armed as do—Burnt 15th Octr. 8—Philadelphia—1, 12, & 2, 9 prs Burnt 15 Octr. 9—New York ♀ do Arm'd. 10—Jersey ♀ do—taken 12 Octr. 11—Connecticut ♀ Burnt 13 Octr. 12—Providence ♀—Sunk 12 Octr in a Squall. 13—New Haven ♀—Burnt 13 Octr. 14—Spitfire ♀ Burnt Do. 15—Boston ♀ Sunk 11 Octr.

N B the Liberty Schooner & a Row Galley at Tyconderoga with those Mark'd * were taken or Destroy'd in 1777, those Mark'd ♀ Carried same Number & weight of Metal as the Philadelphia— the Above Vessels were Command'd by Benedict Arnold.

A VIEW OF HIS MAJESTY'S ARMED VESSELS ON LAKE CHAMPLAIN OCTOBER 11, 1776

1—Carleton—14 Six pounders (Lt. Dacres). 2—Inflexible—18 twelve pounders (Lt. Shank). 3—Maria—16 six pounders (Lt. Stark). 4—Convert—5 nine pounders (Lt. Longcroft). 5—Thunder —6 twenty-four pounders; 18 twelve pounders (Lt. Scott). 6—A Long Boats. 7—Gun Boats. 8—Valcure Island—

N B there were three Longboats with 2 two pounders on Sliders, 17 Gun boats, having one Gun—from Six to 24 pounders. Commander Captn Thos Pringle of the Royal Navy—Sir Guy Carleton wa on board the Maria in Both Actions.

1. Lines plan of the captured American gundalow *Loyal Convert*. Admiralty Collection. *NMM neg 8057*

2. A contemporary watercolour drawing of the schooner *Royal Savage* from the Schuyler Papers, Rare Books and Manuscripts Division, New York Public Library. *New York Public Library*

3. Lines plan of the captured American sloop *Lee*. Admiralty Collection. *NMM neg 6407*

4. Lines plan of the captured American galley *Washington*. Admiralty Collection. *NMM neg 6409*

5. Views of 'the New England Arm'd Vessels' and 'His Majesty's Armed Vessels' after a contemporary watercolour by Lieutenant C Randle, RN. The original annotation is in manuscript, although typeset for clarity here. *Naval Institute Press*

6. Lines plan of the schooner *Maria*. Admiralty Collection. *NMM neg 6440/64*

7. Lines plan of the radeau *Thunderer*. Admiralty Collection. *NMM neg 6406/53*

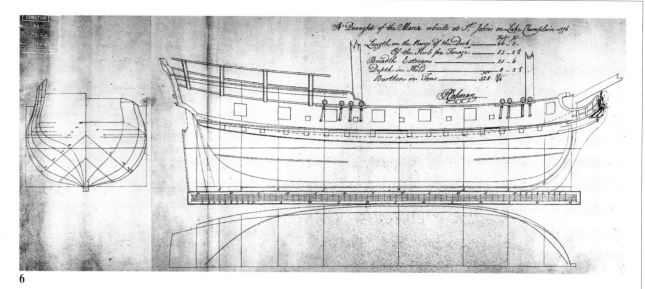

6

mantled and re-erected at St John's. HM Ships *Isis, Blonde, Juno, Pearl, Triton* and the transports *Lord Howe* and *Bute* gave up twenty-four 12pdrs, eight 9pdrs, and eight 6pdrs to add to army weapons available for the ships. This was all achieved in the remarkable time of three months, which included building the powerful radeau (or prame) *Thunderer* at St John's. According to contemporary records, only the schooner *Maria* (6) was formally on the Navy List, the others being Canadian colonial vessels, but they were all commanded by Royal Navy officers of the St Lawrence squadron.

The other schooner was the *Carleton*, while the ship was christened *Inflexible* 'the prowess of which will give us the dominion of Lake Champlain beyond a doubt,' as Captain Charles Douglas, in charge of preparations, correctly predicted. With sixteen 12pdrs and two 9pdrs, ten swivels and 120 men, she was the capital ship of the lake. The *Thunderer* (7) was another powerful vessel with six 24pdrs on the lower deck, six 12pdrs on the quarterdeck and two on the forecastle, plus two 8in howitzers, but as Douglas confessed, 'The Radeau would be more formidable did she carry her Six Battering 24 pounders below a little higher…'. The schooners carried fourteen (*Maria*) and twelve 6pdrs, six swivels each and forty-five men, while the *Loyal Convert* had two 12pdrs on the centreline and six 6pdrs on the broadside (although she went into action with seven 9pdrs). The rest of the

British force comprised about twenty gunboats with a single gun (of between 6 and 24pdr calibre, some army pattern, and some with howitzers), four ships' launches with single 3pdrs on slides acting as armed tenders, twenty-four transport longboats for provisions, and about 450 'Batoes' for the conveyance of troops.

Vessels on both sides were optimised for rapid construction and operations on inland waters, the principal requirement being very shallow draught. This made them poor performers to windward—the *Thunderer* could not beat up to enter the fray at Valcour, for example—though the British had the answer to hand but had ignored it. Lieutenant Schank, who commanded the leewardly radeau, had experimented with drop keels, the ancestor of the modern yachtsman's centreboard, and proposed them during her construction. He was later to persuade the Navy to adopt them in many coastal warships, but in 1776 they were rejected.

A list of 1777 gives the dimensions (deck length, breadth, depth in hold) of the British vessels as follows:

Inflexible—80ft 1½in x 23ft 10in x 9ft, 204 tons, max draught 9ft 6in.

Maria—66ft x 21ft 6in x 8ft 2½in, 129 tons, max draught 7ft 4in.

Thunderer—91ft 9in x 23ft 4in x 6ft 8in, 423 tons, max draught 4ft 6in.

Carleton—59ft 2in x 20ft x 6ft 6½in, 96 tons, max draught 7ft 4in.

Jersey (ex-American)—52ft 6½in x 14ft 9in x 4ft 8½in, 52 tons, max draught 2ft 6in.

7

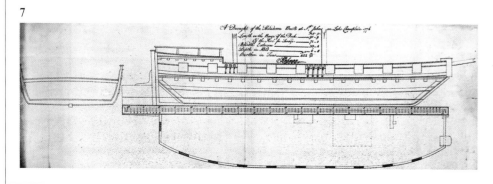

The first naval moves, fall 1775–spring 1776

A NUMBER OF apparently unrelated incidents that took place between the fall of 1775 and the spring of the following year demonstrate the interwoven nature of the forces escalating hostilities beyond all possibility of a negotiated settlement.

In October 1775 a small squadron comprising the armed vessels *Canceau, Halifax, Symmetry* and *Spitfire* under the command of Lieutenant Mowat sailed into the harbour of Falmouth (now Portland, Maine), bombarded the small town and left it in flames (1). A similar fate was suffered by Norfolk, Virginia the following January and there might have been other examples if Rear-Admiral Graves had not been replaced and his policy of 'burning and laying waste the whole country' had not been disowned by the British government. Nevertheless, America was outraged. Congress was debating the establishment of a Continental Navy and when news of the attack arrived it precipitated a decision in favour of purpose-built warships.

Mowat's flagship, the *Canceau* (2), was to have a busy war. A merchantman originally purchased in 1764 for survey work on the North American coast, she was rerated as 'an armed ship' and was to play a prominent part in the struggle for Canada. She was part of the reinforcement for Quebec early in 1776, and Mowat's successor in command, Lieutenant Schank, was largely responsible for the successful assembly of the Lake Champlain fleet that beat Benedict Arnold at Valcour Island.

The Continental Navy, encouraged if not actually initiated by *Canceau*'s earlier activities, was ready for fleet action by early in 1776. The American war effort was seriously hamstrung by the shortage of arms, and especially gunpowder, so a raid on the British stores at New Providence (Nassau) in the Bahamas (3) was undertaken in February. The squadron comprised the ship *Alfred*, flying the commodore's pennant of Esek Hopkins, the brigs *Andrew Doria* and *Cabot*, the sloops *Columbus* and *Providence*, and the schooners *Wasp, Hornet* and *Fly*. The landing was a great success (4)–not least as propaganda –and some seventy cannon and fifteen mortars were captured. On the other hand, Hopkins delayed his

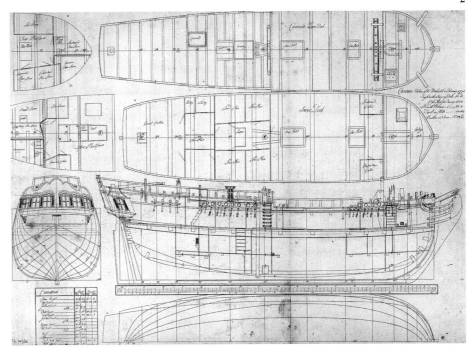

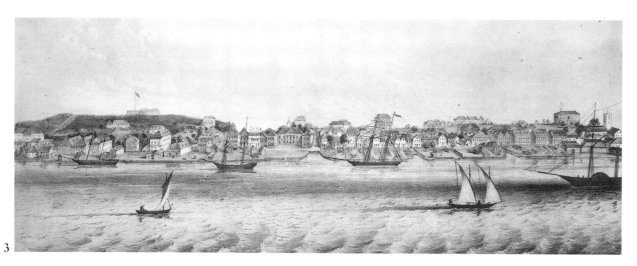

3

attack until daylight—against the advice of his lieutenant John Paul Jones—allowing most of the gunpowder to be spirited away.

American successes in the far-off Canadian campaign provided another source of heavy artillery, and one des-

4

tined to have a major effect on the war. At the end of January 1776 Henry Knox reached Boston with forty-three captured British cannon and sixteen mortars he had dragged all the way from Fort Ticonderoga. Although Washington was still crying out for powder, once these guns were emplaced around the city, the position of the besieged British army, already parlous, became completely untenable. In March after the occupation of Dorchester Heights, Howe, who had taken over from the disgraced Gage, bowed to the inevitable and decided to evacuate Boston. By threatening to burn the city, he was able to extricate his forces without hindrance, but the need for a large harbour in friendly territory to regroup and recuperate led him to Halifax, Nova Scotia (5).

Halifax was far from ideal, lacking provisions, stores and suitable accommodation, but Howe remained there until June when he had news that reinforcements were on their way. The troops were then re-embarked and the fleet set sail for New York, a destination long since divined by Washington, who had already moved the bulk of his forces south from Boston.

5

1. 'The Town of Falmouth, Burnt by Captain Moet, Octbr 1775', engraving from the Boston edition of the *Impartial History of the War* (1781), Vol II. *Library of Congress*

2. Lines plan of the *Canceau*. Admiralty Collection. *NMM neg CU/147/66 CUN 0171*

3. 'To Colonel Sir Francis Cockburn . . . This View of Nassau, New Providence . . . is . . . dedicated', coloured lithograph by R J Hughes (artist) and Thomas Gilkes (engraver). *NMM ref PAH2967*

4. A modern interpretation of the landing on New Providence by the Continental squadron, 3 March 1776. Oil painting by V Zveg, 1973. The ships (left to right) are two captured sloops, the schooner *Wasp* and the sloop *Providence*. *Naval Institute Press*

5. Halifax, Nova Scotia. Published London, March 1766 by R Short, engraved by James Mason after an original by Dominic Serres. *NMM ref PA10292*

1

George III and his navy

2

A T THE time of the American War of Independence, the monarch still played a key role in gov-
erning Great Britain and her colonies. As head of
government, King George III appointed ministers, guid-
ed policy, and fully felt himself to be master and protec-
tor of all his subjects. 'The interest of my country ever
shall be my first care', he had declared in 1759, the year
before he ascended the throne at the age of twenty-two.
And so it was. He was stigmatised by Americans in the
Declaration of Independence as 'unfit to be the ruler of a
free people', but throughout the crises of the American
War he worked calmly and dispassionately with ministers. Having 'no object so much at heart as the maintenance of the British constitution', with much sorrow in
March 1782 he drafted a resignation that was never presented.

This deeply conscientious monarch was also head of
the armed services. Of these, army affairs took prefer-
ence. Having inherited as well the title of Elector of
Hanover, a principality vulnerable to invasion from
France, and rival to the state of Prussia for power in

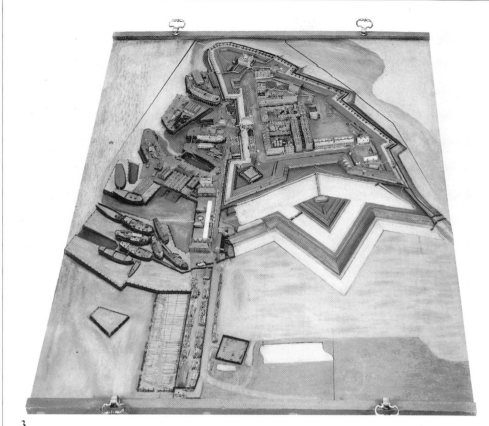

3

In the Royal Navy, George III was deliberately induced to take an interest. As the founder of the Royal Academy, an avid collector of the books that came to form the King's Library in the British Museum, and of the scientific instruments that now form the King's collection in the Science Museum in London, George III had a natural academic inclination towards many things nautical. In 1771 he attended the launch of the *Grafton* at Deptford, but had to be deterred from walking about the yard because the crowd would be particularly great, 'and the shutting the gates and keeping the populace at a distance would possibly occasion complaint and disturbance'.

This natural interest was nevertheless cultivated by Lord Sandwich following his appointment as First Lord of the Admiralty in 1771. They exchanged books—the King's library contained surveys of the dockyards going back to the time of Pepys—and in 1773 Sandwich induced George III to make a four-day visit Portsmouth:

> nothing would give more Satisfaction to the People of all ranks than to Observe His Majesty deigning to cast an eye upon his marine . . . and at the same time satisfy his own curiosity in objects truly worthy the Royal attention.

At Portsmouth he reviewed the fleet (1) and went on board the *Lion* and *Berwick*, building in the yard. He was subsequently sent profile elevations, plans and perspective views of warships of each rate and a model of a Third Rate:

> the timbers are all marked with their proper appellations, & Lord Sandwich flatters himself that

north Germany, military matters were vital to the survival of his continental heritage. Earlier in the century, George I had fought under the Duke of Marlborough in Germany and George II had fought at the Battle of Dettingen in 1743. George III was still nominal head of the British army. In consequence, he weighed deeply the deployments of regiments during the American War, thinking carefully for the security of Great Britain and Hanover before ordering too many of his forces, either German or British, across the North Atlantic.

4

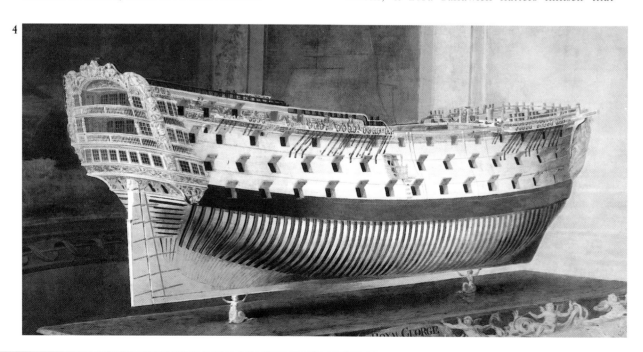

5

nothing can be more likely to give your Majesty a thorough idea of a ships construction than this model. Mr Williams who is the maker of the Model (& who had the honour of attending you before) will be the bearer of it, & will be able to answer any questions concerning it (2).

George was fascinated; he had no doubt the model would 'thoroughly explain the construction of a ship, which the more I reflect the more it shows the perfection to which mechanick is arrived'. To capitalise on this interest, he was then sent the model of a mainmast of a ship, made in exactly the same manner as masts made for service, which could be taken to pieces.

In 1773, possibly with George III in mind, Sandwich was prompted to commission models to be made of each of the six main dockyards (3). These minute and precisely crafted reproductions of the yards were built to a common scale of 40 feet to the inch by two men from each yard. They were completed in 1774 and presented to the King. (All six are now preserved in the National Maritime Museum in London.) A series of paintings of ships followed (4), the King's interest enhanced by the discoveries of Captain Cook and his study of Cook's charts. In 1774 Sandwich even introduced him to the man brought back from Tahiti and sent seed of flax found in New Zealand for him to plant.

Thereafter George III was kept fully informed of improvements in the dockyards (5), and of such setbacks as the shipwrights' strike in 1775, induced by Sandwich's attempt to introduce piecework. He kept accounts of ships building and repairing, and of oak timber in store. In 1778, during the American War, he visited Portsmouth again and on visiting the anchorage at Spithead found that ships were not preparing quickly enough to join Vice-Admiral Byron's squadron at sea. Tactfully he gave notice he would not be leaving Portsmouth until the ships had sailed, which, as he noted joyfully, 'put great alacrity into all of them; . . . I have no object but to be of use, if that is answered I am completely happy.'

1. 'George III reviewing the Fleet at Spithead, 22 June 1773', watercolour by John Cleveley the Younger (1747-1786)
NMM neg D441

2. Model of *Intrepid*, 64 guns, in frame, with the timbers all labelled; believed to be the model Sandwich sent to the King.
NMM neg D7361

3. Sheerness Dockyard model, the first of a series commissioned, possibly with the King in mind, by Sandwich in 1773. It is the most detailed and most skilful of them all.
NMM neg D7824-A

4. Oil painting of a model of *Royal George*, 100 guns, by J Marshall (*fl*1777-1779), signed and dated 1779, one of a series representing the latest ship of each rate presented to the King.
NMM ref BHC3603

5. Oil painting of Deptford Dockyard by Joseph Farrington (1747-1821).
NMM ref BHC1874

2

Parker and Clinton at Charleston, June 1776

1

OR MUCH of the war, the British Government persisted in the belief that the southern states were fundamentally loyalist in their sympathies, and an early priority was an expedition to detach the south from the revolutionary cause. Unfortunately, the need to send a relief force to Canada in the winter of 1775-76 disrupted preparations, and a fleet from England under Commodore Sir Peter Parker (1) and Major General Lord Cornwallis did not finally rendezvous with Clinton's detachment off Cape Fear until May. The loyalist uprising, meanwhile, had been put down at Moore's Bridge on 27 February.

Instead of then concentrating forces for the planned assault on New York, Clinton's orders were vague enough for him to justify an attack on Charleston (or Charlestown as it was usually spelt at the time), the major city of South Carolina (2). The navigation was tricky for large ships, but Parker should have had access to a good chart like this one from Des Barres's great *Atlantic Neptune* portfolio (3); nevertheless, it took two weeks to sound the channels and get the ships over the bar. *Bristol*, the 50-gun flagship, had to take her guns out and reduce her draught to 17ft 6in to achieve this.

The shipping channel was dominated by Sullivan (or Sulivan) Island, on which was a partly completed fort, and this was the first object of attack. Troops intended to take the fort in the rear were landed on Long Island to the northeast by 18 June—top right in the plan (4). Foul winds prevented the ships from attacking until the 28th, and what followed was a disaster. The channel between the islands, supposed to be 18 inches deep at low water turned out to be 7 feet, and Clinton had too few boats for anything more than a demonstration by way of diversion; furthermore, the Americans had already placed artillery facing the landing beach, so the army could do nothing.

Parker's ships came in boldly, the 28-gun *Active* leading the first division of the 50s *Bristol* and *Experiment* and the *Solebay*, 28, but they moored at about 350 yards range, and too far for musketry from their tops and grapeshot

3

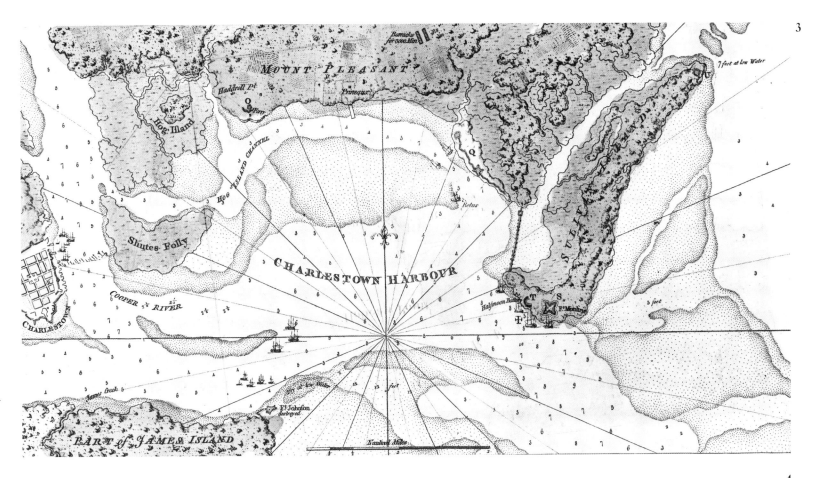

4

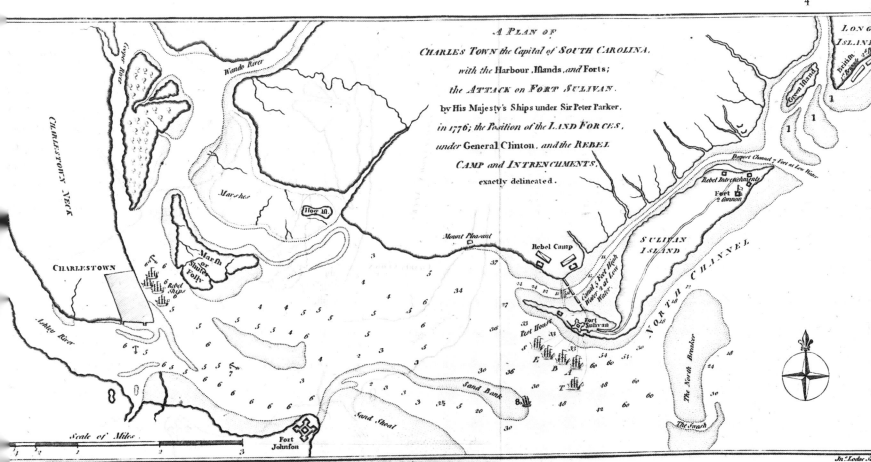

A N:bE View of the Fort on the Western end of Sulivans Island *with the Disposition of* His Majesty's *Fleet Commanded by Commodore Sir Peter Parker Kn:t &c &c &c. during the Attack on the 28:th of June 1776. which lasted 9 hours and 40 minutes.*

A. The Active 28 Guns Capt:n William, B, Bristol Commodore Sir Peter Parker Kn:t &c.&c.&c. of 50 Guns, Capt:n Morris. C Experiment 50 Guns Capt:n Scot. D Solebay 28 Guns Capt:n Simons. E Syren 28 Guns Capt:n Fourneau. F F. The Acteon of 28 Guns Capt:n Atkins and Sphynx of 20 Guns Capt:n Hunt on a Shoal the latter got off but the Acteon was burnt by our felves the next Morning as it was impoffible to get her off. G H. The Thunder Bomb Capt:n Reed with the Friendship Armed Veffel of 28 Guns Capt:n Hope. I I Mount Pleafant. K Hog Ifland. L Sulivans Ifland and Fort. M A Narrow Ifthmus. N. An Armed Hulk to defend the ifthmus. O The Continent P. The Myrtle Grove. Q. The Weftern end of Sulivans Ifland & Fort Erected upon a Peninfula.

LONDON. Engrav'd & Publifhd according to Act of Parliament Aug:t 10th 1776. by W:m Faden Corner of S:t Martins Lane Charing Crofs.

To Commodore Sir Peter Parker Kn:t &c &c &c. This View is Most humbly Dedicated and Prefented by L:t Colonel Tho:s James R:l R:t of Artillery June 30:th 1776.

5

to have any effect. The second division comprising the 28s *Actaeon* and *Syren* led by the 20-gun *Sphynx* fared even worse, all being put aground by incompetent pilots. The bomb vessel *Thunder* was anchored so far out that the mortars were overcharged to achieve the range, which soon destroyed their mounting beds.

The incomplete fort (5), commanded by Colonel Moultrie, was built of palmetto logs with a sandy interior, both of which proved capable of absorbing shot and shell. The fort was said to be armed with powerful French 36pdrs from the *Foudroyant* captured in 1758 and sent ashore by the Navy as non-standard, but only twelve actually faced the ships. The battle raged for nine and a half hours, and at various times the fort seemed to be silenced – largely from shortage of powder as it transpired – and at one point the flag was shot away, to be replaced at no small risk by Sergeant William Jasper, who promptly became one of the first heroes of the revolution.

However, most of the damage was done to the other side. At one point the spring on *Bristol*'s cable had been shot away, and the flagship turned stern-on to the fort; she lost her mizzen mast and the main was repeatedly struck. Parker had had enough but had to await the turn of the tide before withdrawing his battered ships. The second division were refloated, with the exception of the *Actaeon* which was burned by her crew the following morning to avoid capture. A number of observers sent sketches home, and from one of these (6) was engraved by William Faden; it shows the fleet lying in Five Fathom Hole the morning after the attack, with the damage to *Bristol* and *Sphynx* (which lost her bowsprit) quite apparent.

Casualties were heavy on the two 50s: *Bristol* lost 40 dead and 71 wounded, and *Experiment* 23 and 56 respectively, the frigates losing a further 1 dead and 12 wounded. The officers in particular suffered heavily, Morris the *Bristol*'s captain dying from his wounds, and even the Commodore was hit, although his report was noticeably reticent about it: '. . . I received several Contusions at different Times, but as none of them are on any Part where the least Danger can be apprehended, they are not worth mentioning . . .' The rebels were less discreet, and gleefully reported 'the Commodore's Breeches torn off – his Backside left bare . . .' This was the final indignity heaped on a botched enterprise, and too good a propaganda victory to pass up: even as the battered fleet was straggling up to New York, Whig opponents of the war were penning a satirical song, 'by Sir Peter Parker', which included the verse

Now bold as a Turk
I proceed to New York,
Where with Clinton and Howe you may find me.
I've the wind in my tail,
And am hoisting my sail,
To leave Sullivan's Island behind me.

The first major offensive by the British was marked by features that to varying degrees were to dog their efforts for the rest of the war: confused and contradictory strategic direction; subordination of sea power to land concerns, and the consequent misuse of naval assets (particularly using deep-draught warships in confined waters); and poor co-operation between army and navy. Charleston did not auger well for the British war effort.

1. Admiral Sir Peter Parker (1721-1811), oil portrait by Lemuel Abbott. *NMM ref BHC2932*

2. 'A View of Charles Town, the Capital of South Carolina in North America', published by Carington Bowles, London c1775. *NMM ref PAD7576*

3. Charleston harbour chart, engraved by J F W Des Barres, 1777 for *The Atlantic Neptune*. *NMM neg B7865*

4. 'A Plan of Charles Town the Capital of South Carolina, with the Harbour, Islands, and Forts; the Attack on Fort Sulivan by his Majesty's ships under Sir Peter Parker in 1776; the Position of the Land forces under General Clinton, and the Rebel Camp and Intrenchments exactly delineated', engraved by John Lodge, London, February 1780. Published in *Political Magazine* 1 (1780). The positions of the first division are denoted by the initial letters of the ship's names; T is the bomb *Thunder* and 8 is the *Actaeon* aground. *NMM ref PAD5326*

5. 'A N. by E. View of the fort on the western end of Sulivans Island with the Disposition of His Majesty's Fleet commanded by Commodore Sir Peter Parker Kn &c&c&c during the Attack on the 28th of June 1776, which lasted 9 hours and 40 minutes', engraved and published by William Faden, London, 10 August 1776 after an original by Lieutenant Colonel Thomas James, Royal Regiment of Artillery. The letters denote the positions of the ships during the attack: A *Active*, B *Bristol*, C *Experiment*, D *Solebay*, E *Syren* FF *Actaeon* and *Sphynx*, GH *Thunder* covered by the armed ship *Friendship*. *Beverley R Robinson Collection*

6. 'A N.W. by N. View of Charles Town from on board the Bristol Commodore Sir Peter Parker Kn &c&c taken in Five Fathom Hole the day after the Attack upon Fort Sulivan by the Commodore & his Squadron, which Action continued 9 hours & 40 minutes', engraved and published by William Faden, London, 10 August 1776 after an original by Lieutenant Colonel Thomas James, Royal Regiment of Artillery. *Beverley R Robinson Collection*

6

LONDON. Engrav'd & Publish'd according to Act of Parliament Aug.t 10th 1776. by Wm Faden Corner of St Martins Lane Charing Cross.

N.W.b.N. View of CHARLES TOWN from on board the Bristol Commodore Sir Peter Parker Kn.t &c. &c. taken in Five Fathom [Hol]e the day after the Attack upon Fort Sulivan by the Commodore & his Squadron, which Action continued 9 hours & 40 minutes.

[...]les Town, B. Ashley River, C. Fort Johnston, D. Cummins's Point, E. Part of Five Fathom Hole *where all the Fleet rode before & after the Attack of Fort Sulivan*, F. The Station of the headmost Frigate the Solebay, [...] & three quarters from Fort Sulivan Situated to the Northward of G. NB. Cummins's Point D & F. Johnston, C. bears nearly N & S, H. Part of Mount Pleasant, I. Part of Hog Island, K. Wando Riv.r L. Cooper Riv.r [...]s Island, at the Southern Point is Fort Johnston *opposite the Center of Mount Pleasant Three Miles and a ¼ distance*. N. Breakers on Charles Town Bar, O. Rebels Schooner of 12 Guns.

To Commodore Sir Peter Parker Kn.t &c. &c. &c. This View is Most humbly Dedicated and Presented by Lt. Colonel Thos. James R.l R.n of Artillery, Five Fathom Hole South Carolina, June 29th 1776.

Gunpowder—the sinews of war

THE EARLY stages of the American Revolution were hamstrung by the shortage of gunpowder; Washington was continually 'crying out for powder—powder—ye gods, give us powder'. The British had been careful to restrict the manufacture of gunpowder in the colonies, and much of the initial American activity—like the Bahamas raid and the establishment of Washington's schooner fleet—was directed towards redressing this deficiency. By contrast, the British benefited from a well-established supply organisation.

Throughout the eighteenth century, indeed until 1855, guns, ammunition and gunpowder were supplied to Britain's armed forces at home and abroad by the Board of Ordnance. The Board was headed by the Master General of the Ordnance, under whom business was conducted by a lieutenant general, surveyor general, treasurer and secretary. The Master General between 1772 and March 1782 was Viscount Townsend, a politician who sat in the Cabinet and was privy to strategic policy. The Board's central offices were located in Palace Yard, Westminster, and at the Tower of London, with their main magazine at Greenwich, between Deptford and Woolwich on the River Thames.

From this main magazine, supplies were distributed to the forts, regimental and naval depots around the British Isles, and in the form of 'artillery trains' to armies fighting overseas. Naval supplies were distributed to the Ordnance yards close to each of the main dockyards at Chatham, Portsmouth and Plymouth. These were also sent to Ordnance bases overseas, at Gibraltar, Jamaica, Antigua, Halifax and Annapolis in Nova Scotia, St Johns and Placentia in Newfoundland. From these depots they were loaded on board warships as required, to become on board the responsibility of the Gunner who also received his warrant from, and was accountable to, the Board of Ordnance.

The Board secured the bulk of its munitions by contract supply from private manufacturers. The most famous gun foundries were in the north: those of Walker and Company at Rotherham, and the Carron Company at Falkirk. Before being accepted, these cannon were tested at the Board's Royal Laboratory at Woolwich, where the Ordnance Board also cast its own brass guns. Gunpowder was obtained under contract from about ten private powder mills in Kent, Surrey, Essex and Middlesex, the counties close to London, from where it could be transported to Greenwich with relative ease and security. To secure an assured part of its supply, the Board of Ordnance purchased complexes of existing gunpowder mills at Faversham in Kent in 1759 and at Waltham Abbey in 1787.

The private manufacturers of gunpowder purchased their own raw materials—saltpetre, charcoal, and sulphur—and, after appropriate processing of them, combined them in the proportions of seventy-five, fifteen and ten per cent respectively. Charcoal was obtained locally by the controlled burning of carefully selected wood. Sulphur came mainly from Italy. It was purchased in London, and refined by distillation. Saltpetre was imported from India, especially the area around Patna in Bengal, by the East India Company. The Ordnance Board purchased an annual supply from the Company's warehouses in Rotherhithe and issued it in the quantities required to its contractors. Twenty tons of saltpetre was allowed for every 485 barrels of gunpowder. At each mill, the saltpetre was refined twice, sifted and ground.

One military advantage Britain derived from her extension of control over an increasing area of India was the capability of depriving France of a supply of saltpetre from the sub-continent. Without any supply of natural saltpetre, except at a high price from Dutch merchants, the French monarchy had to prepare its own substitute from a mixture of earth, lime and vegetable and animal refuse. By 1774 half of France's requirements were produced at home, and half came from Holland.

Compared to this shortage, the British supply of gunpowder to its armed forces was efficient. The Royal Navy never went short. Quantities were ordered after Parliament approved the estimates for the number of ships to be maintained in commission. The Admiralty gave written instructions to Board of Ordnance of the identity, size and location of every ship to be supplied, when in turn the Board sent written authority to its officers at each port to equip the stated ships. The quantities involved were vast: 540 barrels of powder to every First Rate of 100 guns for foreign service; 490 for Channel service. When necessary, to avoid shortages, supplies were redistributed between depots, for example, from Upnor Castle near Chatham on the Medway around the coast to Portsmouth. Delays in supply there were, arising from the impressment of crews from ships hired by the Board, from detainment with convoys, or from the effects of storms and adverse winds. But these were neither long-term nor owing to structural weakness in the system of supply. On the contrary, repeated wars during the eighteenth century permitted the Board of Ordnance to refine its procedures.

During the American War of Independence, moreover, experimentation by the British scientific community, at the Royal Military Academy and Royal

2

Laboratory at Woolwich (1-3), and in the mills at Faversham, contributed to improvements in methods of testing, and observations on the performance of different quantities of gunpowder with different types of shot, weights and sizes of guns. These in turn contributed to improvements in manufacture, economy of materials, and accuracy of firepower under the direction of trained gunners.

1. Woolwich Arsenal—Laboratory square facing north, anonymous watercolour, mid eighteenth century. *NMM neg C4381A*

2. Woolwich Arsenal—interior, mixing gunpowder, anonymous watercolour, mid eighteenth century. *NMM neg 4589*

3. Woolwich Arsenal—interior, moulding powder cartridges, anonymous watercolour, mid eighteenth century. *NMM ref PA10745*

3

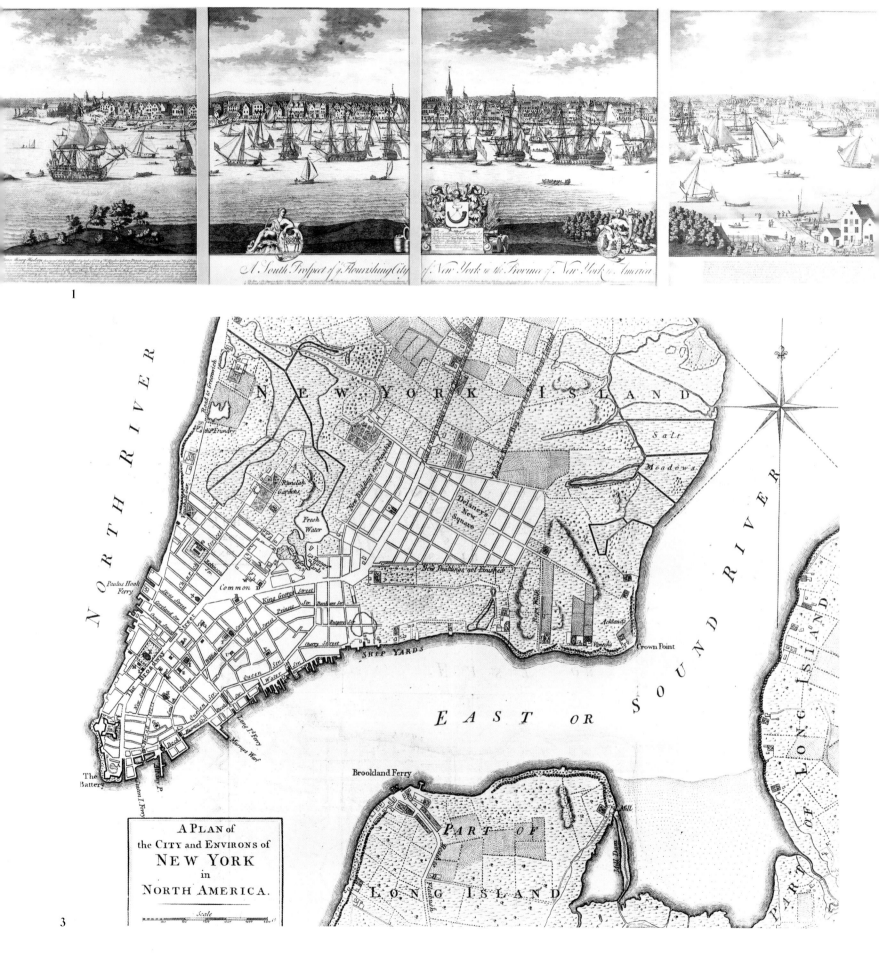

1

3

2

Assault on New York: first phase, June-August 1776

NEW YORK was the most important commercial centre in North America, and at any time before the war its superb harbour would normally have been filled with shipping (1). The harbour was one of the few places south of Halifax that could safely accommodate the whole British North America squadron in perfect safety (2), and it was also a centre of loyalist sentiment. Furthermore, with the British advancing from Canada down Lake Champlain, seizing the southern end of the Hudson promised the chance for a single knockout blow. This was dissipated by administrative

delays and ministerial confusion: Clinton was allowed to waste resources in an abortive attack on Charlestown, and the main reinforcements from Britain did not arrive until August.

Having rested and reorganised his troops at Halifax, General Howe finally sailed on 12 June, but his destination was an open secret. At that time New York City was confined to the lower end of Manhattan (3), and its defences were mainly directed seawards, so a direct assault was unlikely. The Americans were well prepared to defend the high ground of Long Island, the probable

4

5

the fleet made an impressive sight, and was sketched by an officer present on 12 July (4), showing the arrival of the 64-gun *Eagle*, flying the flag of the new naval commander, Lord Howe (5), the general's brother.

While the army was kicking its heels waiting for reinforcements from England, the Navy decided to send a squadron up the Hudson, '. . . to cut off and intercept Supplies coming to New York . . .' *Phoenix* of 44 guns, *Rose*, 20 and the schooner *Tryal*, plus two tenders, broke through the incomplete defences on 12 July and for a month operated with impunity against Washington's lines of communication. He regarded it as a reconnaissance for a possible flanking manoeuvre, and made it a priority to drive them out: indeed, at that time General Clinton was making a strong case for seizing Kingsbridge, in order to trap the whole American army on Long Island, so Washington's fears were reasonable. The best planned attack on the British squadron was by fireships and galleys on the night of 16 August, which burnt the tender *Charlotta* and narrowly avoided setting fire to the *Phoenix* (6). The ships returned to the fleet two days later, once more running the gauntlet of Hudson defences with minimal damage.

invasion route. However, on 3 July Howe began landing troops on Staten Island from 120 transports under the guns of the *Chatham, Centurion, Rose, Swan* and *Senegal*; opposition was non-existent. Moored just inside the Narrows,

In the meantime the long-awaited reinforcements had finally arrived, the main body of eighty-five transports under Commodore William Hotham's convoy dropping anchor on 12 August. Two day later Parker's

6

7

battered squadron from Charleston joined, and the Howe brothers then had 25,000 troops and 350 ships at their disposal—'Such a Fleet', said the Admiral's secretary, 'was never seen together in America before.' A week later the invasion began in earnest, with a shore-to-shore assault across the narrows to Gravesend Bay on Long Island. Although this engraving (7) was done a generation later, it has the main features right. There were 75 flat boats in three divisions, 11 batteaux and 2 galleys, covered by *Phoenix, Rose, Greyhound* and the bombs *Thunder* and *Carcass* (seen in the foreground), and such was the efficiency of the operation under Hotham's direction that 15,000 men and 40 guns were ashore before noon.

The main features of the geography of the area can be seen from this contemporary map (8), and the oppportunities for exploiting the flexibility of British seapower in flanking operations is apparent. Despite some argument to the contrary—particularly from Clinton—General Howe chose a more conventional route. On the night of 26/27 August he attacked the American positions, and although his ensuing victory was tactically brilliant (9) he threw away his advantage by not ordering an immediate frontal assault on the feeble defences of Brooklyn Heights where the Americans had retreated. The casualties of Bunker Hill cast a long shadow.

The Navy's sole contribution to the victory was a demonstration against Red Hook fort, and the fleet lay comfortably at anchor (10) instead of penetrating the East River to enfilade the American positions. On the night of 29/30 August, with a north wind blowing so the ships could not then intervene, Washington withdrew the remnant of his army, some 10,000 men and all but their heaviest equipment, across to Manhattan without interference; thereafter he swore to avoid pitched battles, but he had mastered the art of tactical withdrawl.

1. 'A South Prospect of ye Flourishing City of New York in the Province of New York in America', engraving on four sheets by John Harris after an original by William Burgis, 1717. Prints Collection, Miriam and Ira D Wallach Division of Art, Prints and Photography, New York Public Library. *New York Public Library*

2. 'View of New York with the Entrance of the North and East Rivers', about 1773, coloured aquatint published by J F W Des Barres, London, 1779. From *The Atlantic Neptune*. The southernmost tip of Manhatten Island, the Battery, is in the centre. *NMM neg 6254*

3. 'A Plan of the City and Environs of New York, in North America . . . 1776', etching by P Andrews after an original by John Montresor, published by A Dury, London, 1776. *NMM neg 6252*

4. View of the Narrows between Long Island and Staten Island, showing the British fleet at anchor, with Lord Howe's flagship, *Eagle*, 12 July 1776. From Archibald Robertson's *Sketches of America*. Prints Collection, Miriam and Ira D Wallach Division of Art, Prints and Photography, New York Public Library. *New York Public Library*

5. Lord Howe in later life, oil painting by John Singleton Copley (1737-1815). *NMM neg BHC2790*

6. 'The *Phoenix* and the *Rose* Engaged by the Enemy's Fire Ships and Galleys on the 16 Aug 1776', engraved by J F W Des Barres from a painting by Dominic Serres after a sketch of Sir James Wallace. From *The Atlantic Neptune*. *Beverley R Robinson Collection, Annapolis*

7. 'Disembarkation of the troops at Gravesend Bay under the command of Sir George Collier, RN', engraving by Bailey published by Joyce Gold, London, 30 November 1814. *NMM ref PAD5328*

8. 'A Sketch of the Operations of His Majesty's Fleet and Army . . . in 1776', (detail) engraved and published by J F W Des Barres, 17 January 1777. *The Atlantic Neptune*. *NMM neg B9384b*

9. An analysis of the Battle of Long Island, 27 August 1776, engraved for Stedman's *American War*, London 1794. *Chatham Collection*

10. An original sketch by an English officer on board one of Admiral Howe's fleet while at anchor in New York harbour, just after the Battle of Long Island. A watercolour, possibly by Thomas Davies, purchased from the estate of a descendant of Lord Rawdon. Emmet Collection. Prints Collection, Miriam and Ira D Wallach Division of Art, Prints and Photography, New York Public Library. *New York Public Library*

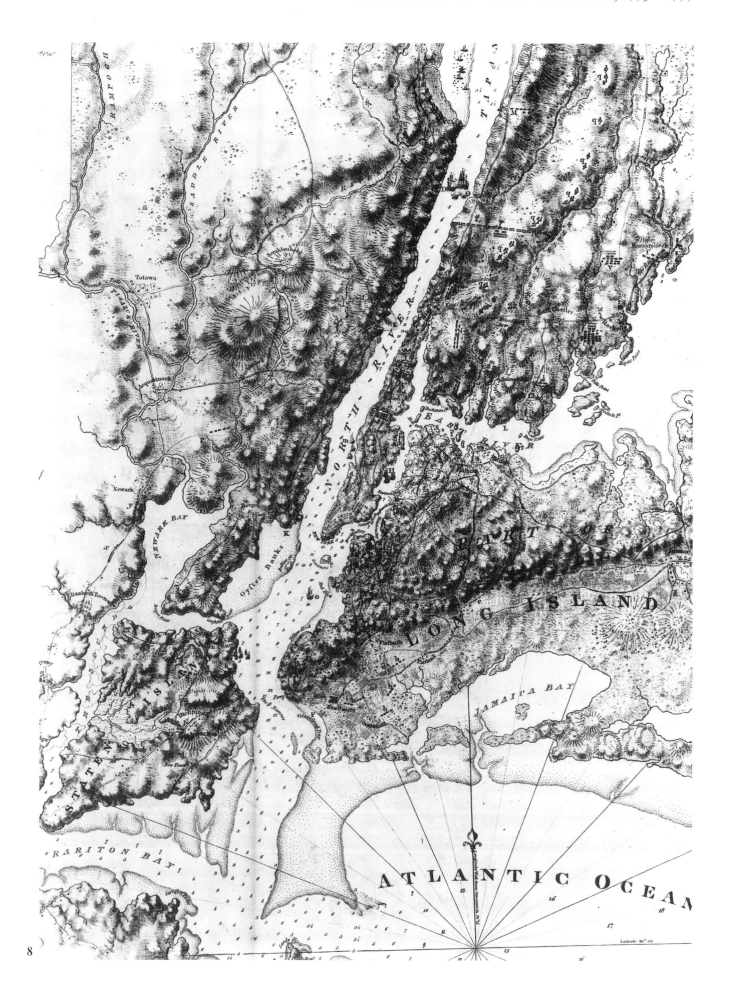

9

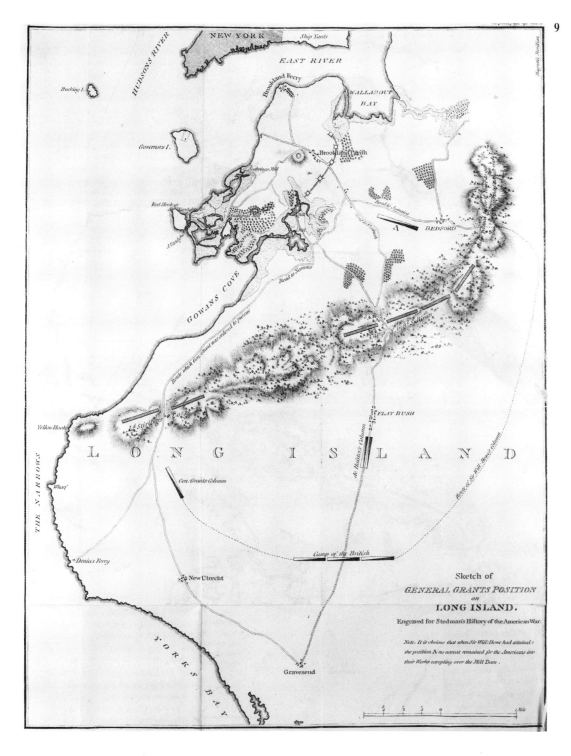

Sketch of
GENERAL GRANTS POSITION
on
LONG ISLAND.
Engraved for Stedman's History of the American War.

Note. It is obvious that when Sir Will. Howe had attained
the position A no retreat remained for the Americans into
their Works excepting over the Mill Dam.

10

Colonial warfare vessels

BEFORE THE entrance of France into the war, the struggle in America was carried on with a very distinct part of the Royal Navy's resources. In peacetime, it was rare for ships of the line to serve on foreign stations, although the more important might warrant a 64-gun ship (1)–the smallest rate regularly allowed in the line of battle–as flagship. Such vessels

1

2

were simply too expensive in manpower and, unless there was an identifiable threat, an unnecessarily powerful asset to have lying abroad. As the American troubles escalated, reinforcements included a few 64s, but the British government was simultaneously faced with the problem of dissuading its European rivals from taking advantage of the situation. The best method was to have a well-prepared fleet at home, and in August 1775 the three North American guardships–*Asia, Somerset, Boyne,* 64s–were ordered to return, to be replaced with 50s and 44s.

These latter, both small two-deckers, were to become the colonial warfare vessels, *par excellence.* The 50-gun ship (2) was in any case the standard colonial flagship, being the smallest vessel equipped with enough accommodation for a flag officer. Their main battery was comprised of 24pdrs like the 64, but with a nominal crew of 350 instead of 500 and a mean draught at about 18ft some 3ft less than a 64. The 'shallowness' of the draught was relative, as Parker's *Bristol* discovered before Fort Sullivan, but the 64 should never have been risked in estuarial waters: the *Augusta* was destroyed in the Delaware in October 1777 while the *Defiance* was wrecked on Savannah bar in 1780. One reason why two-deckers were necessary was the labour-intensive nature of army support work, as Sir Andrew Snape Hamond pointed out:

> You can have no idea of the number of men it takes to attend upon such an army as this; . . . when all the flat boats, galleys, gondolas, horse stages &c &c are mann'd there is scarce men enough left on board many of the ships to move them so that we really want six or eight line of battle ships; not so much perhaps for the use of the ships; as for their large complements of men for the purposes before mentioned.

Also popular for service in North America was the 44-gun ship (3), an obsolescent two-decked design that had effectively been replaced as a cruiser by the new frigate. However, the type staged a revival during the American War, because their 18pdr main battery was considered more than a match for most privateers, and in their usual colonial role–supporting the army–the second deck provided more concentrated firepower for shore bombardment duties. The two-decked layout, tall for its length, made them poor performers under sail, but they were effective in the defensive convoy escort role, as *Serapis* proved when her convoy escaped before she surrendered to John Paul Jones.

3

The other great requirement for the North American station was for small cruisers, initially for blockading a long and heavily indented coastline, and then for the protection of transports and merchantmen against the increasingly effective colonial privateering campaign. At first these tended to be sloops of 10-16 guns (4), like the *Kingfisher* and *Otter* that attacked Norfolk, Virginia in January 1776; these were combined with small Sixth Rates of 20 and 24 guns (5), like the *Glasgow* that fought off Esek Hopkins's squadron, and the larger frigate-built 28s, like the *Active* depicted here (6) or the *Actaeon* lost before Charleston. Eventually, with the building of frigates for the Continental Navy, the standard 12pdr-armed 32 (7), was sent to America in large numbers. By the time a general mobilisation of the Channel Fleet was ordered towards the end of 1776, there were no small cruisers left in Britain fit for sea.

The very smallest warships were also in great demand, for dispatch duties and for operating close inshore. Cutters were the most common British type, mostly hired or purchased rather than purpose-built, but in American waters the local type, the schooner, was usually preferred.

Basic data for typical ships, and a few examples of each that played important parts in the war, are given below:

64-gun ships, like *Eagle, Somerset, Augusta, Nonsuch, Raisonable, St Albans, Yarmouth, Asia*
Typical dimensions: 160ft x 44ft x 19ft, 1370 tons
Armament: 26-24pdrs, 26-18pdrs, 12-9pdrs, 500 men

50-gun ships, like *Isis, Bristol, Chatham, Preston, Centurion, Renown*
Typical dimensions: 146ft x 40ft x 17ft, 1045 tons
Armament: 22-24pdrs, 22-12pdrs, 6-6pdrs, 350 men

4

5

44-gun ships, like *Roebuck, Phoenix, Rainbow, Serapis*
Typical dimensions: 140ft x 38ft x 16ft, 879 tons
Armament: 20-18pdrs, 22-9pdrs, 2-6pdrs, 300 men

32-gun frigates, like *Emerald, Repulse, Flora, Brune, Niger, Juno, Lark, Orpheus, Pearl*
Typical dimensions: 125ft x 35ft x 12ft, 679 tons
Armament: 26-12pdrs, 6-6pdrs, 220 men

28-gun frigates, like *Active, Greyhound, Surprise, Solebay, Cerberus, Lizard, Liverpool, Guadeloupe*
Typical dimensions: 118ft x 33ft x 10ft, 586 tons
Armament: 24-9pdrs, 4-3pdrs, 200 men

20-gun ships, like *Rose, Sphynx, Glasgow, Camilla, Unicorn, Ariel, Squirrel, Galatea*
Typical dimensions: 108ft x 30ft x 10ft, 430 tons
Armament: 20-9pdrs, 160 men

Ship sloops, like *Swan, Martin, Tamar, Kingfisher, Otter*
Typical dimensions: 97ft x 27ft x 13ft, 300 tons
Armament: 14 or 16-6pdrs, 125 men

Cutters, like *Alert*
Typical dimensions: 69ft x 26ft x 11ft, 180 tons
Armament: 10-4pdrs, 45 men

---

1. A 64-gun ship from a portfolio of ship drawings by Edward Gwyn of about 1775.
NMM ref PAG3811

2. A 50-gun ship, watercolour portrait by Thomas Mitchell of about 1770.
NMM ref PAI2613

3. The 44-gun ship *Argo*, launched in 1781, watercolour by Thomas Buttersworth, 1799.
NMM ref PAH9510

4. A ship rigged sloop from a portfolio of ship drawings by Edward Gwyn of about 1775. Although the vessel cannot be precisely identified, a number of designs of the 1760s featured the characteristic lute stern shown in this drawing.
NMM ref PAG3815

5. 'A Sixth Rate on the stocks', oil painting by John Cleveley the Elder (*c*1712-1777), signed and dated 1758.
NMM ref BHC 1045

6. 'The *Active* Frigate, in Stays, in a Light Breeze, off the back of the Isle of Wight', published by Carington Bowles, London, 19 May 1783. Despite the date, the ship depicted is closer in detail to the 28 lost in 1778 than the 32 built in 1780, which emphasises the fact that the subjects of prints are often of a much earlier period than publication date would suggest.
NMM ref PAD7564

7. A pen and ink sketch of a British 32-gun frigate by an unknown hand, but of eighteenth-century, foreign provenance.
NMM ref PAD8512

Assault on New York: second phase, September–November 1776

SEPTEMBER, WITH the campaigning season running out, saw little sense of urgency from the Howe
brothers. Besides being military commanders, they
were charged by the British government with trying to
arrange a negotiated settlement and they never pursued
the war—about which they personally harboured very
mixed feelings—with anything like ruthlessness. Ships

were sent to Hell's Gate, the turbulent waters where Long
Island Sound meets the East River, and two of the islands
were occupied, threatening to cut off Washington's
retreat northward, but when the main offensive opened
it was directed at Kip's Bay, in lower Manhattan (1) on 15
September. Another superbly drilled shore-to-shore
assault followed a tremendous bombardment by *Phoenix*,

1

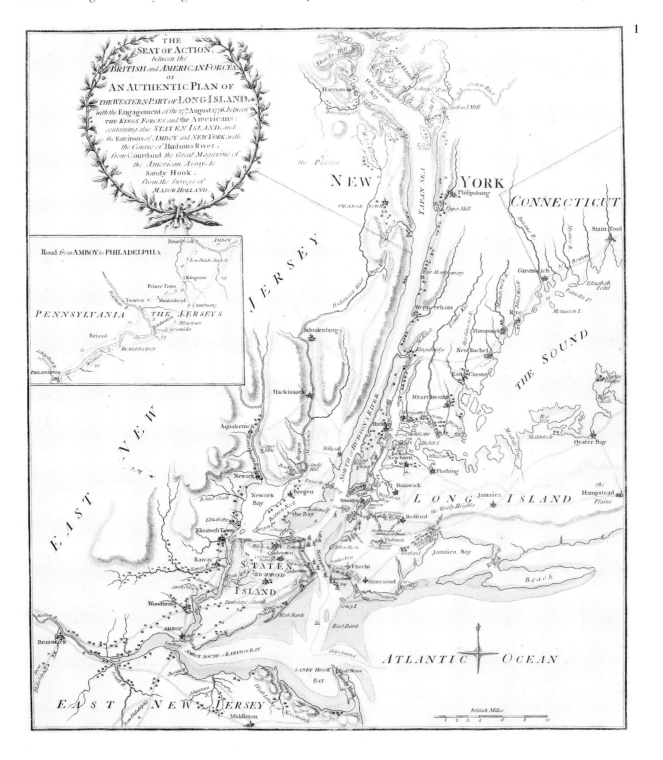

2

Roebuck, Orpheus (which expended 5376lbs of powder in 45 minutes), *Carysfort* and *Rose*, landing almost without opposition; while *Renown, Repulse, Pearl* and *Tryal* staged a diversion in the Hudson. Howe did not immediately press on across the island, and yet again large numbers of American troops were allowed to escape.

Nevertheless, New York was finally taken, and a senior British officer, Lord Percy, expressed a common view that 'this business is pretty near over'. Howe settled down to consolidate his gains. A panorama drawn some years later (2) shows what the city looked like after it had recovered from the disastrous fire of 19/20 September.

To allow free access to the Hudson, the battery opposite on Paulus Hook needed to be eliminated and *Roebuck, Tartar, Emerald* and *Carcass* achieved this without fuss on the 23rd. However, the Navy's most audacious contribu-

tion to the campaign was to be another penetration of the Hudson, but this time as far north as the Tappan Zee. On 9 October Hyde Parker's *Phoenix* led the *Roebuck, Tartar, Tryal* and two tenders up the river, piloted by a man who claimed to know a way through the obstructions emplaced by the Americans. At the last moment the pilot's nerve gave out, and Parker was left to his own devices, so he took the ships close in to the eastern shore where he knew there was deep water—and right under the guns of Fort Washington, as dramatically depicted in Thomas Mitchell's painting (3). The ships suffered 9 killed and 18 wounded, but drove on to capture two of the defending galleys, a schooner and two sloops. When she was careened later the *Roebuck* was found to have two 32pdr shot embedded 4ft below the waterline fired from the elevated battery on the Jersey shore.

2

A View of the City of NEW-YORK from Brooklyn Heights, foot of Pierrepont St, in 1798 by Monsieur

3

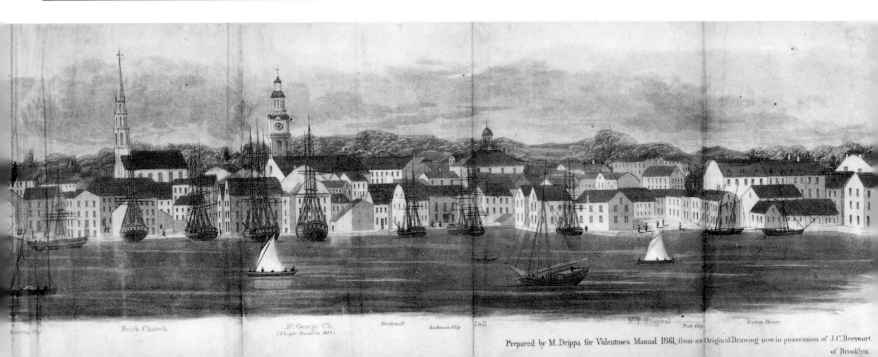

Prepared by M. Dripps for Valentines Manual 1861, from an Original Drawing now in possession of J.C. Brevourt of Brooklyn.

1. 'The Seat of the Action between the British and American Forces or an Authentic Plan of the Western Part of Long Island, with the Engagement of the 27th August 1776 ... From the Surveys of Major Holland', published by Robert Sayer and John Bennet, London, 22 October 1776. The inset shows the road from Amboy to Philadelphia. *NMM ref PAH7766*

2. 'A View of the City of New York from Brooklyn Heights foot of Pierrepoint Street in 1798', for *Valentine's Manual* 1861, hand coloured engraving by M Dripps after an original by C B Julien. *NMM negs 6245-6248*

3. Parker's *Phoenix* (right to left) leads the *Roebuck, Tartar, Tryal* and two tenders past the batteries on the Hudson, 9 October 1776. Oil painting by Thomas Mitchell (1735-1790). *NMM neg BHC0420*

4. 'A Plan of the operations of the King's Army ... in New York and East New Jersey ... from the 12th of October, to the 28th of November 1776. Wherein is particularly distinguished The Engagement on the White Plains, the 28th October.' By Claude Joseph Sauthier; engraved by William Faden, 1777. This version produced 12 April 1793 for Stedman's *American War*, London 1794. *NMM neg A4113*

5. 'A Topographical Map of the North Part of New York Island, Exhibiting the Plan of Fort Washington ... which were Forced by the Troops under the Command of The Rt Honble Earl Percy on the 16th Nov 1776, and Surveyed immediately after by Order of his Lordship, By Claude Joseph Sauthier ...' Engraved by William Faden. This version produced 12 April 1793 for Stedman's *American War*, London 1794. *NMM ref PAF4632*

6. The landing of the British forces in the Jerseys on 20 November 1776 under the command of Lord Cornwallis. A watercolour, possibly by Captain Thomas Davies, of the Royal Regiment of Artillery. Emmet Collection. Prints Collection, Miriam and Ira D Wallach Division of Art, Prints and Photography, New York Public Library. *New York Public Library*

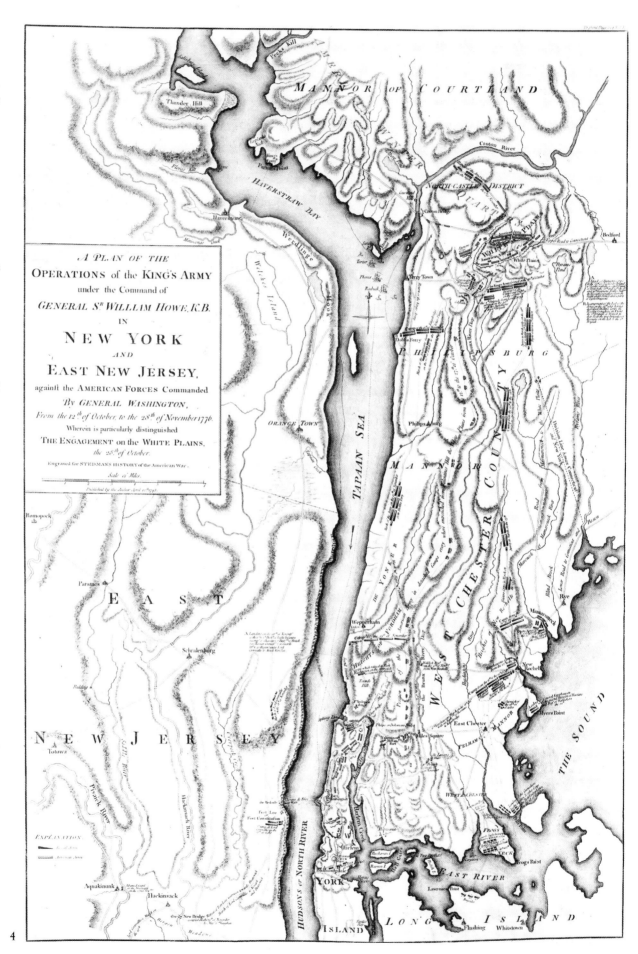

4

One little-known consequence of this action was that the British sank 'a sloop, which had on board the machine, invented by, and under the direction of, a Mr Bushnell, intended to blow up British ships' (General Heath's Memoirs). This was the famous submarine *Turtle*, which had already made one attack on Howe's flagship, the *Eagle*, on 7 September, although the British had scarcely noticed – Howe's secretary noted, 'A slight alarm happened to-night from the Enemy's boats approaching too near;… Their intention was, as we apprehend, to bring down 2 or 3 fire-ships to set adrift in the Fleet.' Unfortunately, there are no known contemporary illustrations of *Turtle*; even the familiar cutaway drawing was only produced in 1875 and is a speculative reconstruction.

During October a campaign of manoeuvre was undertaken against Washington's army, spurred on by a reinforcement of 7000 Hessians who arrived from England on the 16th. Landings in Westchester at Throg's Neck after a hair-raising night passage of Hell Gate, and Pell's Point, forced an American retreat to White Plains, and in the ensuing battle the outflanked Americans were again extricated by Washington without huge losses (4). However, he did leave behind a garrison at Fort Washington, and in the middle of November it was captured (5) with nearly 3000 prisoners taken after a co-ordinated assault in which the frigate *Pearl* gave fire support. The fort had a twin, Fort Lee or Constitution on the opposite shore, and two days later, on 20 November, Cornwallis and 4500 men crossed the Hudson to scramble up the Palisades (6) to the north of the fort. When they arrived, the garrison had retreated, and the British were masters of the lower Hudson.

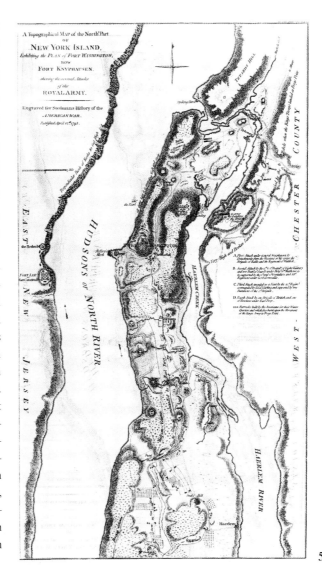

5

6

Rhode Island: a textbook amphibious operation

WITH NEW YORK apparently secured at the end of November an expedition was prepared to capture Newport, Rhode Island, to provide the British fleet with an alternative base. The force of 7000 men in 51 transports with an escort of 15 warships was commanded by the team of Parker and Clinton discredited at Charleston—but this time there were to be no mistakes. Having sailed up the western channel and around Conanicut Island, to avoid the defensive batteries, the fleet anchored off Newport on 7 December. Esek Hopkins's small Continental squadron, including the frigates *Warren, Columbus* and *Providence,* retired up Narragansett Bay to Providence, and on the 8th the British went ashore against virtually no opposition (1).

Throughout the war, as Washington knew to his cost, seapower gave the British forces a degree of mobility he could never match. As the New York campaign had just proved, the British were masters of the techniques of amphibious warfare: mastery built on the hard-won experience of the preceding Seven Years War, where the unprecedented successes at Louisbourg, Quebec, Belle Isle, Martinique and Havana had all depended on seaborne landings. Key to success was planning and organisation. Indeed, the Royal Navy had already discovered the need for what the US Marine Corps in the Second World War came to call 'combat loading'—the preservation of the army's fighting formations during transportation so they could be put ashore in battle order. Division of responsibility was also worked out in this war, it being the Navy's task to put the troops safely ashore, from where the army took over.

For the Rhode Island operation, the transports were

1

 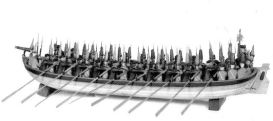

2

arranged in four divisions, each commanded by a naval lieutenant and every unit distinguished by its own pennant. The first division, of light infantry, grenadiers, and artillery, were the assault troops and intended to form the first wave to land; the second division comprised the British Third and Fifth Brigades, the third was made up of the Hessian Corps, and the fourth was the cavalry. The landings began at 8am and, with the exception of 400 men of the 22nd Regiment sent directly to Newport, all these units were ashore by 3pm.

Another lesson of the Second World War was the need for specialist landing craft, and it was the eighteenth-century predecessors of these that allowed the British to put troops ashore so quickly. After the abortive raid on Rochefort in 1757, a special type of flat-bottomed boat—'flat-boats' for short—was developed. These were usually 36ft by 10ft, rowed by ten seamen a side, and carried two rows of soldiers facing inward down the centre (2); there were also smaller 32ft sixteen-oared versions, and depending on size, flat-boats could carry forty to sixty troops. The internal fittings were removable so the boats could be stacked on the decks of transports. The carriage of artillery was a problem—as can be seen from the boats in the foreground of the painting (1)—and specially large craft with a lowering bow ramp were built at Staten Island for the New York campaign.

Troops embarked from the transports and the flat-boats were then organised into echelons reflecting the army's order of battle and formed up into parallel lines. To aid deployment, boats had numbers painted on their bows and flew small flags denoting the units they carried. There were never enough of such craft, and the naval officers who had charge of them became adept at landing troops quickly to return to the transports for the next wave.

Opposed landings required fire support, and the boats themselves could be fitted with small guns, but the massed fire of supporting warships was far more effective. This became so clear during operations like Kips Bay that the Royal Navy fitted out a shallow draught merchantman with sixteen 24pdrs especially for shore bombardment duties. This ship, the *Vigilant*, was kept very busy in the subsequent campaigns.

1. 'The occupation of Newport, Rhode Island, December 1776', black and watercolour pen and ink by Robert Cleverley (1749-1809), signed and dated 1777. The artist was an eyewitness to the event, serving at the time as captain's clerk in the *Asia*.
NMM neg 2891

2. Contemporary models of flat-bottomed boats carrying troops.
NMM neg 2892

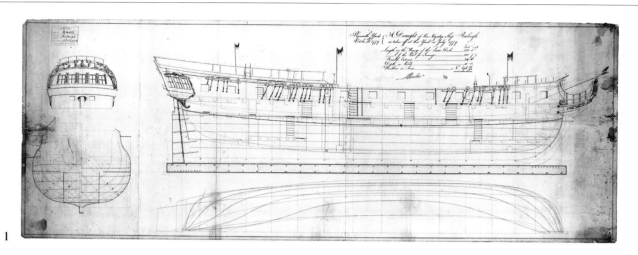

1

The Continental Navy

CONGRESS HAD been considering a naval force since at least August 1775, and took the first steps to purchase two vessels in October in order to intercept British transports, with a further, larger, pair authorised later in the month. These became the brigs *Cabot* and *Andrew Doria* (sixteen 6pdrs each) and the ships *Alfred* and *Columbus* (twenty and eighteen 9pdrs respectively, plus ten 6pdrs). Before the end of the year, regulations for the new navy had been drafted and a Marine Corps established, but the decisive move was the construction of thirteen frigates ordered on 13 December 1775–five each of 32 and 28 guns and three 24s, all to be completed by the end of March following. This was wildly ambitious: in the previous war the British had built a few frigates from softwoods in this timescale as an experiment, but they had well organised and vastly experienced dockyards, and the unseasoned timber

made the resulting ships very short-lived.

In the event, none was completed by March, but overcoming amazing shortages of skills, materials and–above all–guns, their builders got some of them to sea during 1776. Perhaps most remarkable of all was the quality of the ships as naval architecture. Very few merchant ships ever reached the size of a frigate, so there was no direct experience in the colonies of this scale of ship-building, yet most of the ships were highly regarded by their opponents. The 32-gun *Providence* captured in 1780 was judged too 'full and burthensome' to make a man of war, but other captured frigates like *Raleigh* (1) were happily accepted into British service. In general, these early frigates were somewhat larger than their British sisters, but smaller than the largest French cruisers, and their hull forms followed British models. Main batteries, even for the smaller rates, usually comprised 12pdrs, but

2

shortages sometimes resulted in rather mixed armaments. In fact, the colonial shipbuilding industry was sufficiently competent—and confident—to build a ship of the line, but this ship was transferred on completion to the French navy as *America* in 1782.

Unfortunately, it was easier to build good ships than to forge an efficient naval service, and even when they could evade the blockade most of the frigates were soon captured or destroyed in action. Lack of *esprit de corps* can be seen in the action in which the 32-gun *Hancock* was lost, despite an earlier success in which, with the smaller *Boston*, she had captured the 28-gun *Fox*, the first major Royal Navy warship to surrender to an American on the high seas. Manley of the *Hancock* did not see eye to eye with McNeill of the *Boston* and little cooperation was forthcoming when on 7 July 1777 they ran into a British squadron consisting of the 44-gun *Rainbow* and the 32-gun *Flora*. Francis Holman painted a series of three oils showing the course of the action for Captain Brisbane of the *Flora*, two of which are reproduced here (2 and frontispiece). In the first *Flora* is engaging *Hancock* while *Boston* tacks out of the battle (both American ships have lateen sails on their ensign staffs, which accords with British intelligence reports on their rig); the *Fox* is escaping to the left while the two-decked *Rainbow* comes up under all plain sail. In the second (frontispiece), the faster *Flora* has tacked to pursue, and eventually retake, the *Fox*, while *Rainbow* goes after the *Hancock*. McNeill was court-martialled for not supporting his senior officer and Manley was censured for the loss of his ship, but renamed *Iris* the *Hancock* became a very highly regarded cruiser in the Royal Navy.

Although this first generation of frigates were not as radical as the *Constitution* class of the 1790s, the originality of American thinking is apparent in some of the later vessels. The big 970-ton *Confederacy*, built at Norwich, Connecticut, in 1778, for example, was a galley-frigate, with a complete tier of oar-ports on the lower deck. In many ways, she was a return to a concept abandoned half a century earlier, but on a massive scale. The ship, captured in 1781, was unusual enough to attract the artist Edward Gwyn, who included a portrait of the ship in his portfolio (3). However, she did not impress her captors, who found her weakly built and suffering premature decay, the ship being broken up shortly after reaching England in 1782.

However, the most unusual American warship of this period was the Dutch-built *Indien*, which as the *South Carolina* was to enter the service of that state after a very convoluted history. She was designed by the Chevalier Boux, who had been trying for years to interest the French navy in his ideas for very heavily armed frigates—indeed when captured in 1783 she was carrying twenty-

3

eight French 36pdrs, ten 12pdrs and two 9pdrs, more than a match for a British 64. There is a plan of the ship in Admiral Paris's famous portfolio *Souvenirs de Marine*, but there is also a naïve painting thought to represent the ship (4). Some historians would like to see a link between this immensely powerful vessel and the 'pocket battleship' concept of the *Constitution* and her sisters. Some experience with building large vessels was gained during the war when a single 74-gun ship of the line was built, but this ship never served the American Navy.

Most of the states also had their own navies, New Jersey and Delaware being the exceptions, and some of these forces predated the Continental Navy by a few months. Massachusetts and South Carolina boasted significant numbers of seagoing cruisers, but the prime concern for most of the local navies was coast and river defence, for which galleys and gunboats were the best weapons—as the Royal Navy found to its cost in the Delaware and Hudson.

4

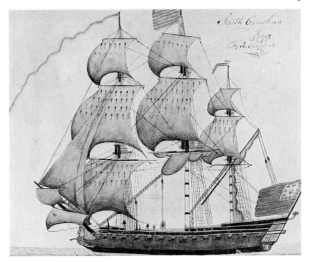

1. Frigate *Raleigh*, lines plan as taken off at Plymouth, July 1779. Admiralty Collection.
NMM neg 2400

2. *Flora* and *Rainbow* engaging *Hancock*, *Boston* and *Fox*, 7 July 1777. Oil painting by Francis Holman (d 1790), done in 1779 for Captain Brisbane of the *Flora*. *Peabody Essex Museum, Salem MA neg 20,038b*

3. A portrait of a frigate from the sketchbook of Edward Gwyn. The unique design of the ship, and the agreement between the drawing and the surviving Admiralty draught in such details as the number of gun- and oarports makes certain its identification with the *Confederate*, ex-*Confederacy*.
NMM ref PAG3813

4. Painting by Jonathan Phippen, dated 1793, of the *South Carolina*. *Peabody Essex Museum, Salem MA neg 15637*

Guerre de course

FOR CENTURIES attack on the enemy's trade had been a well understood strategy of maritime warfare, a strategy enshrined in the French term *guerre de course.* For the nascent states of America, with a large seafaring population, an extensive coastline of inlets, bays and estuaries that defied total blockade (1), but no existing naval forces, such an approach was inevitable. Decades of evading the Royal Navy's anti-smuggling patrols produced natural raiders, and the capture of British merchantmen became the primary mission of privateers and official naval forces alike.

Privateers were free-enterprise warships, armed, crewed and paid for by merchants who gambled on the dividend of a valuable capture. Both the Continental Congress and individual states granted licences, and there were also the similar 'Letters of Marque' which were issued to ships going on normal cargo-carrying voyages that might take a prize if the opportunity arose. It is known that during the course of the war Congress granted privateering commissions to nearly 1700 vessels, carrying an aggregate of 15,000 guns and employing over

58,000 men. The numbers grew from 34 in 1776 to a maximum of 550 in 1781, and among the states Massachusetts was the most active, followed by Pennsylvania, Maryland and Connecticut; apart from about 100 tiny galleys and boats, the main types used were about evenly divided between schooners and sloops on the one hand, and larger brigs and ships on the other. Vessels like the *Oliver Cromwell* (2), of 248 tons, and 24 guns (6pdrs), were at the top end of the spectrum, although there were a few significantly bigger privateers. Allowing for duplication, the efforts of individual states and those commissioned abroad, it is calculated that some 2000 vessels took part in the privateering war.

Although many see the small fleet that George Washington commissioned during the siege of Boston as the beginnings of a national navy, it was conceived with a specific raiding purpose in mind. His army was desperately short of military stores, and especially gunpowder —90 per cent of all American gunpowder used before 1777 was brought in by sea—while the British were regularly supplied by storeships that were next to unarmed

1

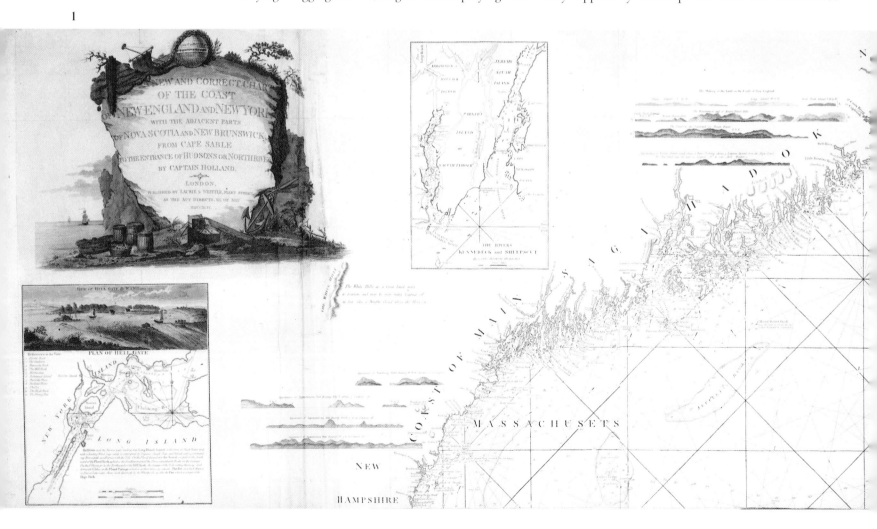

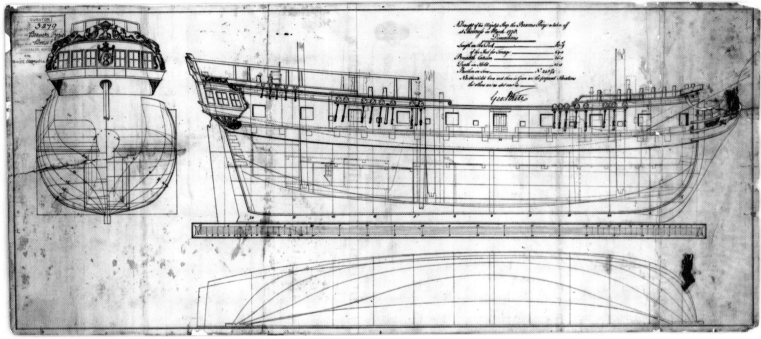

2

and rarely convoyed. A handful of Marblehead fishing schooners, armed with four or six tiny 4pdrs and 2pdrs, made a number of spectacular captures, perhaps the

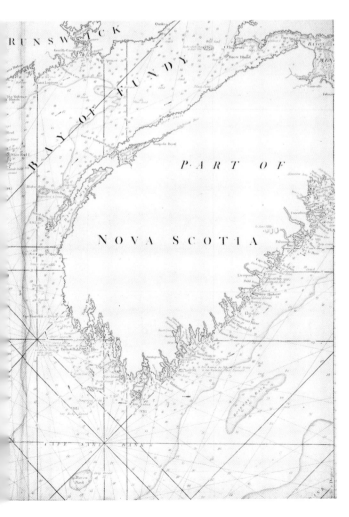

most valuable being the ordnance transport *Hope*, whose manifest included 75 tons of powder, taken by the *Franklin* on 17 May 1776. Her master, James Mugford, was killed in the bloody repulse of a British boat attack shortly afterwards, and is reckoned to be portrayed in the cameo inset of a naïve portrait of the *Franklin* thought to be the work of Thomas Russell, the first lieutenant (3). The schooner flies an ensign of a green pine tree on a white ground, the flag flown by the floating batteries around Boston, and regarded as the earliest specifically naval ensign of the rebellious colonies. It usually carried the slogan 'Appeal to Heaven' on the reverse.

Typical of their exploits was an attack by the schooners *Harrison* and *Washington* on a storeship off the Massachusetts coast on 23 November which was driven off by the frigate *Tartar*; but the *Harrison* slipped back the following day, boarded and set fire to one transport, which was then at anchor within sight of Boston light and the British fleet. She was pursued by the sloop *Raven*, 14 guns, but escaped after a three-hour chase. A painting of this episode (4) seems to conflate these two actions by portraying two schooners attacking the anchored storeship.

Not content with operations off their own coast, the Americans decided to take the fight to their enemy's doorstep. Lambert Wickes led the way, with the 16-gun brig *Reprisal* which cruised very succesfully in the Irish Sea in the spring of 1777 in company with the brig *Lexington* and cutter *Dolphin*. He was followed by Gustavus Conyngham, a merchant master stranded in France who was able to obtain a commission and fit out firstly the lugger *Surprise* and then the cutter *Revenge*. His

3

achievements included a much publicised capture of a mail packet (5), and he rapidly became a bogey figure to the English. In truth, American commerce raiders were far more daring than their French and Dutch predecessors, operating in coastal waters long regarded as sacrosanct, and sparking panic and indignation in proportion —eleven ships were taken in five days in June 1777, for example, between Kintyre and the northern Irish coast. Diplomatic pressure was exerted to have American pri-

vateers expelled from French ports, with occasional success, but France generally turned a blind eye to these activities.

Most of the best British cruisers were already on the North America station by 1777, and local defence was mostly in the hands of the old and slow ex-merchantmen employed as guardships. Nevertheless, it was a dangerous business and on 19 September the *Lexington* became the first overseas loss to the Continental Navy when she was captured after a long fight by the 10-gun naval cutter *Alert* (6).

For captured American seamen, the prospects were grim. The relatively lucky ones went to shoreside prisons like Forton at Portsmouth or Mill at Plymouth, but most dreaded were the prison hulks (7). These superannuated warships were a common method of confinement in Britain for both convicts and prisoners of war, and similar measures were taken in America. Several hulks were moored off New York, in Wallabout Bay, the most notorious being the *Jersey*, a converted 60-gun ship. She was described by one inmate, Ebenezer Fox, thus:

Her external appearance was forbidding and gloomy. She was dismantled; her only spars were the bowsprit, a derrick that looked like a gallows, for hoisting supplies on board, and a flagstaff at the stern. The port-holes were closed and secured. Two tiers of holes were cut through her sides, about two feet square and about ten feet apart, strongly guarded by a grating of iron bars.

4

6

A source of propaganda at the time, and an emotive issue ever since, the treatment of prisoners on both sides would never have satisfied the Geneva Convention, but the prison ships left a particular scar in the American psyche.

Such were the risks of privateering, but were there rewards? John Adams believed that commerce warfare was 'a short, easy and infallible method of humbling the English'. In this he was wrong, like many of Britain's enemies from the French in the 1690s to the Germans of 1940, but raiding certainly had a major impact on both commerce and grand strategy. In the latter case, the need to arm and/or convoy military storeships placed an even greater burden on stretched naval resources, while captures sent insurance rates sky-high. Lloyd's calculated that American privateers took about 2200 British ships that were not ransomed or recaptured, in a war in which some 3400 mercantile vessels were lost in total. This is a high proportion, but to put it in context, roughly the same total was lost in the War of the 1690s when the British merchant fleet was only half the size. There was no parliamentary outcry, so while losses were heavy, they were not the dominant influence some felt they could be.

4. Washington's schooners attack a British storeship off Boston. Watercolour by Lt William Elliott, RN.
Naval Institute Press

5. Conyngham's *Revenge* capturing the Ostend packet, 2 May 1777. Engraved by Reinier Vinkeles after an original by Jacobus Buys, published in the Netherlands, 1786. Although Conyngham became famous for his exploits in the cutter *Revenge*, the packet was actually captured by his earlier command, the lugger *Surprise*.
NMM neg A2775

6. *Lexington* captured by *Alert*. Published by Pennant, *London to Dover*, Vol XX.
NMM neg A64

7. Anonymous grey pen and wash drawing of a prison hulk thought to date from about 1810.
NMM ref PAG8260

7

1. 'A New and Correct Chart of the Coast of New England and New York with the adjacent parts of Nova Scotia and New Brunswick from Cape Sable to the Entrance of Hudsons or North River by Captain Holland; View of Hell Gate by W A Williams 1777 (inset); Plan of Hell Gate (inset); The Rivers Kennebeck and Sheepsant (plan) by Captn Joseph Huddart (inset).' By W A Williams, published 1794 by Laurie & Whittle.
NMM ref PAH2940

2. *Beaver's Prize* ex-*Oliver Cromwell*, lines plan. Admiralty Collection.
NMM neg 3279/48

3. 'Schnr. *Franklin* of Boston, Mass, Capt Jas. Mugford, Master', watercolour by Thomas Russell, First Lieutenant, 1776.
Peabody Essex Museum, Salem, MA neg 9766

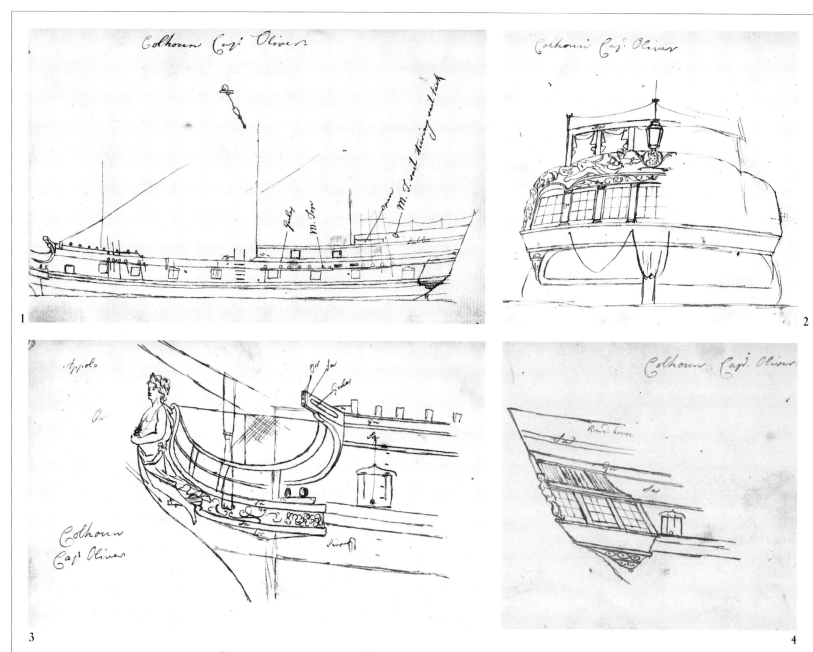

A forgotten incident in the trade war

BESIDES DEPICTING major battles, marine artists were often called upon to immortalise far more trivial events that nevertheless had meaning for those involved. The sketchbooks of Thomas Luny (1759-1837) contain preparatory drawings covering a number of such half-forgotten incidents, including one commissioned by Captain William Oliver of the merchantman *Colhoun*, a big, well-armed ship probably built for the West Indies trade (1-4).

This ship was one of a convoy of about sixty ships from the Windward Islands which was pursued by the Continental ships *Raleigh*, 32 and *Alfred*. On 5 September 1777, having outsailed her consort, *Raleigh* attacked the most exposed escort, the sloop *Druid* of 14 guns, which

put up a stout resistance and the American frigate broke off the action. One sketch (5) suggests that the reason the *Raleigh* sheered off was the intervention of the *Colhoun*, and this was clearly a source of sufficient pride that her captain had one of the country's leading marine artists prepare a picture. Not so the naval officers concerned: neither the log of the *Raleigh* nor the *Druid* mention the involvement of a merchant ship.

Luny, seen here in a rather self-effacing self-portrait (6), clearly took his commission seriously, noting that the *Colhoun* should 'have a single Reef in her topsails, & to hoist close upp', presumably after consulting Oliver. He also noted, accurately, that the *Druid*'s stern was too broad, having been a New York merchant packet before

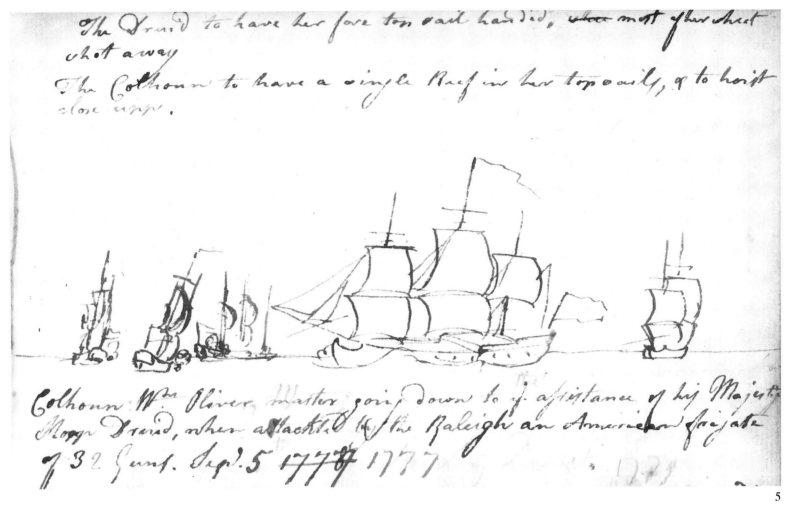

The Druid to have her fore top sail handed, ~~when most of her sheet~~ shot away

The Colhoun to have a single Reef in her top sails, & to hoist close upp.

Colhoun W.m Oliver, Master going down to y.e assistance of his Majesty.s Sloop Druid, when attackt by the Raleigh an American frigate of 32 Guns. Sep.t 5 ~~1778~~ 1777

5

naval service, and numerous other details about the action, including the loss of the sloop's main topsail.

The sketches of the ship were drawn on 3 September 1779, clearly from life. As a representation of the event, it is rather more convincing than the logs, both of which are 'economical with the truth'.

1-4. Thomas Luny (1759-1837) Sketchbook, 75 leaves of brown pen and ink sketches, c1780. Sketches of the *Colhoun*, merchantman. *NMM ref PAE9626-9629*

5. Sketch for a painting of the action of 5 September 1777. *NMM ref PAE9630*

6. Self portrait of the artist? *NMM ref PAE9739*

1

The occupation of Philadelphia, summer 1777

WASHINGTON'S SURPRISE winter campaign of 1776-77, and the stunning victories of Trenton and Princeton, pushed the British out of most of the territory they had occupied in New Jersey. For 1777, therefore, Howe decided on a renewed attempt to crush the Continental Army by offering to attack Philadelphia, the seat of Congress and the nearest thing to an American capital (1, 2). At the same time

Burgoyne's plan for a renewed advance down the Hudson was approved by the British Government, and Howe was expected to send a force northward to link up at Albany. Thus a fatal confusion was introduced into the British grand strategy since Howe had neither the forces nor the time to pursue both objectives.

In fact, because of the delays that seem endemic in eighteenth-century administration, reinforcements

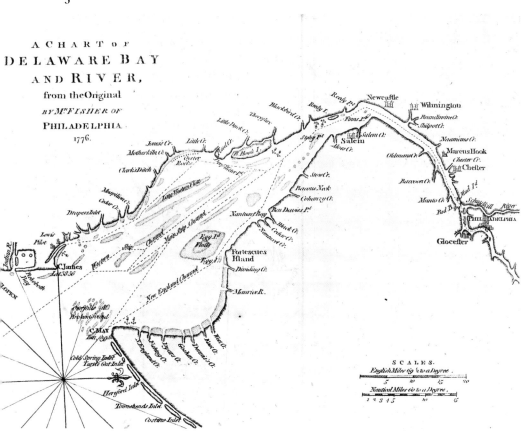

3

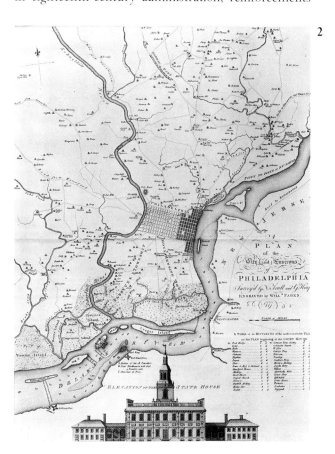

2

from England did not reach New York until the middle of June. Many expected an overland advance, but Howe decided once again to exploit the Royal Navy's command of the sea and on 23 July an armada of 267 ships set sail and, as far as American intelligence sources were concerned, disappeared for a month. Washington was faced with a number of alternative targets, but in August he learned that the fleet was in the Chesapeake. Howe had intended to sail up the Delaware (3) but the blockading squadron had informed him that it was too heavily obstructed so he diverted to the Chesapeake. After a nightmare voyage of calms and adverse winds in which

all the horses died and a significant proportion of the army became sick, another textbook landing was carried out on the Elk river at the Head of the Bay—but the long passage had destroyed the hoped-for element of surprise. Nevertheless, Howe was able to win the battle of Brandywine on 10 September, outmanoeuvre Washington, and enter Philadelphia on the 25th (4). Among the prizes was the continental frigate *Delaware* of 24 guns.

The task for the Navy was then to open up the Delaware, which would greatly shorten the army's lines of communication and allow the fleet a safe anchorage.

4

1. 'An East Perspective View of the City of Philadelphia, in the Province of Pensylvania, in North America, taken from the Jersey Shore, 1778', coloured engraving and etching published by Carington Bowles, London, 1 January 1778.
NMM neg A1424

2. 'A Plan of the City and Environs of Philadelphia, surveyed by N Scull and G Heap', engraved and published by William Faden, London, 12 March 1777.
NMM neg A852

3. 'A Chart of Delaware Bay and River, from the Original by Mr Fisher of Philadelphia 1776', published in *Gentleman's Magazine* 49 (London 1779).

4. 'A Plan of the City and Environs of Philadelphia, with the Works and encampments of His Majesty's Forces under the Command of Lieutenant General Sir William Howe, KB', published by William Faden, London 1 January 1779.
NMM neg A1332

5. 'The Course of the Delaware River from Philadelphia to Chester, Exhibiting the Several Works erected by the Rebels to defend its Passage, with the Attacks made upon them by His Majesty's Land & Sea Forces', published by William Faden, London, 30 April 1778. A very detailed chart showing not only the attacks described above (on the southeastern, Jersey, shore), but also the subsequent successful attack on Fort Island in which the bombardment vessel *Vigilant* and blockship *Fury* worked their way behind Hog Island, allowing Fort Mifflin (inset) to be bombarded from two sides. The inset lower right shows one of the 'stockadoes' that were used in large numbers to block the river, and were blamed for shifting the sandbars that *Augusta* so unexpectedly ran onto.
Beverley R Robinson Collection, Annapolis

6. *Augusta* and *Merlin* aground and on fire, Delaware River, 23 October 1777, by Lieutenant William Elliott, RN, an eyewitness to the event. Published London, 17 February 1787.
Naval Institute Press

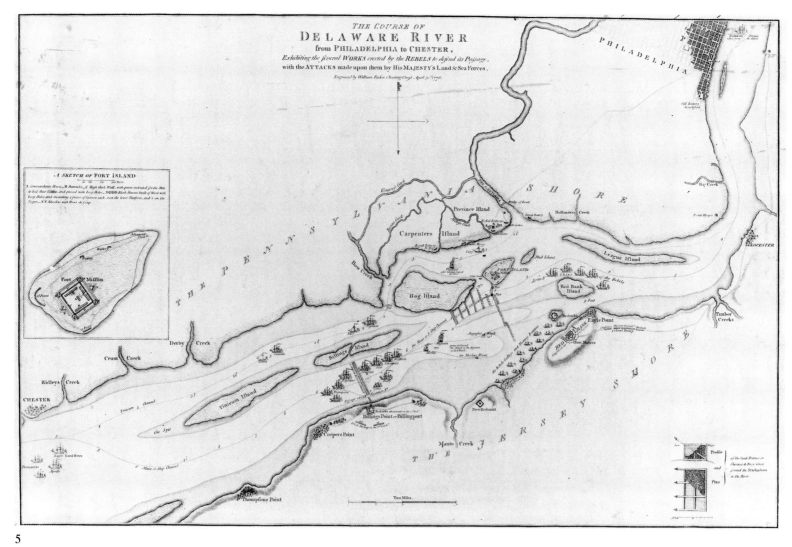

THE COURSE OF
DELAWARE RIVER
from PHILADELPHIA to CHESTER,
Exhibiting the several WORKS *erected by the* REBELS *to defend its Passage,*
with the ATTACKS *made upon them by His* MAJESTY'S *Land & Sea Forces.*

Engraved by William Faden Charing Cross. April 30.th 1778.

5

The experienced Hamond, commander of the blockading force for the last year, was given the task, which began in early October with the clearance of a channel through obstacles between Billing's Island and the Jersey shore (5). Gun batteries and the row galleys of the Pennsylvania state navy put up quite a fight, but the overwhelming strength of the British forces soon began to tell. However, the Royal Navy suffered a serious reverse when the 64-gun *Augusta* and the sloop *Merlin* went aground supporting a failed Hessian attack on Red Bank fort. Despite frantic efforts to refloat the ship, *Augusta* was still hard aground on the morning of 23 October and drew heavy fire from all the American gunboats and batteries; she caught fire aft and eventually blew up with a blast that 'felt like an earthquake in Philadelphia'. The cause was never established, but burning wadding from her own guns igniting stowed hammocks was the most popular theory. The *Merlin* was also abandoned and set on fire (6).

A further month of heavy fighting followed before the first British supply vessel reached Philadelphia. Most of the defending American ships were captured or destroyed in the process, but in return the main British Army had been immobilised for two months, and the campaigning season of 1777 was effectively over. Howe's army wintered in the relative comfort of the city while Washington took post in the grim surroundings of Valley Forge.

6

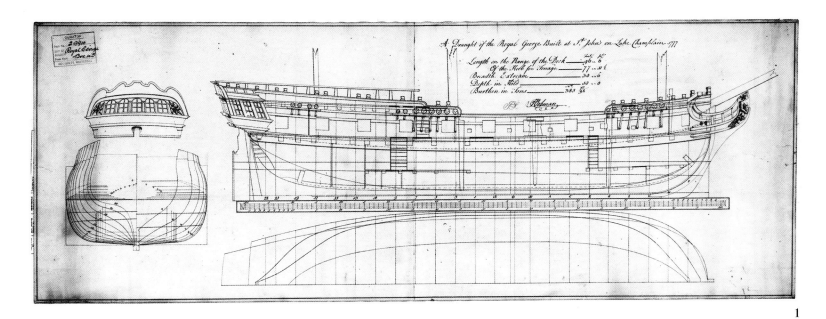

1

The road to Saratoga,
May–October 1777

T HE NAVAL contribution to Burgoyne's ill-fated campaign was largely confined to its earlier stages. The British fleet had dominated Lake Champlain since the October battles around Valcour Island, and during the winter its superiority was increased by the completion of a powerful new flagship, the 386-ton *Royal George*, armed with twenty 12pdrs and six 6pdrs (1). Because spring comes late to these northern parts, the expedition could not get underway until May, the fleet then comprising 44 gunboats, 4 large provision boats, 23 longboats, 3 twelve-oared barges, 26 cutters, 260 batteaux, 10 flat-boats, as well as the larger ships from the previous year's campaign and the three American prizes.

The first object was the capture of Fort Ticonderoga, which lies on a promontory between the Lakes Champlain and George (marked 'A' in 2). By manhandling heavy artillery up on to the heights opposite—previously regarded as unscaleable—the Americans were forced to withdraw. James Hunter's watercolour (3) was apparently done just before the British attack on 6 July and shows the fort in the middle distance with Mount Independence to its left. The viewpoint is the north shore and the boom ('F' in 2) can be seen stretched across the inlet protecting a both a communicating bridge and a small American squadron—the high-peaked lateen yards of the row galleys are particularly evident. Following the capture of the fort, these five remaining vessels were pursued and destroyed by the British.

Burgoyne then moved beyond the sphere of direct

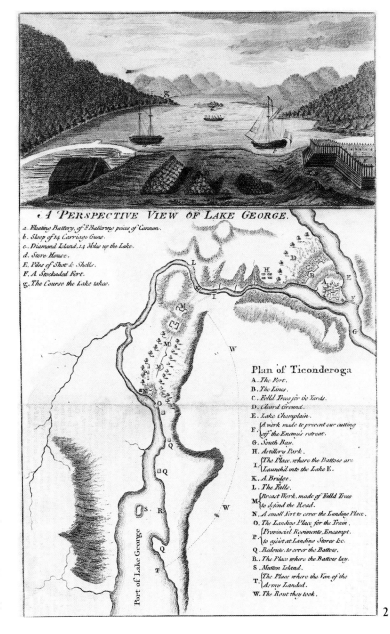

2

3

4

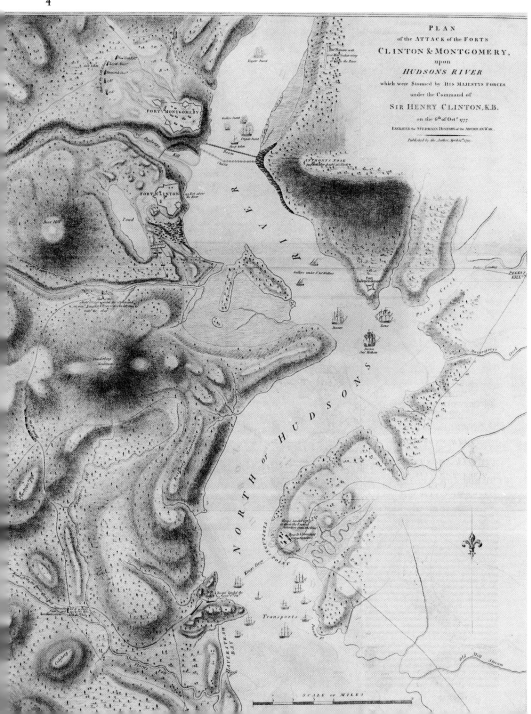

naval support, and his lines of communication back to Champlain were very exposed. Indeed, raids by three American detachments destroyed several of his gunboats and 150 batteaux, making retreat problematical, if not impossible. American forces were rapidly rallying to General Gates, and Burgoyne's position was becoming more parlous by the day.

With the main army under Howe at Philadelphia, Clinton at New York did not have sufficient forces for a decisive intervention. The best he could do, after receiving 3000 recruits from Britain, was to launch an amphibious attack up the Hudson, once again superbly organised on the naval side by Hotham. On 6 October surprise assaults at the end of the bayonet carried Forts Montgomery and Clinton (4), and the British were able to advance as far north as Esopus, destroying river craft and military stores; the retreating Americans themselves were forced to burn the frigates *Washington*, 32 and *Congress*, 28 and about thirty smaller craft. The huge boom chain across the river at Fort Montgomery (5) was removed by the British and sent to protect Gibraltar.

Clinton announced to Burgoyne: '*Nous y Voila*, and nothing now between us but Gates. I sincerely hope this little success may facilitate your operations . . .' It did not, and after Burgoyne's attempts to breakthrough were bloodily repulsed, his depleted army was forced to surrender on 17 October at Saratoga.

---

1. Lines plan of the 26-gun *Royal George*. Admiralty Collection. *NMM neg 2994/45*

2. 'A perspective view of Lake George: Plan of Ticonderoga . . .', coloured etching, c1777. *NMM ref PAD5329*

3. 'A View of Ticonderoga from a Point on the North Shore of Lake Champlain', by James Hunter, 1777. *British Library Map Library K.Top. CXXXI.107.b*

4. 'Plan of the attack of the Forts Clinton & Montgomery . . . on the 6th of Oct 1777. Drawn from the Surveys of Verplanck, Holland & Metcalf, by John Hills, Lt 23rd Regt and Asst Engineer', published by William Faden, London, 1 June 1784. This version produced for Stedman's *American War*, London 1794. *NMM neg A4114*

5. Chain boom on the Hudson between Fort Montgomery (A) and Anthony's Nose (B). Key: a—floats to chain, b—boom in front of chain, c—chain. Inset S: c—chain, f—floats. From Justin Winsor (ed), *A Narrative and Critical History of America* after an original in Ruttenber's *Obstructions to the Navigation of the Hudson River*. *Chatham Collection*

5

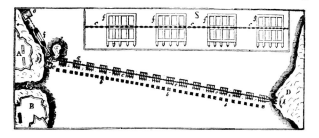

Part II   AMERICA AND THE WEST INDIES 1778-1783

THE FAILURE of deterrence, and the defeat of Burgoyne, changed the nature of the war. Sandwich advised the Cabinet that Britain should seek to inflict a signal defeat on France that would put an end to her support of the rebels. Leaving strong forces in the West Indies, and at Halifax, he would have concentrated efforts in home waters and in the Mediterranean.[22] The strategy adopted, however, was to be a compromise. A state of war was not even acknowledged to exist until France proclaimed it in July. An attempt was made to reach a settlement with the Americans, Lord Carlisle being sent to New York to negotiate. London was even willing to acknowledge American independence if the structure of trade were retained, and if the Royal Navy remained the exclusive naval force of the Empire. The sailing in April of Vice-Admiral d'Estaing from Toulon with eleven ships of the line bound for America, however, and the dispatch of units of the French army to co-operate with Washington, ensured that the Americans had no need to make concessions. Consequently, although Philadelphia was abandoned, the war continued. Less attention was given to the American theatre, but efforts continued to be made to snatch an American victory out of European stalemate. The scope of the war was widened to include operations in the West Indies and Asia, and in European waters the policy was to maintain the naval resources to meet any threat from France.

The appointment of General Lord Amherst to the Cabinet with responsibility for the development of British strategy proved to be an inadequate solution to the problem of strategic direction because of his age, and his overriding concern for his task of commander-in-chief of the home forces in England. He was preoccupied with the responsibility to meet the threat of invasion. His advice, however, against abandoning the American theatre altogether without first reaching an agreement with the Americans, was sound enough.

Unless the potential of the rebels was contained, there was a danger they would take the offensive against British interests in the Carribean. Germain continued to believe that loyalists in the American colonies could prevail if provided with support.

The strategic mistakes in London were compounded in New York. Lord Howe and his brother were both given permission to return home, but Lord Howe retained his command until his relief arrived. General Clinton assumed command of the forces ashore. Instead of concentrating the army, and seeking to control enough hinterland so that supplies could be obtained locally, with the hope of forcing the Continental Army to seek a general action on the glacis of British defences, Clinton's strategy became one of dispersal. Small detachments were used to harry the population in the hope that they would withdraw their support for Congress. These isolated detachments depended entirely on the Royal Navy for their amphibious movement within the theatre, and for defence against attack from the sea.

Whether or not the Americans obtained their independence, the West Indies sugar islands were bound to remain colonies of one or other of the European powers, and to support the financial position of their possessor. The forces France had moved to the islands far outnumbered British garrisons, so immediate offensive action was necessary to prevent the French picking off British possessions one by one. Lord Mulgrave, a member of the Board of Admiralty, suggested that at the outbreak of war a force be sent from New York to seize St Lucia, and perhaps St Nicolas Mole in Haiti. To Lord Howe's complaint of the weakness of his squadron, Sandwich replied: 'The object of the war being now changed and the contest in America being secondary consideration, our principal object must be distressing France and defending… His Majesty's possessions.'[23]

Operationally and strategically, the Amer-ican theatre was symbiotically tied to the West Indies. Bad weather meant that campaigning in the northern colonies was impossible in the winter, and in the Indies in the summer hurricane season. Ships and soldiers could be moved from one to the other, provided command of the sea were retained. That, however, was a proviso which proved to be beyond the capability of the Royal Navy to guarantee at all times. Besides the demands on its resources in America for support of the army, the navy had to maintain in Europe the forces it needed to contain the French threat at home, and to be ready to send detachments to follow French squadrons when they sailed to the West or East Indies, and to America. France was in a position to set the strategic agenda.

The Admiralty's failure to stop d'Estaing's sailing for America, or even to give adequate warning, seriously compromised British forces in America. Fortunately, Clinton had decided to bring the army north from Philadelphia by land, for otherwise the transports might have been caught at sea by the arrival of the French. Howe's command was significantly inferior to the French squadron fresh out of dockyard hands. Howe was the Royal Navy's premier tactician and had prepared his captains with improved signals and fighting instructions, but he could not risk action at sea. He took up a strong position anchored off Sandy Hook which, when he arrived on 11 July, d'Estaing felt unable to challenge. Instead, he steered for Rhode Island to co-operate with American forces attacking the British garrison at Newport. It had been forced to retreat from its outposts, and to scuttle the station's ships, their crews being formed into support troops. To relieve the garrison, Howe took the forces under his command up Long Island Sound. D'Estaing decided against fighting at anchor,

---

22. Advice Given about the Change of The War in America, March 1778, *Sandwich* I p359.

23. Admiralty Papers 2/1334, 22 March 1778.

and sailed, with Howe retreating before him. He outmanoeuvred d'Estaing, but did not have the strength to force action.

In June the Admiralty had belatedly detached from the Channel Fleet a battle squadron under Vice-Admiral John Byron with orders to sail to New York in pursuit of d'Estaing. It was badly damaged by a storm, however, and scattered. On 11 August, a storm also struck Howe's and d'Estaing's ships. Two French ships of the line, *Languedoc* and *Marseillais* were dismasted, and during the night they were closely attacked by two British 50-gun ships *Renown* and *Preston*, but they were driven off in the morning. Three days later another 50, HMS *Isis*, engaged the 74-gun *César* in a running battle during which both ships were badly shot-up.

Howe returned to New York, where he was able to refit, and d'Estaing to Rhode Island, but just before Howe sailed to challenge him again, d'Estaing sailed to Boston. He was aware that Howe was being reinforced, and his principal interest was in refitting his ships for the autumn West Indies campaign. Missing a chance to cut off and destroy the American army which was forced to abandon Newport, Howe sailed to intercept d'Estaing but failed to seize a fleeting chance to attack him in the entrance of Boston harbour. At the end of September he turned over command to Byron.

By then the effort to blockade the American coast had in effect been abandoned, and Byron's instructions placed operations against d'Estaing as his first duty. Germain had ordered in February that the futile efforts at catching American ships at sea be abandoned and instead amphibious raids should be directed against American coastal towns. General Clinton described this as 'War by Conflagration'. It was not a popular policy amongst most British officers, many of whom questioned its expediency both in the short or longer terms, but starting with New Bedford a number of American towns were deliberately put to the torch. On 5 May 1779 six warships under the command of Commodore Sir George Collier sailed from New York to escort twenty-eight transports carrying 1800 soldiers under Brigadier Edward Mathew, to raid the ships and warehouses of Elizabeth River in Chesapeake Bay. Property worth as much as £1

million was destroyed, and Fort Nelson was razed.

More operationally dangerous than the raids were the attempts to secure loyalist support by occupying ground with small detachments. On 3 November 1778 1000 soldiers were embarked for Pensacola, and on the 7th 2000 sailed for St Augustine in order to begin the invasion of Georgia from the south. At the same time, Commodore William Hotham sailed from Sandy Hook with seven warships to escort fifty-nine transports with 5000 soldiers under orders to capture St Lucia.

On 7 September the French had seized the opportunity presented by their superior military establishment in the Leeward Islands, and captured Dominica. Rear-Admiral Barrington with his small squadron which included two ships of the line was to windward at Barbados awaiting the arrival of the forces from New York. When Hotham arrived, however, the British were able to go on the offensive. Hotham was the officer who had organised the amphibious operations at New York, and with equal efficiency he put his force ashore on St Lucia and rapidly occupied it.

D'Estaing had sailed from Boston on 3 November 1778, bound for the West Indies. He had actually captured several of Hotham's transports at sea. Now he arrived at St Lucia with twelve of the line to Barrington's two, and five 50-gun ships. Barrington felt obliged to take up a strong position anchored close to the island with the transports inside the line. D'Estaing found he could not penetrate the line, but was able to put ashore 9000 French infantry. Brigadier Medows's brigade, however, beat off three assaults, inflicting casualties of 30 per cent.

On 11 November Byron had followed d'Estaing with ten ships of the line, bound for Antigua. His arrival gave the British naval command of the Leeward Islands, and ensured that St Lucia remained in British hands. Eight more ships of the line were sailed for the West Indies in December and joined Byron in February. But the French Marine had also sent four ships under the Comte de Grasse, *Lieutenant Général des Armées Navales*, two more arrived in April 1779, and in June Commodore la Motte-Picquet arrived at Martinique with five more from Brest, giving the French a predominant naval force in the West Indies. The French moved

quickly and captured both St Vincent and Grenada. Byron's squadron was given a rough time when he attacked in general chase what he thought was only a part of the French squadron at Grenada. He was lucky to be able to withdraw his battered ships. Having lost command of the sea, and needing all the soldiers available to garrison the remaining British possessions, Byron was not able to take any forces back to New York. Instead it was d'Estaing who was able to strike at the time and place of his choosing. The entry of Spain into the war in April 1779 prevented the Admiralty being able to restore naval control of the American theatre.

The danger of the strategy of dispersal was demonstrated when a post was established at Stony Point across the Hudson, only to be surprised and taken by storm in July 1779. At the same time, another isolated post which had been established at Castine, Maine, on the Penobscot was invested by a rebel army dispatched by the Commonwealth of Massachusetts. This time, however, a British squadron under Commodore Collier arrived in time not only to relieve the garrison, but to panic the Americans into destroying all but two of their thirty-five ships, *Hunter* and *Hampden* having been captured earlier, and fleeing into the forest.

On Byron's sailing south, the elderly, and incompetent, Rear-Admiral Gambier was left in command of the North American station, to be replaced by Vice-Admiral Marriot Arbuthnot on his arrival in New York 25 August 1779. The latter proved to be too elderly and without tact. General Clinton found it impossible to co-operate with either. Quarrels between commanders-in-chief added to the inability of British forces in America to develop an effective strategy.

In September 1779 d'Estaing suddenly appeared off the coast of Georgia with thirty-three warships and 4000 soldiers, whom he landed. HM Ships *Experiment*, 50 guns, and *Ariel*, 20, and two storeships with the £30,000 payroll for the British garrison at Savannah, were surprised and captured. On Arbuthnot's advice, the post at Newport was evacuated in October, on the grounds that its occupation by the Americans posed little threat to the British at New York and that with his reduced forces he could not stop d'Estaing going there to renew the siege. But d'Estaing's assault on Savannah was beaten off with heavy loss, and he returned with his squadron to Brest. More successful was a Spanish assault on west Florida, leading to the surrender of the British post at Mobile on 12 March 1780. The last British post in West Florida, Pensacola, fell on 9 May 1781 to an amphibious expedition mounted from Cuba.

Arbuthnot had brought with him four ships of the line and 3800 of the 6000 reinforcements Clinton had been promised. Clinton decided

that an assault should be made again on Charleston, and on 20 March 1780 Artbuthnot, with his flag in HMS *Roebuck*, with HM Ships

Renown and *Romulus* sailed into Charleston Harbour. Making a night amphibious move outflanking the American defences, Clinton

The importance of the West Indian sugar islands to the European powers dictated a change of strategic emphasis as soon as France entered the war on the side of the North America colonists, and thereafter the Caribbean became the principal theatre of operations. However, because the hurricane season made the area dangerous in summer, and storms made winter campaigning risky in the north, it was possible to alternate fleets between the West Indies and American stations during the course of a year. It should be noted that British and French nomenclature for the islands differed: the British called the northern end of the Caribbean chain the Leeward Islands, with those from Dominica south the Windwards, whereas the French called the whole chain the Windward Isles, reserving Leewards for San Domingo and Jamaica. NMM neg B7866

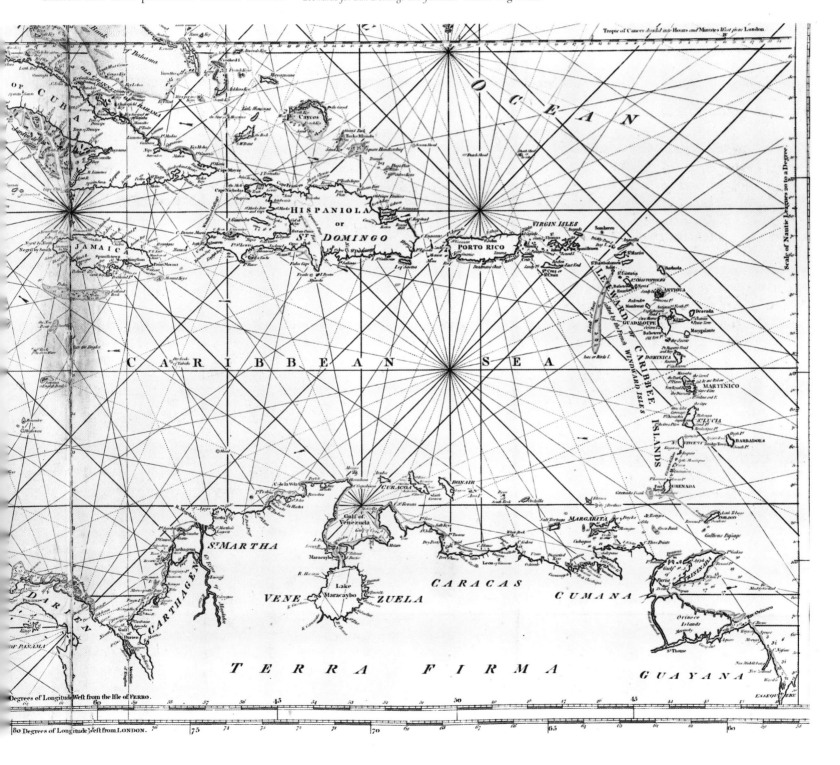

landed north of Charleston on the Ashley River. The town, which was isolated on a peninsula, was besieged. Arbuthnot broke into the inner harbour and seized American works north of the town. The American commander, Major General Benjamin Lincoln, surrendered on 12 May before an assault had to be made.

In February 1780 Admiral de Guichen sailed from Brest with fifteen ships of the line and 16,000 soldiers for operations in the West Indies. When he arrived, French naval forces in the Leeward Island outnumbered the British, but Admiral Rodney soon arrived with four ships from Gibraltar which, with the seventeen already there under the command of Rear-Admiral Sir Hyde Parker (Captain Hyde Parker's father), gave him enough to seek battle. The French were found at Martinique on 17 April, but to Rodney's frustration, his captains failed to understand his tactical intentions. Instead of concentrating on the enemy rear, they stretched out to engage the enemy along its entire line, according to standard practice. The result was a dispiriting draw, and violent recriminations. The French, however, did not have enough strength to take the offensive because de Guichen was working within operational instructions to avoid battle except when the odds were strongly in his favour. The balance of power changed from week to week as ships arrived from Europe, and squadrons departed. When Rodney learnt that a French squadron under Chevalier de Ternay d'Arsac was expected at Rhode Island, he sailed north to New York.

Although in scale of operation a side show, the attempt launched from Jamaica early in 1780 to seize control of a route across the Central American isthmus through Nicaragua was important because it was intended as part of an effort to detach Spain from the French alliance by offering a separate peace, and by threatening to take key parts of her empire. Horatio Nelson, as a young captain, played an important part in the campaign, and was one of the few who did not die of disease. Conditions were so unfavourable for campaigning that nothing could be made of the limited success which he obtained.

On 8 June Arbuthnot and Clinton, with the bulk of the soldiers, had returned from Charleston to New York to meet an expected return of the French to North America.

General Cornwallis was left in command in the Carolinas. In March the Cabinet had decided to send a reinforcement of six ships of the line under Rear-Admiral Thomas Graves, but it was not until the end of June that London had learnt that the destination of the French squadron was Rhode Island, where the French arrived on 11 July. Its occupation by the French was a serious blow. Clinton believed that an amphibious landing, if undertaken before the French consolidated their position, could make their post untenable but Arbuthnot refused to co-operate.

On 14 September Admiral Sir George Rodney arrived without warning at New York with ten ships of the line, and assumed command despite Arbuthnot's attempt to maintain his independence. The conflict between the leaders, however, was enough to prevent Britain's temporary naval superiority being put to good use before Rodney's return to the West Indies in mid-November. He left orders that if de Ternay sailed for the southward Rear-Admiral Graves was to be detached with eight or ten coppered ships of the line, and frigates.

With Rodney's withdrawal, the scattered British posts returned to their state of vulnerability. Yet Clinton continued to increase their number. In October 1780, Major-General Leslie had sailed to Chesapeake Bay with 2500 soldiers to destroy American supply depots at Petersburg, Richmond and other places in Virginia, and then to establish a post. He found the population hostile. A covert operation to seize West Point on the Hudson, with the help of the American Brigadier Benedict Arnold, failed, and in the aftermath of that fiasco, Arnold, now in British service, was given command of another expedition bound for the Chesapeake.

The vulnerability of these detachments was emphasised again when in January 1781 the French ship of the line *Eveille* and two frigates escaped from Newport and sailed for the Chesapeake. Graves pursued with three ships, but they encountered bad weather; *Culloden* was driven ashore, *Bedford* was dismasted, and *America* was badly damaged. Arnold moved most of the small ships attached to his force, which he used for amphibious movement, into the Elizabeth River out of reach of the French, but HMS *Romulus* was captured. That was the limit of the French effort, and the squadron

returned to Newport. On 19 February, however, Washington gave orders to Major-General the Marquis de Lafayette to march with an elite force of light infantry into Virginia.

After the end of two years of war, French finances were all but exhausted. The Continental Army was demoralised, and in February 1781 Vergennes urged the Americans to make peace. Because the Continental Army was showing strong signs of demoralisation, rather than reinforce de Ternay, Vergennes decided that French naval forces should be sent to the West Indies under de Grasse. It was intended that, when the hot season arrived, he should head for Rhode Island, possibly to evacuate the Comte de Rochambeau, the commandant of French land forces at Newport.

The first attempt of the French squadron at Newport to isolate the British in the Chesapeake and co-operate with the forces ashore proved abortive. On 8 March Captain Destouches, who had succeeded to command after de Ternay's death, sailed with seven of the line, a 44 and a *flute*, and with 1120 embarked soldiers. He was followed by Arbuthnot with his entire force, also seven of the line, a 50, and several frigates, and brought to action off the mouth of Chesapeake Bay. Destouches proved the better tactician, but in the end withdrew leaving the British in command of the coast.

Another isolated force, General Lord Cornwallis's detachment, having been baffled by General Nathaniel Green, in the Carolinas, marched out of Wilmington, North Carolina, on 25 April 1781 to fight its way northwards towards Virginia. Clinton had not approved of Cornwallis's decision, but provided what support he could, and decided to make a permanent establishment on the Chesapeake. Although Cornwallis regarded Yorktown as virtually indefensible from the landward, he began to fortify it because Arbuthnot and Clinton believed that it should be developed as a base for the navy.

Washington's orders to Lafayette had been the beginning of the movement which led to the defeat of Cornwallis at Yorktown. In May 1781 Rochambeau received advice that a large French squadron under de Grasse which had sailed from Brest in April for the West Indies should be able to undertake operations on the American coast in July or August. Through captured documents the British were soon able to deduce that a combined naval and military operation by the French and Americans would be mounted, but could not determine whether it would be against New York or Cornwallis.

Rodney failed to intercept de Grasse on his arrival because he was engaged in looting the Dutch warehouses at St Eustatius of the munitions British merchants had been dispatching under neutral colours to the rebels. This was to cost him dearly in the law courts, which were ready to support the interests of property over those of the state. He did send Rear-Admiral Samuel Hood with the bulk of the fleet to lie windward of Martinique, but then redeployed them so close to the island that when de Grasse arrived he was able to slip into harbour. Outnumbering Hood, he was able to overpower the small garrison at Tobago. Rodney caught up with him there, but did not press action. Probably his real reason was his ill health, and exhaustion. When de Grasse departed for America, Rodney detached Hood with fourteen ships of the line to follow, and himself returned to England with the escort for the West Indies convoy.

The small size of Hood's squadron was to be a decisive factor in the defeat at Yorktown. Rodney might have given him a stronger force had he thought it possible that de Grasse would be so bold as to cancel the sailing of the French West Indies convoy, and take the entire French battle squadron with him. The importance to Britain of her maritime trade would have made it unthinkable for a British admiral to have taken a similar measure.

Arbuthnot reacted to the news that de Grasse was on his way by moving his squadron over the bar into New York Harbour, and Clinton sent a letter to Rodney, requesting that he proceed to the support of British forces in America. In London it was assumed that this was what would happen. Hood was to prove himself a highly effective tactician, but he was at the bottom of the flag list, having been specially promoted so that he could take the relief squadron to the West Indies. Consequently, when Arbuthnot finally gave up his command at the beginning of July and returned to England, it was the lacklustre Graves who commanded during the most critical hour in British affairs in North America.

Washington had learnt much in six years of war, and was ably supported by Lafayette, and by de Grasse who arrived with twenty-six sail of the line and seven frigates at the entrance to the Chesapeake on 29 August 1781. Three thousand soldiers were put ashore to join the siege operations before the lines at Yorktown. Clinton did not act decisively to threaten Washington's rear, only sending Arnold to burn New London, Connecticut.

Graves gathered the ships under his command which were fit for sea, and arrived off the mouth of the Chesapeake on 5 September. His ships were fully manned and copper-bottomed, but some were in desperate need of repairs, and HMS *Terrible* was leaking so badly that she had eventually to be burnt at sea, but he had only nineteen of the line, seven frigates and a fireship. He fought a classic battle against odds, and despite the harsh criticism he received from Hood, he can be credited with having achieved a tactical draw. In the circumstances, however, Cornwallis's army was doomed if French control of the Chesapeake could not be broken.

The squadron at Newport was now commanded by *Lieutenant Général de la Armée Navale* de Barras who had been sent from France to replace de Ternay who had died during the winter. De Barras had consented to carry Washington's siege train to the Chesapeake, and was able to slip into the bay on 10 September.

Graves felt unable to force action, and returned to New York to repair damage. He sailed again on 19 October with twenty-five ships, three 50s and eight frigates, with 7149 soldiers embarked, to attempt to fight his way into the bay, still against the odds. On the way south, however, he learnt that Cornwallis had been forced to ask for terms of surrender.

The defeat at Yorktown was so demoralising that the British lost the will to restore Royal authority in America, but the war continued for another year. Vergennes cautioned that, though 'history offers few examples of a success so complete, one would be wrong to believe that it means an immediate peace; it is not in the English character to give up so easily'.[24] Although Washington would have liked to retain the use of the French fleet to make possible an assault on Charleston, de Grasse returned to Martinique, and was followed by Hood. Hood's force was inferior, but he skill-fully disposed his fleet at anchor to defend St Kitts. The island, however, fell to French soldiers, and Hood slipped his cables by night and stood out to sea. De Grasse then proceeded to take control of Nevis, Demerara and Essequibo, and then in accord with a commitment to Spain, preparations were completed for an attack on Jamaica.

His triumph was to be short. With Rodney's arrival on 25 February, ultimately with seventeen ships of the line, the British regained a small superiority at sea. When de Grasse sailed on 7 April, Rodney followed. De Grasse sent his troop convoy into Guadeloupe and tried to avoid action, but several of his ships collided with each other, and battle could not be avoided. Near a group of islets called the Saintes, Rodney achieved a notable victory, partly occasioned by the accidental cutting of the French battle line in several places. A total of seven ships were captured, and de Grasse himself was taken prisoner. Jamaica was saved from capture.

Before news of the victory reached London, however, the aftermath of Yorktown had led first to the resignation of Germain from the ministry, and in late March to the fall of the North Administration. King George refused to let North make peace with the Americans, but in the end he had no choice but to invite the Marquis of Rockingham to form an administration, and Rockingham was committed to ending the war. Admiral Keppel became First Lord of the Admiralty, and ordered Rodney's replacement by a nonentity, Admiral Pigot, before news of the Saintes reached London. The victory briefly led it to consider compensatory conquests of West Indian islands, and reinforcement of Jamaica against a renewal of the Franco-Spanish threat, but the naval reality was that there were not the transports and victuallers available for anything of the sort. Those available were to be fully employed by Sir Guy Carleton, who replaced Clinton in command of the American theatre, in transporting the garrisons of St Augustine, Savannah, Charleston and New York, and the 40,000 loyalist refugees, to Nova Scotia. The preliminary peace accord with the Americans was signed at the end of November 1782.

---

24. Doniol IV p688.

1. An 80-gun ship, watercolour portrait by F J Emeric. Despite the Dutch flags, the ship has all the features of a French design. *NMM ref PAH9406*

2. *La Bretagne*, 110 guns, watercolour portrait by F J Emeric, 1782. The caption gives the dimensions (in French feet) as length on deck 185ft 6in, maximum breadth 50ft, depth in hold 25ft, height of battery amidships 5ft 6in; the quoted armament is as in the table above. *Peabody Essex Museum, Salem, MA neg 16647*

3. French 64-gun ship, engraving by Nicholas Ozanne. *NMM ref PAD7439*

4. A small French 8pdr-armed frigate of about 1770, watercolour by 'OLM'. *NMM neg A102*

2

The French Navy

THE FRENCH navy of 1778 was a far cry from the service that had been so soundly defeated in the Seven Years War. The fleet that was almost totally destroyed in the battles of 1759 had been rebuilt in the massive construction programmes of the late 1760s associated with the administration of Choiseul. Spain undertook a similar effort so that by 1770 the combined Bourbon navies were larger than Britain's. Following a hiatus in the first half of the 1770s, shipbuilding was again stepped up after 1775, when the French battlefleet comprised one 110-gun ship, one 90, five 80s (three very large with 24pdr upper deck batteries), twenty-six 74s, twenty 64s and six 56- or 50-gun ships that could stand in the line in an emergency. A very large programme planned after 1775 did not come to fruition, and only eleven battleships—nine of them 64s—were added before the outbreak of war, but the dockyards were well stocked with timber and stores, so the French navy began the war against Britain better prepared than on any previous occasion.

For much of the mid-century France had eschewed the three-decker and the characteristic French battleship was a large two-decker of 80 or so guns—the *Soleil Royal* of 1749 was so big that on displacement terms she was probably the largest ship in the world at the time. The 80-gun ship itself was divided into two types, with a bigger variant designed as a flagship (1): d'Estaing's *Languedoc* was one of these, and so sizeable that she is often called a 90 in contemporary accounts. As many a historian has pointed out, these ships had significantly

1

greater firepower than the small 90-gun three-deckers that were so common in the British fleet, but in battle their psychological effect came as a surprise to the French. After Ushant in 1778, a crash programme of four 110-guns ships was pushed through the dockyards, and the 90-gun *Ville de Paris* was rebuilt as a 104-gun ship, in which guise she served de Grasse as his flagship at the end of the war.

The largest ship in the navy in 1778—and until after the war—was the *Bretagne*, which had just been rebuilt and acted as the flagship of the Brest fleet (2). She was some 20ft longer than the *Ville de Paris*, which was herself somewhat larger than the *Victory*, the newest First Rate in the Royal Navy.

Perhaps surprisingly for a navy that specialised in large two-deckers, the French retained a large force of 64-gun ships (3), whose 24pdr main batteries made them a weak spot in a battle line otherwise armed with the powerful 36pdr (because the French pound was heavier, this was the rough equivalent of 39 pounds English). In truth, the British also had fair numbers of similar ships, but in both navies the 64s suffered losses out of proportion to their numbers, indicating their vulnerability. The usual French armament was as follows (number of guns-calibre in pdr):

3

Guns	Lower deck	Middle deck	Upper deck	Quarter-deck/ Forecastle	Typical ships
110	30-36	32-24	32-12	16-8	*Bretagne*
90	30-36	32-24	28-12	-	*Ville de Paris* (before refit)
80	30-36	32-24	-	18-8	*Languedoc, Couronne*
80	30-36	32-18	-	18-8	*Duc de Bourgogne*
74	28-36	30-18	-	16-8	Standard ship
64	26-24	28-12	-	10-8	Standard ship
50	24-18	26-12	-	-	Standard (one or two had 24pdrs)

In terms of quality, there had never been much doubt about the superiority of French ships of the line, which were significantly bigger than their British counterparts and therefore more likely to achieve the best compromise between sailing qualities and gun power. However, in the early part of this conflict, British squadrons exhibited considerable speed advantages, thanks to their widespread adoption of copper sheathing, which more than compensated for the traditional superiority of longer French hulls. The British found these proportionally longer hulls rather lightly built and lacking in girder strength.

The French navy had been quick to adopt what came to be called the 'frigate form' for cruisers, in which an unarmed lower deck, placed about the level of the waterline, gave reduced topside height over two-deckers for better windward performance, but a height of battery that allowed the guns to be fought in all weathers. Like their battleships, French frigates were very large and usually carried twenty-six 12pdr or 8pdr (4) main batteries, with 6pdrs or less on the quarterdecks, but from 1780 onwards a few 18pdr ships were built in response to British equivalents.

4

2

D'Estaing in America: the French view

1

W HEN THE fleet of the Comte d'Estaing (1) sailed from Toulon in April 1778 on board was Pierre Ozanne, a talented draughtsman with a feel for ships and the sea. His elder brother was draughtsman to the French Navy, with good connections at court, and Pierre's appointment was clearly intended as an early form of official war artist. The series of superb watercolours he produced chronicles the highlights of d'Estaing's campaign, both in North America and the West Indies, with a degree of eyewitness authority not vouched to most artists.

The first of the series (2) shows the French fleet making its landfall off the Delaware on 8 July, with 'B' marking Cape Henlopen and 'C' the entrance to the Bay. It comprised the 80-gun *Languedoc* (flagship) and *Tonnant*, the 74s *Cèsar, Zèlè, Hector, Protecteur, Marseillais* and *Guerrier*, the 64s *Vaillant, Provence* and *Fantasque*, the 50-gun *Sagittaire*, and four frigates. It missed its main target, Admiral Howe's small squadron, which had sailed a week earlier, but trapped the 28-gun *Mermaid* ('C', to the left), which ran herself on shore to avoid capture.

However, news of the imminent arrival of the French

3

4

task force had prompted the evacuation of Philadelphia, but Clinton, who had succeeded General Howe as commander of the land forces, wisely decided to withdraw by land to New York, which therefore became d'Estaing's next destination. With only six 64s and three 50-gun ships, plus a handful of frigates, Howe could not offer battle at sea, but he brilliantly arranged his ships in an anchored line just inside Sandy Hook to enfilade the channel leading into New York harbour. After a number of hard-fought rearguard actions, Clinton's army arrived at the Hook and had been ferried across to New York before d'Estaing arrived on 11 July. Ozanne's second view (3) depicts the French fleet at anchor on the following day. The long sandy spit can be seen in the

middle ground, its end marked by a lighthouse, with the British fleet visible beyond. Forcing a way past a line of anchored ships, with springs on their cables to direct fire, was a tough assignment, and d'Estaing was persuaded by local pilots that there would be insufficient water over the harbour bar to allow an attack.

Ten days later, the French set sail, to reappear at the end of the month off Rhode Island, as the result of a plan for its recapture agreed with Washington. On 8 August d'Estaing led the main squadron past the batteries of the eastern entrance (4), having previously sent detachments up the Narragansett channel ('F') to the west of Coanicut Island ('D'), and another up the Sekonnet channel to the east of the main island. To avoid certain

5

6

7

capture, Captain Brisbane set fire to his frigates *Flora, Juno, Lark* and *Orpheus* and the sloop *Falcon* off Newport ('A' far right), to join the sloop *Kingfisher* which met a similar fate in the Sekonnet passage.

Having received some reinforcements, Howe appeared the following day and d'Estaing put to sea in pursuit. Howe outmanoeuvred his opponent, and Ozanne shows the moment on the afternoon of the 11th (5) when the French turned onto a close-hauled line and it became clear that they could not gain the weather gage, and so gave up the chase. A heavy gale then dispersed and dam-

aged both fleets, and when it abated on the 13th the only contact between the fleets was a number of single-ship engagements between Britsh 50s and larger French vessels—the *Preston* with the damaged *Marseillais* and *Isis* with the *Cèsar*, but the biggest potential prize of all was d'Estaing's flagship. She was dismasted in the storm, and was discovered in the evening by the *Renown* under a jury rig made up of only her boat sails (6). *Renown* tacked back and forth under her stern where only a few chase guns could reply, and so certain seemed her fate that d'Estaing had his confidential papers thrown overboard.

However, with un-Nelsonic forebearance, Captain Dawson of the *Renown* lay to in the night, but instead of being able to finish the job the next morning he encountered other French ships who came to the rescue of their admiral.

In the next few days, d'Estaing was able gather his battered ships together, and the whole battlefleet—minus the *Cèsar*, which had not returned from her clash with the *Isis*—was represented by Ozanne on 17 August (7). Repairs at sea had given the *Languedoc* (fifth from left, 'A') a temporary rig of topmasts, and a jury rudder, also constructed from a spar. *Marseillais*, less heavily damaged, has a jury foremast (fifth from right, 'B'). With the fleet is the captured sloop *Senegal* (third from right), taken by the *Hector*, and the bomb *Thunder* was captured at the same time by the *Vaillant*.

In the meantime, the siege of Newport continued, but d'Estaing decided to take his fleet to Boston for repair, and withdrew the French army at the same time. This was regarded as little short of desertion by his American allies, who were forced to lift the siege on 30 August, and d'Estaing's welcome in Boston was unfriendly in the extreme. Ozanne's final view of this first stage of the campaign shows the main body of the fleet in Nantasket Road (8): the ship at the far right is the *Vaillant* ('D'), getting out her masts for transfer to *Protecteur* (right forground, 'C'), which in turn is transferring her masts to the flagship, *Languedoc* ('B'). Workshops were set up on Long Island ('E') and the various batteries set up in anticipation of a British attack are marked 'F'.

Although it was contemplated, no British attack was forthcoming. Lord Howe, after a brilliant campaign against the odds, sailed for home, swearing never to serve again until a change of government; his successor, Admiral John Byron, was given different priorities, and thereafter the main British concern became the West Indies.

Little had been achieved by this first French intervention in America, and on 3 November d'Estaing's refitted fleet sailed south to Martinique to pursue France's real interests.

---

1. Portrait of Charles Henri Comte d'Estaing, Lieutenant-General and Vice-Admiral of France, engraving by Coulet after an original by d'Haisne. *NMM ref PAD3020*

2. The French squadron entering the Delaware and chasing the frigate *Mermaid*, 8 July 1778, watercolour by Pierre Ozanne. *Library of Congress, Washington DC ref 609826-262-904*

3. The French squadron moored off New York, blockading the English squadron and intercepting ships wishing to enter, 12 July 1778, watercolour by Pierre Ozanne. *Library of Congress, Washington DC ref 609826-262-899*

4. The French squadron entering Newport under the fire of the batteries and forcing the channel, 8 August 1778, watercolour by Pierre Ozanne. *Library of Congress, Washington DC ref 609826-262-900*

5. Moment in the afternoon of 11 August 1778. A gale makes battle impossible, and the signal to disengage is made, watercolour by Pierre Ozanne. *Library of Congress, Washington DC ref 609826-262-901*

6. The *Languedoc* dismasted by a gale during the night of the 12th attacked by an English warship in the afternoon of 13 August 1778, watercolour by Pierre Ozanne. *Library of Congress, Washington DC ref 609826-262-902*

7. The *Languedoc* remasted at sea, also the *Marseillais* refitted with the spare spars of the squadron, 17 August 1778, watercolour by Pierre Ozanne. *Library of Congress, Washington DC ref 609826-262-903*

8. The French squadron moored at Boston remasting the ships, watercolour by Pierre Ozanne. *Library of Congress, Washington DC ref 609826-262-905*

8

1

2

West Indies 1778–St Lucia

WITH THE French entry into the war the West Indies immediately became a major theatre of operations. Indeed in this war there were bigger fleets engaged here than in any conflict before or since, and more major sea battles were fought here than even in European waters. It was a very clear statement of the economic importance, both real and perceived, of these islands at the time.

The outbreak of war took some by surprise. The British frigate *Minerva* on a cruise in the West Indies was approaching what her captain took for a harmless merchantman when the French frigate *Concorde* opened fire; unprepared and shattered by an explosion the British ship surrendered (1).

The first significant move came from the French in September when, by a surprise attack from Martinique,

3

4

they captured their northern neighbour, Dominica from the British. However, south of Martinique was the more important French-held island of St Lucia, which became the target of a British expedition. This consisted of some 5000 troops sent under escort of Commodore Hotham (with two 64s and three 50s) from New York, which had joined the local British commander, Rear-Admiral Samuel Barrington (2), with his two ships of the line, at Barbados. Barrington immediately took the combined force to St Lucia and landed the soldiers there on 13 December (3). The next day they captured the

defences of the bay known as the Carénage, whose northern end was marked by a steep promontory, La Vigie. This happened only just in time.

The French fleet under d'Estaing, also having come from North America with twelve ships of the line, had just arrived at Martinique, and it arrived off St Lucia with 7000 troops aboard before sunset of 14 December. The next day found the much smaller British naval force (with two frigates and a 20-gun post ship taking their places with the ships of the line and 50s) anchored in a line across the mouth of the bay, with the fifty or so

5

6

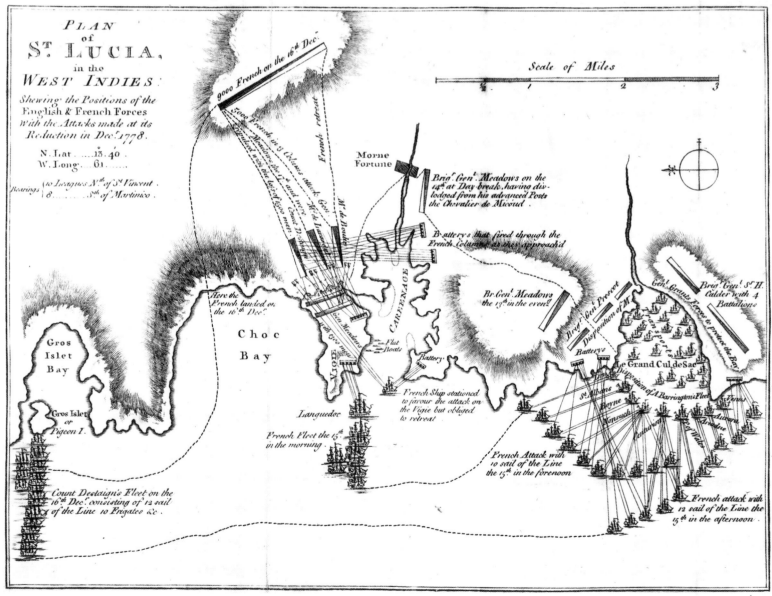

7

transports inside them (4). d'Estaing made two runs along the seaward side of the British line but failed to make much impression (5, 6), not much helped by uncertain and unfavourable winds which hindered him closing the inferior force. Barrington achieved a smaller version of the stand-off that Hood would manage at St Kitts just over three years later. The French abandoned the attempt to attack by sea, and instead tried a land attack on La Vigie (7). This proved much more costly than the naval contest to the French, whose attempt on the steep slopes of the promontory was beaten off with the loss of some 850 men. The surviving French soldiers were re-embarked whilst Barrington strengthened his defences. On the 29th d'Estaing left and a day later the remaining French forces on St Lucia surrendered. Henceforth, the island would prove to be a useful base to the British, in particular in 1782 when Rodney's fleet was based there just before intercepting and defeating de Grasse at the Saintes. Barrington and his military colleague, Major-General James Grant, had scored a striking and important success by their prompt and decisive action against considerable odds.

Hamilton delin.   *Thornton sculp.*

ST LUCIA *in the* WEST INDIES *taken* Possession *of by* ADMIRAL BARRINGTON Monsieur de Micoud *and the* Inhabitants *having* Capitulated *the* 30.*th of* December, 1778, *being the day after* COUNT D'ESTAIGN *left the* Island *much disconcerted*

8

1. 'Combat de la Frégate Français la *Concorde* contre la frégate Anglaise la *Minerve* (22 Aout 1778)', steel engraving by Chavane after an original by Th Dubois, published by Diagraphe et Pantographe Gavard, Paris, no date. *NMM ref PAF4638*

2. Admiral Samuel Barrington (1729-1800), undated stipple engraving by William Ridley after an original by John Singleton Copley (1737-1815). *NMM ref PAD3049*

3. 'Vue de l'Ile Sainte Lucie, Prise le 31 Decembre 1778 par l'Admiral Barrington', engraved and published by Antoine Suntache after an original by Charles Forest, no date. It shows the assault boats full of troops following the ships of the line into the bay. *NMM ref PAD5343*

4. 'Barrington preparing to receive the French attack on the shipping in the Grand Cul de Sac in St Lucia, 14 Dec 1778', watercolour thought to be the work of Dominic Serres the elder (1722-1793). *NMM ref PAF5787*

5. Barrington's action at St Lucia 15 December 1778, oil painting by Dominic Serres the elder (1722-1793). The procession of French ships passing down the anchored British line is very clear. *NMM ref BHC0422*

6. Barrington's action at St Lucia 15 December 1778, oil painting by Francis Holman (fl1760-1790). The viewpoint is outside the French line with the British within. *NMM ref BHC0423*

7. 'Plan of St Lucia in the West Indies: shewing the positions of the English and French forces with the attacks made at its Reduction in Decr 1778', engraving by T Bowen, from the *Gentleman's Magazine* 49, London, 1779. *NMM ref PAD5341*

8. 'St Lucia in the West Indies taken possession of by Admiral Barrington, Monsieur de Micoul and the Inhabitants having capitulated the 30th of December 1778 being the day after Count D'Estaing left the island much disconcerted', etching by Thornton after an original by Hamilton, no date. *NMM ref PAD5342*

1

Ships of the battlefleet

B Y THE time France entered the war in 1778, a distinct division of labour had emerged among the ships of the Royal Navy. The main types employed in North America have been covered in an earlier section, 'Colonial warfare vessels', and those retained for war with the other European powers were essentially the units of the battlefleet.

The largest, most powerful and most costly ships to build, maintain and operate, were three-deckers carrying 90-100 guns. Largest of all were the First Rates of 100 guns and upwards (1), which were almost exclusively employed as fleet flagships. Because they represented such substantial investments, there were never many, and for most of the American War only three—*Royal George, Britannia* and *Victory*—were available. They needed deep water, a lot of room to manouevre, and the support of a sophisticated dockyard for maintenance, so were rarely risked outside home waters. British First

2

3

Rates were smaller than their French and Spanish equivalents and the *Royal George*, ordered in 1746, was the first to exceed 2000 tons; by way of comparison, the French 110-gun *Ville de Paris*, captured at the Saintes in 1782, measured 2347 tons by British rules.

The real power of the British battle-line resided in the Second Rates of 90 or 98 guns (2), of which there were sixteen in 1775. They were cheaper to build, maintain and man than the prestige First Rates, and in many ways they were the equivalent of the very large two-decker 80-gun ships favoured by France and Spain—in fact, because the latter carried more of the heavier calibres their broadside weight of fire was actually superior. However small and relatively weak in firepower, the Second Rate was still a three-decker, and the British firmly believed in their superiority in battle: the higher command of the third deck gave them a tactical advantage, as well as a depressing effect on enemy morale. They were also resilient: in the April 1780 battle off Martinique, *Sandwich* was engaged for 1½ hours, received 80 hits in the hull, but was still able to manouevre. Furthermore, the relative economy of 90s made it possible to risk them overseas, and most of the West Indies and American squadrons after 1778 were led by Second Rates, beginning with Byron's *Princess Royal*, and including Hood's *Barfleur*, Graves's *London* and Rodney's *Sandwich*—indeed, there were five 90/98s at the Battle of the Saintes.

The Royal Navy's extensive commitments could only be covered by numbers of ships, which led to a consistent and almost unbroken policy which not only resisted growth in the individual sizes of ships but also preferred the smallest and cheapest type that could do the job. In this respect the 98, an 'economy' three-decker, is a characteristic British ship type. Unfortunately, if quan-

4

5

The prospect of war with France produced one of the Royal Navy's few technical initiatives of the eighteenth century, when a decision was taken to introduce a big new frigate type armed with 18pdrs. There were two classes: a 38-gun ship armed with twenty-eight on the main deck (4), and a 36 with two less. Not only were these vessels significantly more powerful than their equivalents in other navies as designed, but were also among the first to be fitted with carronades. *Flora*, 36, was the first completed and in her action with the French frigate *Nymphe* the performance of one of her forecastle 18pdr carronades—manned only by the bosun and a boy—was so impressive that the widescale adoption of the new short-barrelled guns was speeded up. The few 18pdr frigates completed before the end of the war were mostly employed on battlefleet scouting duties, the *Arethusa*, for example, with the Channel Fleet, and the *Flora* with Rodney in the West Indies.

The battlefleet also required small craft for inshore reconnaissance and the carriage of dispatches, the most popular British type for this purpose being the cutter (5). Developed on the English Channel coast, they had a reputation for involvement in dubious activities like smuggling, for their sharp lines, light clinker-built hulls and a broad spread of canvas made them especially fast and weatherly. They were initially hired by the Navy in wartime, but in the 1770s purpose-built naval versions began to be built. One of these, the 10-gun *Alert*, captured the Continental brig *Lexington* in 1777.

Basic data for typical ships, and a few examples of each that played important parts in the war, are given below:

100-gun ships, like *Royal George, Britannia, Victory*
Typical dimensions: 178ft x 52ft x 21ft, 2065 tons
Armament: 28-42pdrs (later reduced to 32pdrs to increase rate of fire), 28-24pdrs, 28-12pdrs, 16-6pdrs, 850 men

90-gun ships, like *Barfleur, Princess Royal, Formidable, Sandwich, London*
Typical dimensions: 177ft x 50ft x 21ft, 1934 tons
Armament: 28-32pdrs, 30-18pdrs, 30-12pdrs, 2-6pdrs (from 1778 some had an extra 8-6pdrs, to become 98s), 750 men

74-gun ships, like *Culloden, Cornwall, Invincible*
Typical dimensions: 170ft x 47ft x 20ft, 1658 tons
Armament: 28-32pdrs, 28-18pdrs, 18-9pdrs, 550 men

38-gun frigates, like *Arethusa, Minerva, Latona*
Typical dimensions: 141ft x 39ft x 14ft, 928 tons
Armament: 28-18pdrs, 10-6pdrs, 270 men

Cutters, like *Alert*
Typical dimensions: 69ft x 26ft x 11ft, 180 tons
Armament: 10-4pdrs, 45 men

tity has a higher priority than quality, there must a penalty, and in the case of the Second Rate, that penalty was in sailing qualities and seakeeping. Since speed is largely a function of waterline length, short designs like the 98 tended to be slow; furthermore, because the height between decks was more or less fixed by the size of human beings, they were relatively tall for their length, which made them leewardly. In fact, the Second Rate suffered an unenviable reputation in the fleet for dismal sailing and clumsy handling.

The most numerous member of the battlefleet was the 74-gun ship (3), a two-decker whose lower profile made it more weatherly than three-deckers but carrying the same lower deck battery of 32pdrs as all but the largest First Rates. This made the 74 an ideal compromise between firepower and sailing qualities, so by 1775 it was virtually the 'standard' battleship, with fifty-seven in service. They were introduced into British service in the 1750s—in concept, a replacement for the old top-heavy and leewardly 80-gun three-deckers—but similar, and generally larger, vessels had existed in the French and Spanish navies for a decade. They were very widely used in every theatre after 1778, and performed so well that by the end of the war there was a widespread feeling that nothing smaller should be allowed in the line of battle—with the 24pdr-armed 64s excluded, and the cumbersome 42pdrs of First Rates replaced, this would give a homogeneous main armament of 32pdrs throughout the battlefleet. However, in 1775 there were still thirty-two 64s in service, and more under construction, so this ideal was not achieved until well into the Napoleonic Wars.

1. A three-decker with a double figurehead, probably the *Royal George* of 1756, drawing by Thomas Mitchell and published by William Mitchell. *NMM ref PAI2612*

2. A 90-gun ship, watercolour portrait by Thomas Mitchell of about 1770. *NMM neg 481*

3. A 74-gun ship in the Solent, watercolour by Dominic Serres, about 1770. *NMM neg D2525*

4. A pen and ink sketch of a British 38-gun frigate by an unknown hand, but of eighteenth-century, foreign provenance. *NMM ref PAD8513*

5. A naval cutter from a portfolio of ship drawings in grey pen and ink and wash by Edward Gwyn of about 1780. *NMM ref PAG3810*

West Indies 1779 — Grenada

AT THE begining of 1779 Vice-Admiral Byron (1), who possessed the somewhat discouraging and unfortunately prophetic nickname of 'Foul Weather Jack' arrived at St Lucia with reinforcements from North America, and replaced Barrington in command. Early in June, whilst Byron was away escorting a homeward-bound convoy out of the West Indies, d'Estaing sent a force to capture St Vincent, and then sailed himself to capture Grenada, which surrendered on 4 July (2). Thirty merchant ships with their rich cargoes were captured in port.

D'Estaing had recently been reinforced and had twenty-five of the line. Byron, with twenty-one of the line and a troop convoy, came hastening to Grenada, and appeared off the island early on 6 July. The British commander did not know his adversary had been rein-

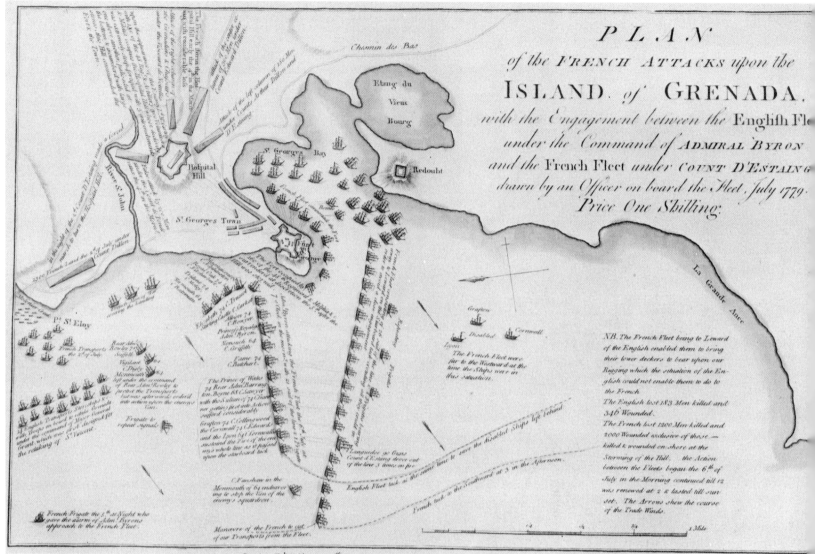

3

forced (indeed he believed the French had fewer ships than himself), and his fleet was not sailing in any particularly good order. As the French fleet emerged from its anchorage, in somewhat straggling fashion, Byron thought he saw an opportunity and signalled 'general chase' to his fleet. This was to encourage them to fall on their enemy as rapidly as possible, and without grouping for mutual support. With the French navy of twenty years earlier or later it might well have worked, even against the numerical odds; but in the case of the well trained and equipped force of the late 1770s, rebuilt after the disasters of the Seven Years War and a decade before the Revolution sapped its strength and morale, it was a bad mistake.

Barrington's three ships were well in advance of the rest of the British fleet and were badly knocked about before the rest came up, trying, with difficulty, to form a line under fire now that they could see the greater strength of the French. Eventually the British were in a rough line, paralleling that of the French, but not before

three ships of their rear had become separated from the rest, come far too close to the enemy, and been crippled by French fire (3).

It was fortunate for Byron that his enemy did not seize the opportunity to capture these damaged ships. As so often happened, the French admiral was too cautious. His fiercest subordinate, Suffren, stated: 'had our admiral's seamanship equalled his courage we would not have allowed four dismasted ships to escape'. Byron withdrew, his ships having suffered much greater damage than his enemy, though mostly in their rigging. French casualties were heavier than British (almost the same number of dead, 183 British, 190 French, but the French had 759 wounded as opposed to the British 239), but there was no doubt that they had won the victory, even if they had failed to take full advantage of it.

On 18 December 1779 small detachments of the British and French fleets, the former at St Lucia under Rear-Admiral Hyde Parker (nicknamed 'Vinegar', and lost at sea before the end of the war, he was not the Hyde

Parker who commanded at Copenhagen in 1801) and the latter under Lamotte-Piquet at Martinique were involved in a sudden little skirmish caused by the unexpected approach of twenty-six French storeships escorted by a frigate (4). The British managed to emerge from their anchorage first with five of the line and a 50-gun ship, and succeeded in taking nine storeships and driving four ashore. However, by then three French ships of the line had emerged from Fort Royal to cover the entry of the rest of the convoy. First one, then another two British ships began to engage the French trio, but were getting too close to the enemy port defences and were called off.

1. The Honourable John Byron (1723-1786) when a captain, oil painting by Sir Joshua Reynolds (1723-1792).
NMM ref BHC 2592

2. 'La Valeur Recompensee, a le prise de la Grenade le 4 Juillet 1779', French engraving by P Laurent after an original by Demarne, published by Boyer, Paris, no date.
NMM ref PAG8865

3. 'Plan of the French Attacks upon the Island of Grenada, with the Engagement between the English fleet under the Command of Admiral Byron and the French Fleet under Count D'Estaing, drawn by an Officer on board the Fleet, July 1779', engraved by J Luffman and published by J Harris, London, 21 September 1779.
Chatham Collection

4. 'Combat naval d'une division français contre une escadre anglais, 18 Decembre 1779', steel engraving by Chavane after an original by A L Rossel de Cercy (1736-1804), published by Diagraphe et Pantographe Gavard, Paris, no date.
NMM ref PAF4640

4

Florida and Central America 1779–1781

IN SEPTEMBER 1779 a small naval force of a 44-gun ship, two frigates, a 20 and some small craft under Captain Luttrell attacked the Honduras coast. He had with him a small detachment of soldiers, some British settlers from Belize, and a number of the local 'Mosquito' (Maya) Indians, long-term British allies, plus his own sailors and marines. After a couple of unsuccessful efforts (the first purely naval) the fort of Omoa was taken by storm on the night of 19/20 October. This was done under the cover of a bombardment by the ships and so effectively that only two fleeing defenders were wounded. A popular incident with historians was the story of a well-armed sailor encountering an unarmed Spanish officer and offering him a cutlass to defend him-

self (1). Two Spanish ships were captured in the harbour and the total amount of treasure taken was some $3,000,000. The British garrison, however, was beyond support and had to be withdrawn a month later.

Another attempt on Spanish Central America in March 1780 was far less successful. An ill-considered attempt to invade Nicaragua up the San Juan River foundered in the face of the very unhealthy climate (2). Thanks, partly, to the exertions of a young Captain Horatio Nelson (3), who had accompanied the soldiers up-river, Spanish advanced positions were taken (4). The main Spanish fort on the river was captured on 29 April but by this time too many troops had died from fever or dysentery (Nelson had already been invalided down-river

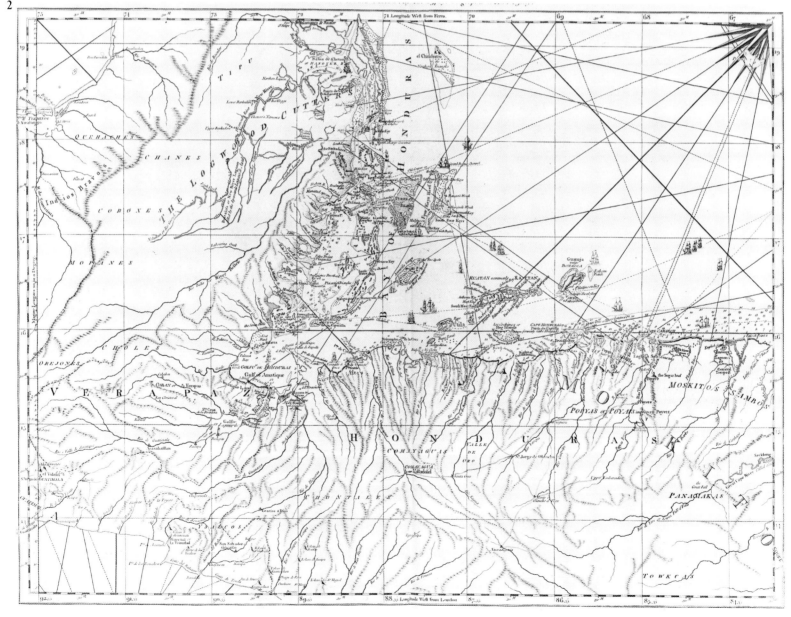

from this, the first of his always unfortunate involvements in amphibious warfare) for there to be any alternative to withdrawal.

Spain achieved much greater results later in the year in its attacks upon British posts in West Florida. By early 1781 only Pensacola (5), the main British base with its garrison of 1200, remained. The Governor of Cuba, Galvez, landed on 9 March to besiege it. Blockaded by an allied squadron which included French line of battle ships, and with no naval support of its own, General Campbell surrendered Pensacola on 9 May.

1. 'Gallant behaviour of an English Sailor in offering a sword to an unarmed Spaniard to defend himself, at the taking of Fort Omoa, in the Bay of Honduras, October 20th 1779', etching by Record after an original by Metz. Engraved for Raymond's *History of England.* NMM ref PAD5354

2. 'The Bay of Honduras. By Tho. Jefferys, Geographer to His Majesty', published by Robert Sayer, London, 20 February 1775. The abolition of British timber cutting rights in the area to the north of the bay was one of Spain's war aims. NMM neg D8285

3. Captain Horatio Nelson (1758-1805), oil painting by Jean Francis

Rigaud (1742-1810), dated 1781. The fort of San Juan appears in the background, representing at this point in his career his most famous exploit.   NMM ref BHC2901

4. 'Storming a post at San Juan', engraving by William Henry Worthington after an original by William Bromley, published by Robert Bowyer, London. NMM ref PAD5359

5. 'A Chart of the Bay and Harbour of Pensacola . . .', engraved and published by J F W Des Barres, London, 1 August 1780. From *The Atlantic Neptune.* NMM neg B4610

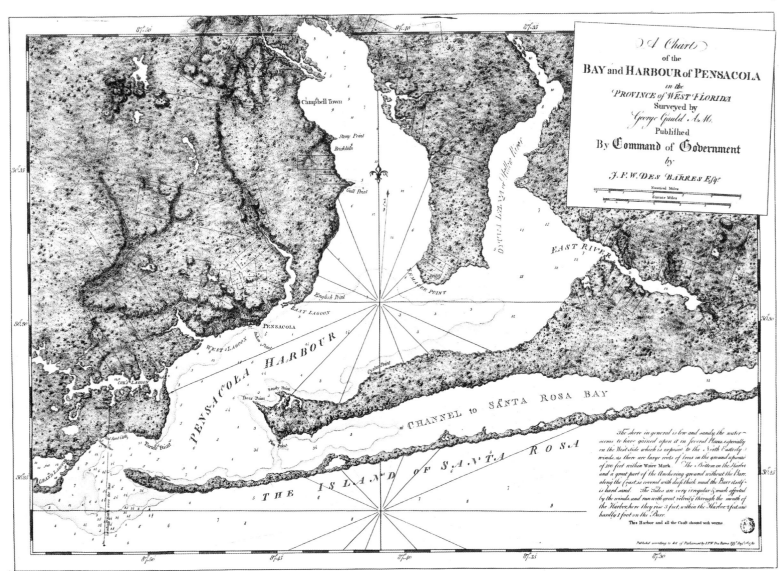

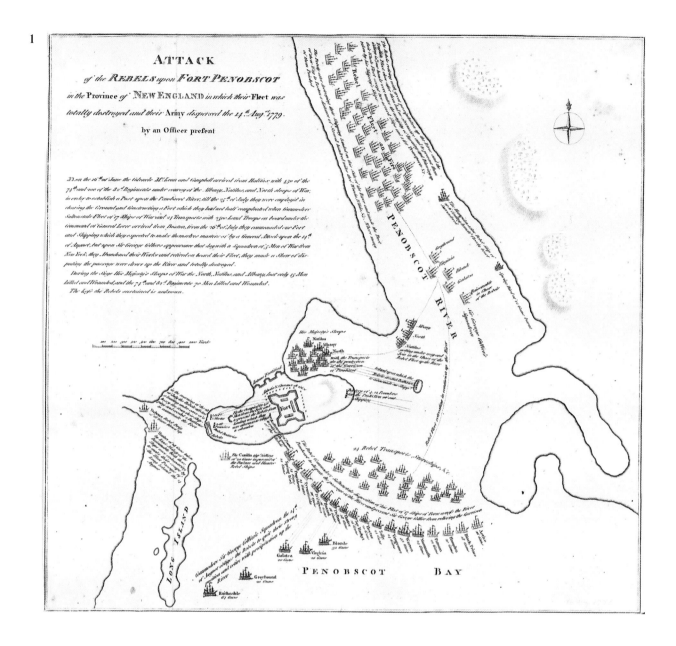

Penobscot fiasco, August 1779

DESPITE REDUCED land and sea forces the British continued a policy of dispersal during 1779, one example being the post set up by troops from Nova Scotia at Castine, Maine in June. It was intended to prevent the rebels from collecting timber supplies from the area, and was enough of an irritant to persuade the Commonwealth of Massachusetts, with virtually no reference to Congress, to mount a major expedition against the place. In fact, it was the state's biggest venture of the war, comprising 1000 militia in nineteen transports, convoyed by seventeen warships, including the continental frigate *Warren*, under the command of Dudley Saltonstall—characterised by John Paul Jones as 'sleepy'.

The British forces were only 450 men protected by three small sloops, *Nautilus, North* and *Albany*, commanded by the infamous 'Mad' Mowat, who burnt Falmouth in 1775; but in a miniature reprise of Barrington's action at St Lucia, Mowat's anchored ships beat off the first attack on 24 July (1). The Americans eventually landed but, given their inexperience in siege warfare, were only ready for a final assault on 13 August. That evening strange sails were seen in the bay, which turned out to belong to a much superior squadron under Sir George Collier—the *Raisonnable*, 64, frigates *Blonde, Virginia* and *Greyhound*, and the smaller *Camilla, Galatea* and *Otter*.

Collier (2) was an experienced, pugnacious and energetic commander who had spent the previous months in

3

large-scale and devastating raids in Chesapeake Bay, but on hearing that Castine was threatened had hastened north and arrived in the nick of time. Sweeping up the bay in general chase on the following day (3), his ships took the *Hunter* and destroyed the *Defence,* the rest of the American flotilla retreating up the Penobscot river in disarray. Lacking pilots, the British anchored for the night, but when pursuit was continued the next day there was only the *Hampden* left to capture–more than thirty ships had been beached and burned by their crews (4) and all survivors–soldiers and sailors–fled into the backwoods.

It was the greatest American naval defeat of the war.

1. 'Attack of the Rebels upon Fort Penobscot in the Province of New England in which their Fleet was totally destroyed and their Army dispersed the 14th August. 1779. By an Officer present'. From Paul de Rapin-Thoyras, *Rapin's Impartial History of England . . .* published, London, 18 December 1784.
NMM ref PAG8866

2. Sir George Collier (1738-1795), Vice-Admiral, stipple engraving by John James Hinchcliffe.
NMM ref PAD3027

3. Sir George Collier's squadron in Penobscot Bay, 14 August 1779, engraved by Baily and published by Joyce Gold, London, 1 November 1814.
NMM ref PAD5344

4. 'Destruction of the American fleet at Penobscot Bay, 14 August 1779', oil painting by Dominic Serres (1722-1793).
NMM ref BHC0425

4

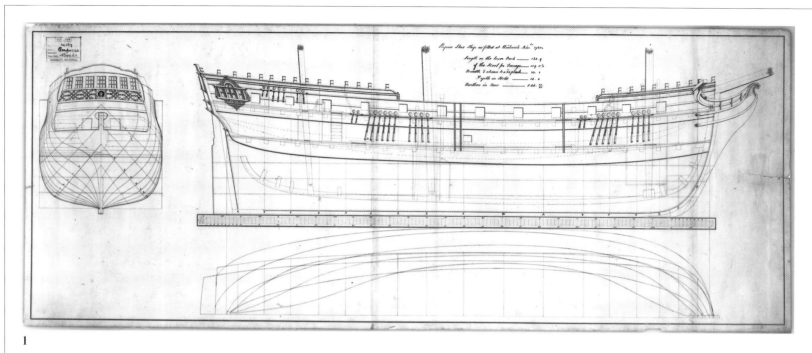

1

Supplying the British army in America

2

URING THE American War of Independence, 'every biscuit, man, and bullet required by the British forces in America had to be transported across 3000 miles of ocean'. The most formidable obstacle to this problem of supply, apart from the Atlantic Ocean, was the inability of the British Cabinet to think in terms of logistics. There was a simple interrelation and interaction between strategy, logistics and shipping, and the effect of geography, but Ministers responsible for strategy were blind to it. They thus ordered movements of whole armies without comprehending that those orders could only be carried out if the shipping transports were available.

In London, understanding of this problem was handicapped by the physical separation of the boards responsible for hiring transports both from one another and from the Cabinet meeting in Whitehall. This obstacle to communication was never solved. Indeed, at the very end of the war, Sir Charles Middleton at the Navy Board only learned of the Cabinet decision to evacuate the army from North America from a newspaper.

The problem of actual hire of transports was intensified by the fact that at the beginning of the war the four boards responsible for transportation had to compete with one another for the shipping available. The Treasury hired army victuallers; the Navy Board hired the transports for troops as well as for the delivery of naval stores (1) to the dockyards and fleet overseas; the Ordnance Board hired ships to carry artillery men, ammunition, arms, ordnance and engineering stores and equipment; and the Victualling Board hired victuallers to supply the fleet. Only in March 1779 was this situation rationalised. The Treasury lacked the facilities and personnel with the technical skills to manage the hire of transports and, partly as a result of the appointment to the Navy Board of the assertive Middleton, the responsibility for army victualling was transferred to the board of which he was Comptroller.

However, the amount of shipping available for hire at any one time was itself limited. After 1780 the Navy Board repeatedly attempted to bring this shortage to Cabinet notice, but in vain. The tonnage already under hire to the Board was retained across the Atlantic, preventing its re-use, and this board was handicapped from hiring more ships because the weakness of its credit did not permit it to offer freight rates that could compete with the rates paid by the Ordnance and Victualling Boards. The Navy Board's shortage was never comprehended as a problem by the Cabinet. Indeed, this failure of understanding placed the British war effort continually on the edge of disaster because the transports actually secured were always subject to delays before they reached their destinations from the impressment of their crews, unfavourable winds, storm damage, and the gathering or slow sailing of convoys.

Initially the British army in America was expected and had to live partly from what it could obtain from local coastal regions. Its failure to capture and hold an area from which to draw supplies, including firewood and horse forage, created an immediate supply crisis. By 1778 the Treasury, initially responsible for the supply of provisions, had brought together a fleet of 115 army victuallers with a total tonnage of 30,052 tons. But in 1779, when the Navy Board took over the maintenance of army victuallers, it found that the responsibility extended not only to the supply over 38,000 regular troops in America and 7000 in Canada, but included 10,500 en route to or in the West Indies, 369 in West Africa, nearly 5000 at Gibraltar, and over 2100 in Minorca.

By December 1781 the Navy Board had 369 ships under hire as transports—157 for troops (2) and 212 to convey their victuals. This number was only exceeded in July 1776 when the Navy Board hired 416 transports with a capacity of 128,427 tons to carry the British army of more than 27,000 troops to America. Most of these ships were obtained by advertisement in the London newspapers and measured, surveyed, appraised and fitted out at the Royal dockyards, especially at Deptford.

Troop transports carried infantry, cavalry, camp equipage, army clothing, horses (3), quartermaster stores, Indian presents, as well as various other items required by the armed forces. Camp equipment included such material as tents with poles and pegs, mallets, drum cases, powder bags, hatchets, scythes, picket posts and ropes, water buckets, kettles, canteens, haversacks and camp colours.

Troops were put aboard in the ratio of 100 soldiers to 200 tons of shipping. In such ships, tall men could neither stand up between decks, nor sit up straight between berths. Men were packed like herring, six to a four-man berth. Lying down together was impossible unless they all laid spoon fashion, so that when one turned over they all had to do the same. Overcrowding and personal frictions made the transatlantic voyage an ordeal. An experienced German mercenary claimed 'the most

strenuous campaign cannot be as trying as such a voyage'. A Guards officer described life on board as 'continued destruction in the foretops, the pox above-board, the plague between decks, hell in the forecastle, the devil at the helm'.

1. Sheer draught of the naval transport *Porpoise*, a big converted Swedish East Indiaman of 646 tons purchased in 1780. By the time the colonists had organised a serious privateering effort, it became essential to give such vessels a significant defensive armament, and this ship carried eighteen 6pdrs. Admiralty Collection.
NMM neg 4167

2. 'Bâtiments de transports anglais embarquant des effets militaires', engraving by J J Baugean, Plate 32 from *Collection de Toutes des Especes de Batiments . . .* (fifth edition, Paris 1826). The habit developed of numbering hired transports and the number was then painted on the hull for identification purposes, as with the '61' on this vessel's quarter. The lateen rigged vessel alongside, from which a gun is being embarked, suggests an Italian port.
NMM ref PAD7408

3. Horses required special facilities if they were to survive long voyages, and this cross-sectional model shows some of the features—the broad staging to help with hoisting them inboard, and the stalls below deck where they were secured in canvas slings to prevent their being thrown around by the movement of the ship.
NMM ref SLR0508

3

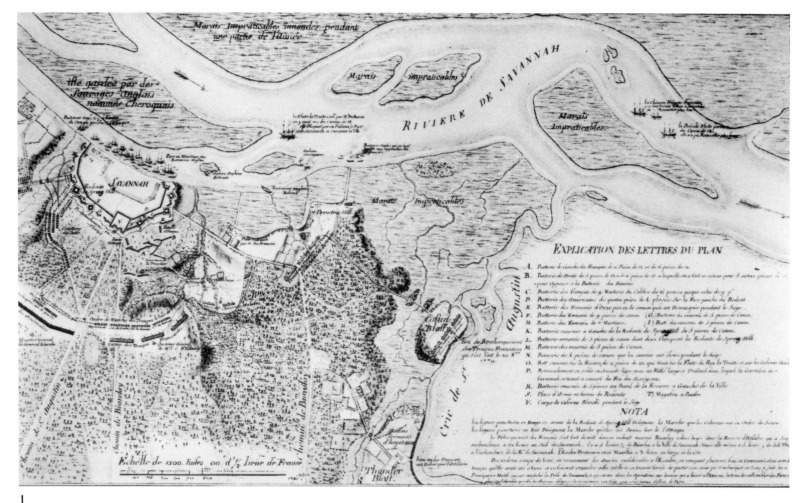

1

Siege of Savannah, October 1779

A PERFECT DEMONSTRATION of the flexibility of seapower was the effect on the British of the uncertainty surrounding d'Estaing's plans for his fleet after the conclusion of his successful spring 1779 campaign in the West Indies. It was rumoured that an invasion of Jamaica was on the cards, and when the French fleet appeared off Georgia, the British had no idea where he might strike—in panic troops were with-

drawn from the Hudson Highlands back towards New York and Rhode Island was abandoned; it was even thought Halifax might be his target.

The arrival of thirty-three ships with 4000 French troops before Savannah on 3 September was a total surprise. The 50-gun *Experiment*, the *Ariel*, 20, and two store-ships were captured, the booty including the British army's complete payroll and—more importantly to

2

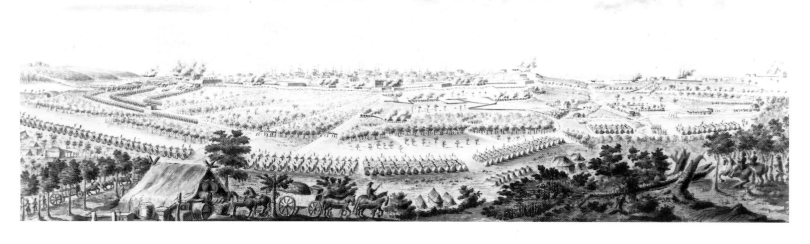

d'Estaing—a wealth of naval stores. Savannah had fallen to the British at the turn of the year through a combination of land forces from Florida and a naval expedition under Hyde Parker, so although the city was surrounded by marshlands and creeks (1), it was not impregnable. The city was formally summoned to surrender on 16 September, but, having been joined by 1500 Americans, d'Estaing began the siege of Savannah's 2400 recalcitrant defenders on the 23rd. The British had blocked the channel immediately before the city, so French warships could not get close enough for an overwhelming bombardment, so investment from the landward side was the only option.

The French were masters of siege warfare, and Ozanne depicted well the formal lines of trenches and encampments before the city (2). But it was an art that required time—time that d'Estaing could not afford, because his fleet was being rapidly reduced by disease,

mostly scurvy, that was causing thirty-five mortalities a day. The siege was making little progress, so he ordered a frontal assault, and on the morning of 9 October three French and two American columns advanced over nearly 500 yards of open ground against well prepared positions. American colours were temporarily planted on one redoubt, but the attack was beaten back with very heavy casualties—about eight hundred of the allies being killed to a mere sixteen British (3). D'Estaing himself was wounded leading the assault, and over the vigorous protests of the Americans, he immediately re-embarked his army and sailed for France, leaving his allies to retreat into South Carolina.

Although he achieved some success in the West Indies, and inspired a number of panicky British retreats, d'Estaing's direct contribution to the cause of American independence was, at the very least, disappointing.

1. 'Siège de Savannah . . . 1779', water-colour by Pierre Ozanne. *Library of Congress, Washington DC ref 609826-262-11899*

2. 'Vue de la Ville de Savannah, du Camp, des Trancheês et de l'attaque Octobre 1779', watercolour by Pierre Ozanne. *Library of Congress, Washington DC ref 609826-262-11898*

3. 'Plan of the Siege of Savannah, with the joint Attack of the French and Americans on the 9th October 1779 In which they were defeated by his Majesty's forces under the command of Major Genl. Augustin Prevost. From a Survey by an Officer', engraved for Stedman's *History of the American War*, 20 January 1794. The original was made by John Wilson, an engineer in Campbell's 71st regiment, and engraved and published by William Faden in 1784. *Chatham Collection*

3

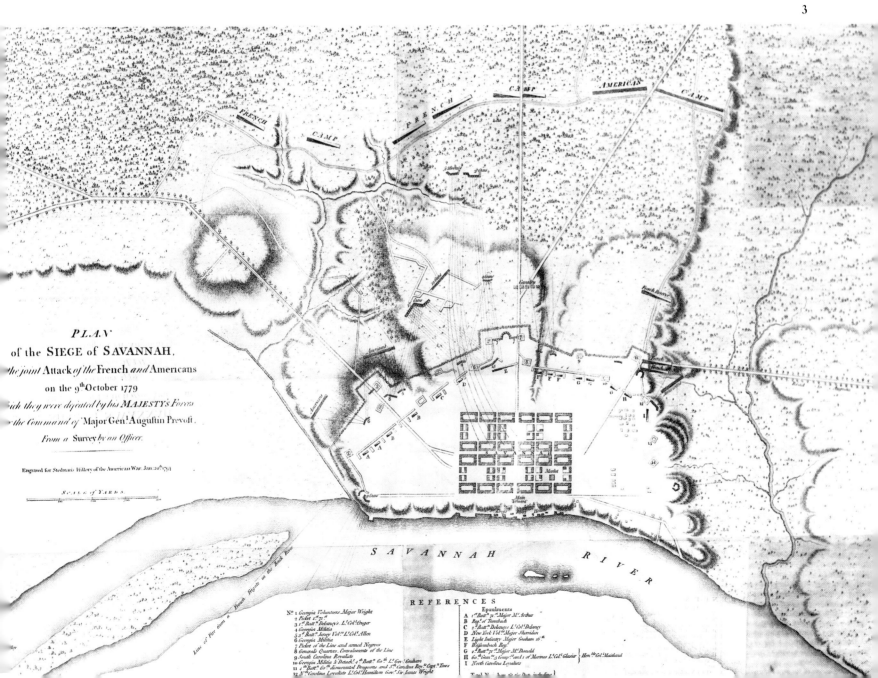

PLAN
of the SIEGE of SAVANNAH,
the joint Attack of the French and Americans
on the 9th October 1779
which they were defeated by his MAJESTY'S Forces
the Command of Major Genl. Augustin Prevost.
From a Survey by an Officer.

Engraved for Stedman's History of the American War. Jan: 20th 1794

SCALE of YARDS.

1

2

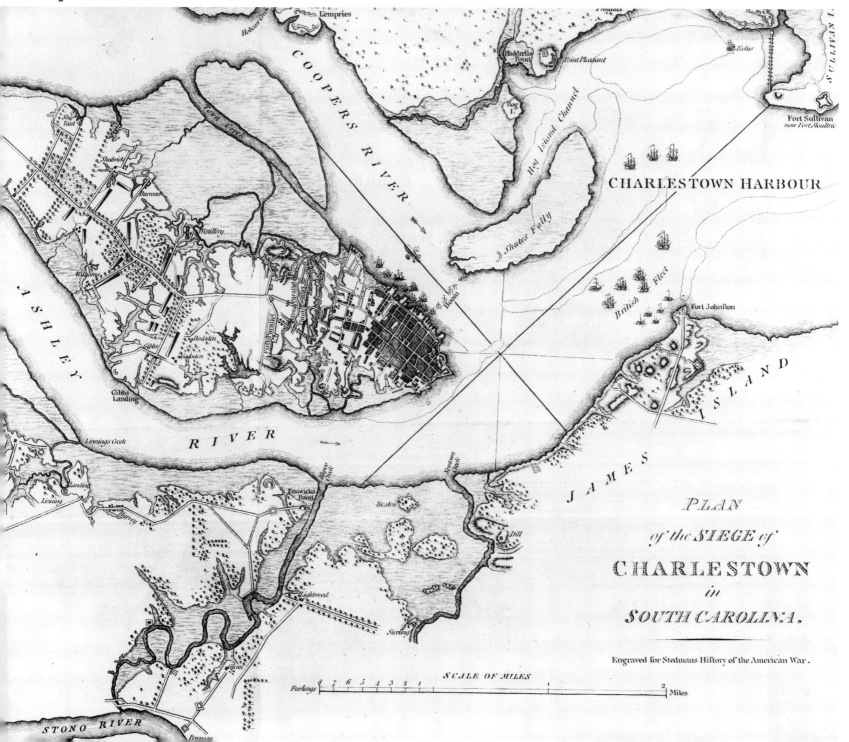

PLAN
of the SIEGE of
CHARLESTOWN
in
SOUTH CAROLINA.

Engraved for Stedmans History of the American War.

Capture of Charleston, 1780

ONCE IT was clear that Savannah was saved and d'Estaing really had taken his fleet back to France, Clinton embarked on another British military adventure in the south. His target was Charleston (1), which he had failed to take in 1776; but in the interim he had learnt much about what was called at the time 'littoral warfare', or amphibious operations, and the whole campaign was much better planned. The area around the city was watery and carved up into many islands, and Clinton intended to use the mobility endowed by his naval resources to slowly envelop the city and trap its defenders, rather than attempt another forcing of the harbour that had proved so disastrous the first time. Although Admiral Arbuthnot, the overall naval commander was old and difficult, Clinton was lucky to have the extremely capable services of George Keith Elphinstone (later Lord Keith) for close support of the army.

After a stormy passage in which ordnance transports went missing and most of the expedition's horses died, about 7500 men were landed on 11 February to begin the process of occupying the south side of the harbour across the marshlands of John and James Islands. Naval vessels first crossed the bar on 20 March and the Americans then blocked the entrance to Cooper River, but Clinton advanced up the western side of the Ashley, and on the 29th elite units conveyed in seventy-five flat-boats made a surprise landing on the peninsula to the north of the city. Charleston was invested on 1 April, and on the 9th the navy ran the gauntlet of Fort Moultrie that had proved their nemesis in 1776. The transport *Aeolus* (top right in '2') ran aground and had to be burnt, but *Roebuck, Romulus*, four frigates and an armed ship got through. Having failed to break into the Cooper river, the navy spent the next month clearing the north shore fortifications in a series of clinically efficient amphibious attacks, and with all communication then cut off Charleston surrendered on 12 May.

Among the ships captured were the whole of Commodore Whipple's squadron—*Providence*, 28, *Boston*, 24, and *Ranger*—a French corvette and several South Carolina state vessels (3). American prisoners included seven generals and 6000 men, with over 400 guns. It is reckoned the worst American defeat by a foreign enemy before Bataan in 1942.

2. 'A Plan of the Siege of Charlestown in South Carolina', engraved for Stedman's *History of the American War*, London 1794.
Chatham Collection

3. 'A Sketch of the Operations before Charlestown, the Capital of South Carolina, 1780', engraved by Abernethie for David Ramsay's *History of the Revolution of South Carolina*, Trenton, 1785.
NMM neg X1933

1. 'A View of Charles-Town, the Capital of South Carolina. From an Original Picture painted of Charles Town, in the year 1774', painted by Thomas Leitch, engraved and published by Samuel Smith, London, 3 June 1776.
NMM ref PAI0325

West Indies, 1780

THE BALANCE of power in the West Indies during 1780 was to see-saw back and forth as successive French and British squadrons arrived from Europe. The initial British superiority was lost at the end of March when de Guichen's fleet of sixteen of the line and four frigates brought in a huge convoy of eighty-three merchantmen. His first plan was to attack St Lucia (1), but he was foiled by the timely appearance off the island of Rodney with four ships of the line, making the British total twenty (2). The French switched their attention to Barbados, but after some initial skirmishing Rodney was finally able to bring de Guichen to action off Martinique on 17 April.

Rodney (3) was one of the growing number of British admirals who knew that battles between roughly equal numbers in line ahead were unlikely to produce a decisive result. He was fresh from a crushing victory over a Spanish fleet at the so-called Moonlight Battle achieved by general chase, and he had a plan for the French: he intended to concentrate on the rear part of the line, and defeat it in detail with overwhelming force, before the van could tack to its rescue. Unfortunately, Rodney was no great communicator, and his captains plainly did not understand his intentions. As the British fleet edged down the leading ship, *Stirling Castle*, made sail for the head of the French line and the whole van division followed suit, the resulting battle turning into the ship-to-ship slogging match Rodney had sought to avoid (4). The result was inconclusive, and although the French suffered twice the casualties, there was no alteration in the balance of power. Rodney was furious, and the recriminations were long and tedious, but whether the cause was his own inadequate briefing or too rigid a signal book, is still a moot point. There were other, equally inconsequential clashes between the fleets in May, but the only result was purely negative, in that de Guichen's planned invasion of St Lucia was prevented.

Despite the appearance of a Spanish squadron in June, the Bourbon allies were unable to capitalise on their superiority because of widespread sickness throughout both forces. However, the extreme difficulty of operating wooden sailing fleets in West Indian conditions was even more emphatically underlined for the British, when an October hurricane devastated the whole command. Rodney had taken some ships north to America, but he could not denude the Leeward Islands entirely in the circumstances, and the storm destroyed the *Thunderer*, 74, *Stirling Castle*, 64, *Phoenix*, 44, three frigates and six smaller ships. This was not the end of the loss because another twelve two-deckers and a frigate were dismasted or otherwise seriously damaged, including the *Egmont* (5), *Hector* and *Bristol* (6); one of their number, the *Berwick*, 74, was driven clear across the Atlantic and eventually made landfall at Milford Haven in west Wales.

With no major dockyard in the whole of the West Indies, Rodney's fleet was more effectively crippled than the French had achieved in two years of warfare.

1. 'A View of Pigeon Island and Gros Islet Bay in the Island of St Lucia, distant about half a League', coloured aquatint and etching by Francis Chesham after an original 'drawn from nature' by Lt Charles Forrest, June 1781, and published by William Faden, London, 1 March 1786.
NMM ref PAH3025

2. 'A View of Pigeon Island and Part of Island of St Lucia, Taken March 25 1780 at Eleven oClock AM', engraved by Francis Chesham after an original 'drawn from nature' by Lt Charles Forrest, late of the 96th Regiment, and published by William Faden, London, 10 March 1784. It depicts the British fleet under Hyde Parker preparing to repulse de Guichen.
NMM ref PAH3026

3. Admiral Lord George Brydges Rodney (1719-1792), 1st Baron Rodney, oil painting by Jean Laurent Mosnier (1743-1808).
NMM ref BHC2970

4. 'Engagement off Martinico between Admiral Rodney & Monsieur Guichen, Apr 18 1780', engraving published by James McGowan, London, 28 April 1781.
NMM ref PAD5360

5. 'To Sir Peter Parker . . . This Representation of the distressed situation of his Majesty's Ship *Egmont* . . . when dismasted in the Great Hurricane, Oct 6th 1780 near the Island St Lucia . . . by . . . William Elliott', mezzotint engraved by Valentine Green, published by Lt William Elliott, Gosport, 30 April 1784.
NMM ref PAG8417

6. 'To Sir Peter Parker . . . This Representation of the distressed situation of his Majesty's Ships *Hector* and *Bristol* . . . when dismasted in the Great Hurricane, Oct 6th 1780 near the Island St Lucia . . . by . . . William Elliott', mezzotint engraved by Valentine Green, published by Lt William Elliott, Gosport, 30 April 1784.
NMM ref PAG8418

3

4

5

6

1

West Indies 1781 – St Eustatius

GEORGE BRYDGES Rodney is one of the least attractive of the great British naval commanders – grasping and nepotistic enough for it to be particularly noticed in a nepotistic and grasping age, and, unusually, a particularly bad judge of character. Despite this he undoubtedly had a great tactical talent, but by 1781 he was an old man, frequently crippled by attacks of gout and near the end of his strength. He was, however, still capable of decisive action.

The neutral Dutch island of St Eustatius had benefited mightily as a centre of smuggling contraband, including arms, to the North American rebels. Many British merchants were heavily involved. On 27 January 1781 Rodney and his military colleague General Vaughan received the welcome news that hostilities were to commence against the Netherlands with an attack on that island, and within three days an expedition sailed. On 3 February, before the threat of twelve ships of the line, the island was immediately surrendered, the haul including over 150 merchantmen in harbour (1, 2). A convoy of thirty ships which had left a couple of days earlier was pursued, and, still unaware of the outbreak of war, captured with its escort, the *Mars* (3).

Rodney then spent a long time supervising the packing up and despatch back to Europe of the loot — valued at around £3,000,000 at the time — when he should have been trying to counter French moves. It seems like poetic justice that the French fleet captured most of the returning convoy with the proceeds from St Eustatius when it reached European waters.

Hood, meanwhile, had been left to blockade the four French ships of the line left in Martinique. On 22 March he found himself, with eighteen of the line, opposed by twenty French ships of the line under de Grasse from Brest, accompanying a convoy. He was therefore outnumbered, but did have the advantage that all his ships were coppered. However, he was too far to leeward to get really close to the French. Long range fire was exchanged: 'Never, I believe, was more powder and shot thrown away on one day before,' said he (4). His four rearmost ships got more closely engaged with twice the number of Frenchmen, but, though damaged, were not crippled, and the action ended indecisively. The next day Hood tried to get to windward of the French without success, and the two fleets then separated.

2

3

4

De Grasse then planned to take St Lucia, but his attempt at landing was beaten off by the strong defences. He then moved on to Tobago (5), to which he had already sent a landing force. The British defenders capitulated on 2 June after a small naval force under Rear-Admiral Drake had been forced to retreat in the face of superior numbers. Rodney attempted to restore the situation by sailing to Tobago with his entire fleet, but it arrived two days too late. On 9 June the two hostile fleets sighted one another, but neither felt able to engage the other, and Rodney therefore lost his last chance to stop de Grasse before he sailed to the Chesapeake.

1. 'Vue De L'Ile de Saint Eustache Prise Dans L'Entiere Entendue Conquise par le Vice Admiral Rodney . . .' 3 February 1781, etching by Charles Forest.
NMM ref PAD5363

2. 'A View of the English Fleet before St Eustatius at the time of its Surrender to Sir George Brydges Rodney Bart. on the 3rd of February 1781', anonymous grey wash and graphite drawing, undated.
NMM neg 1730

3. Dutch etching of the capture of the Dutch *Mars* and her convoy by *Monarch*, 74, *Panther*, 60, and the frigate *Sibyl* on 4 February 1781.
NMM ref PAD5364

4. The battle between the fleets of Hood and de Grasse off Martinique, 29 April 1781, anonymous sketch in black and wash, grey pen and ink, undated.
NMM ref PAH9521

5. 'A Map of the Island of Tobago, drawn from an Actual Survey, By Thos Bowen, 1779 [sic]', published in the *Gentleman's Magazine* 48, London, 1778.
Chatham Collection

5

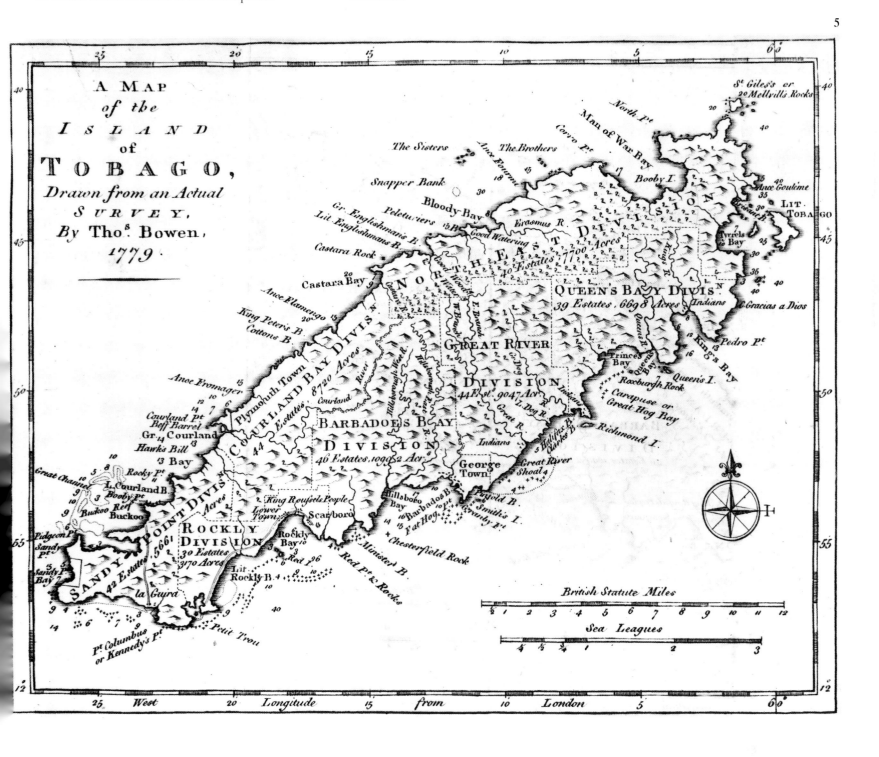

A MAP of the ISLAND of TOBAGO, Drawn from an Actual SURVEY, By Thos. Bowen, 1779.

1

Struggle for the Chesapeake, 1781

AFTER THE success at Charleston, the chronic inability of their commanders, General Clinton and Admiral Arbuthnot, to co-operate lost the British the opportunity to destroy the powerful French army and fleet at Newport during 1780, even after the arrival of Rodney's squadron gave them real superiority. After Rodney had returned to the West Indies in November, Clinton sent a raiding force under Benedict Arnold to the Chesapeake area, where it rapidly captured Richmond and proceeded to wreak havoc in the surrounding countryside. In January 1781, however, the French *Eveille*, 64 and two frigates escaped from the Newport blockading squadron and sailed south, but Arnold was forewarned and withdrew his small craft up the Elizabeth River. They did surprise the 44-gun *Romulus* in the Chesapeake and captured a few merchant ships in February (1), but their greatest success was adventitious: the pursuing squadron was hit by bad weather and two ships of the line were badly damaged, and the *Culloden*, 74, was wrecked.

2

A more serious French attempt was made in March when seven of the line and some smaller vessels under Destouches set sail carrying 1100 troops. To avoid the British squadron they made a detour out into the Atlantic, but with hulls foul from long months of idleness at Newport, they sailed slowly and before they could enter the Chesapeake blundered into Arbuthnot's 'pursuing' squadron on 16 March. Marriot Arbuthnot (2) was not one of the Royal Navy's great admirals, and in the ensuing fight was outmanouevred, although not outfought, by Destouches, who suffered twice the casualties. The British squadron was not well drilled, and although inflexible signals might be blamed (3), Arbuthnot's captains certainly did not understand his intentions. The French, however, abandoned the Chesapeake to the damaged British squadron, who prevented Arnold's force from being trapped, so the battle off Cape Henry was a kind of strategic victory.

In the meantime, Cornwallis's southern army had run into serious guerilla opposition while campaigning in the Carolinas, and although it won a series of bloody but strategically meaningless victories, it was in danger of being expended through attrition to no serious purpose. Cornwallis decided to head for Virginia to join up with the expeditionary forces around the Chesapeake, by then a major focus of British activity (4)—on 25 April at Cape Fear he set out on the road to Yorktown.

Both sides expected a large French fleet under de Grasse to arrive from the West Indies in the summer, and Washington had already set in motion his land forces to trap the British. Rodney sent Rear-Admiral Hood with a strong reinforcement to America, but being junior Hood could not galvanise the new naval commander, Rear-Admiral Thomas Graves (5), into action

British Line of Battle

Under the command of Vice Adm.r Arbuthnot when in Action with the French Fleet under the command of Mon.r De Touches off the Chesapeake 16 March 1781

The America to lead with the Starb.d & the Robust with the Larb.t tack on Board

Ships in the Line Names	Commanders of D.o Names	Signal Pendants	Distinguishing Vanes &c.a Colours	where hoisted	N.o of Guns	Men
America	Capt.n Thompson	Fore		main	64	500
Adament	Johnson	mizen T S yard		D.o	50	350
Bedford	Affleck	main		D.o	74	600
London	{ Rear Adm.l Graves / Captain Graves }	mizen T S yard		Mizen	98	760
Royal Oak	{ Vice Adm.l Arbuthnot / Captain Swiney }	main		Fore	74	650
Europe	Child	mizen T S yard		main	64	500
Prudent	Burnell	main		Fore	64	500
Robust	Crosby	Fore		D.o	74	600
		Total Number of			562	4460
Frigates &c.a						
Iris	Capt. Dawson	mizen		main	32	220
Pearl	Montague	mizen T S yard		D.o	32	220
Guardelope	Robinson	Fore T S yard		D.o	28	200

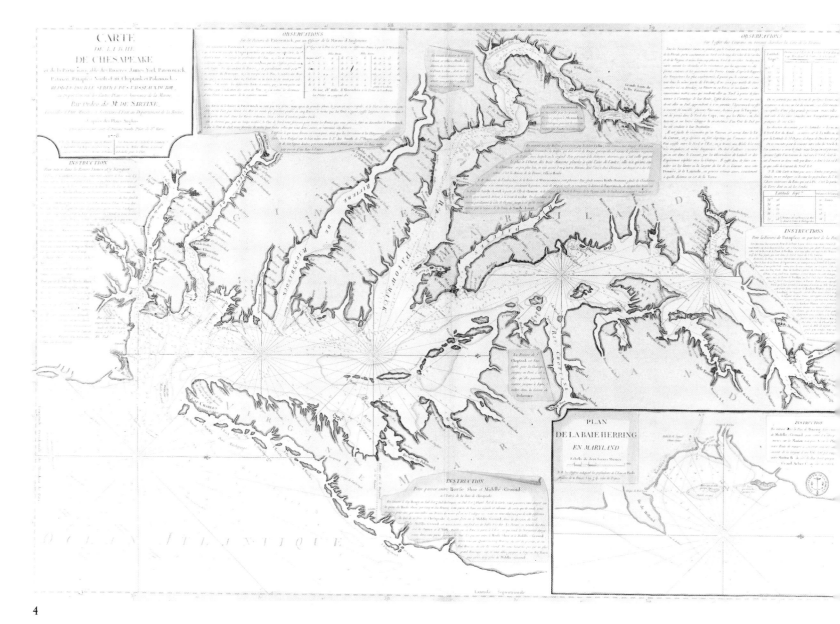

4

5

until it was too late. De Grasse duly arrived on 29 August, with twenty-six sail of the line and eight smaller ships, landing a further 3000 troops to add to those besieging Yorktown. More importantly, he blockaded the mouths of the James and York rivers, cutting Cornwallis's communications by sea, and he then anchored inside the mouth of the Chesapeake in Lynnhaven Bay.

The Battle of the Chesapeake, 5 September

The British fleet of nineteen of the line plus a 50 finally arrived on 5 September, and de Grasse elected to fight at sea rather than at anchor as Barrington had done at St Lucia. Although he could take a significantly superior twenty-four ships of the line to sea, it was an extremely risky manouevre, since it meant working out of the bay in relative disorder in the face of a well formed British fleet (6). Many critics have echoed Hood's view that here was a golden opportunity to destroy the French vanguard before the remainder could come into action, but Byron's experience at Grenada had demonstrated the risks of assaulting a superior squadron in general chase. Instead, Graves ordered his van squadron to wear round together as it approached the Middle Ground shoal, which reversed the previous order of sailing (7).

The fleets then came together on gently converging courses (8), and there followed an inconclusive two-hour cannonade which did not involve the rear of either line before the fleets disengaged. Damage and casualties were roughly equal on each side, and for the next few days both fleets lay to in sight of one another (9). Hood, angry and unco-operative at the time, later claimed that the British fleet should have entered the Chesapeake after the battle and barred the entrance, as he was to do shortly at St Kitts. By this time it was known that Washington was marching on Yorktown and the seriousness of Cornwallis's predicament should have been realised, but Graves felt his fleet was in no condition for decisive action —indeed, on the 10th the badly damaged *Terrible* was abandoned and burnt. On the previous day de Grasse had slipped away to join in Chesapeake Bay the newly arrived squadron from Newport, which was carrying the French army's siege train.

Tactically, the Chesapeake had been an insignificant naval battle, but its strategic consequences were far-reaching. Graves could do little except retire to New York to refit, and the fate of Cornwallis's army was sealed.

1. 'Prise du Romulus dans la Baye de Chesapeak. Par Mr Le Cardeur de Tilly', contemporary French coloured engraving (artist unknown).
NMM ref PAD5365

2. Marriott Arbuthnot (?1711-1794), Admiral of the Blue, engraved by H R Cook after an original by J Rising, published by Joyce Gold, London, 30 April 1810.
NMM ref PAD3022

3. Arbuthnot's line of battle in the engagement with Des Touches, 16 March 1781, with coloured signal pendants, etc. Illustrations from Daniel Woodhouse's journal in HMS *America*.
NMM ref JOD/40

4. 'Carte de la Baie de Chesapeake . . .' Official French naval chart of Chesapeake Bay after English originals, printed by order of M de Sartine, the Navy Minister, 1778. The text includes much pilotage information, including instructions for entering the bay between the Horse Shoe and Middle Ground shoals. Cornwallis's army was confined to York and Gloucester on either side of the York River (second from left of the rivers flowing down into the main bay).
Beverley R Robinson Collection

5. Rear-Admiral Sir Thomas Graves (?1747-1814), oil painting by James Northcott (1746-1831).
NMM ref BHC2722

6. 'Position of the English and French fleets Immediately previous to the Action on the 5th Sepr 1781', engraved for Stedman's *History of the American War*, London 1794.
Chatham Collection

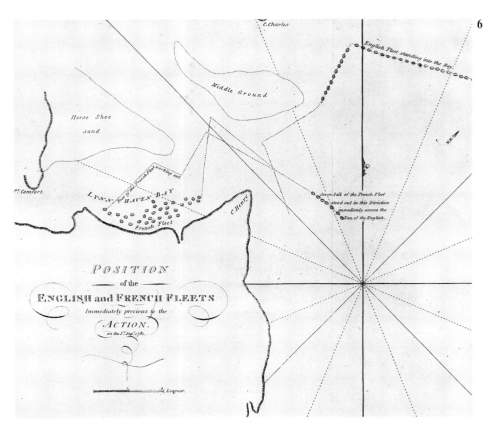

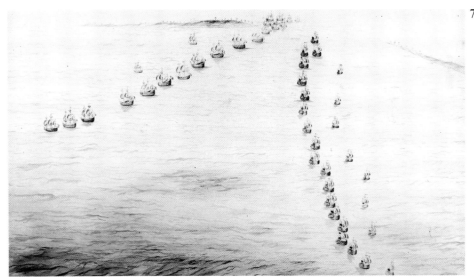

7. 'A View of the French fleet of 24 . . . coming round Cape Henry out of the Chesapeake, while the English fleet of 19 . . . were standing in to Attack them, the 5th September 1781.' Anonymous contemporary drawing in grey wash.
NMM neg 8980

8. 'A View of the English fleet of 19 . . . attacking the French fleet of 24 coming out of the Chesapeake, the 5th September 1781.' Anonymous contemporary drawing in grey wash.
NMM neg 8981

9. 'A Representation of the Sea Fight on the 5th of Sepr 1781, between Rear Admiral Graves and the Count De Grasse' , from William Graves, Two Letters . . . Respecting the Conduct of Rear-Admiral Graves in North America, London, 1782. This is a later, slightly modified variant, published in the *Political Magazine* VI, London, 1784. It is probably the most accurate depiction of the actual manoeuvres in the battle and tallies closely with French accounts.
Beverley R Robinson Collection

9

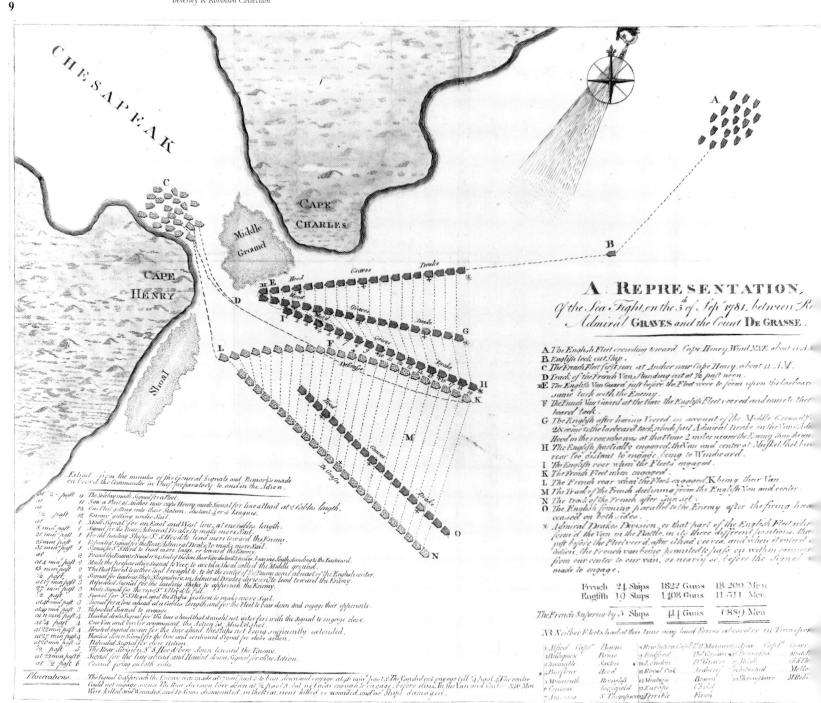

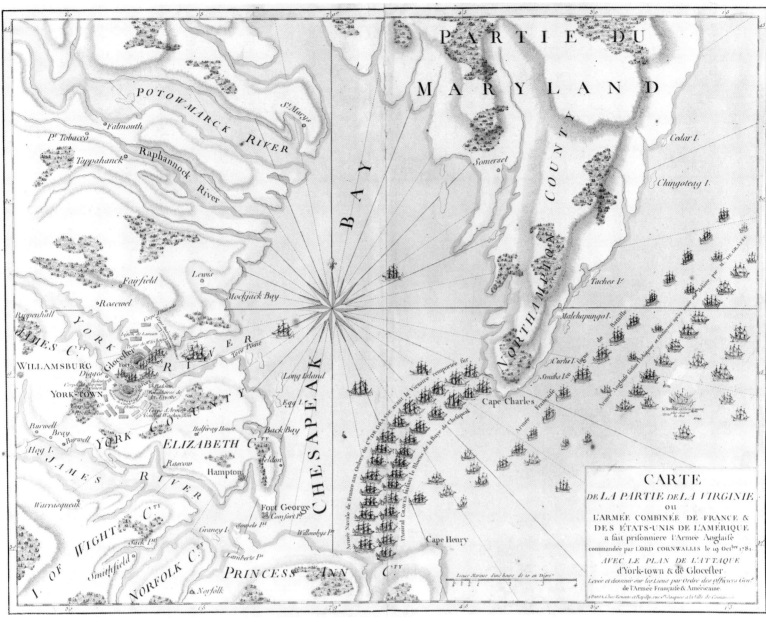

Within the map:

PARTIE DU MARYLAND

NORTHAMPTON COUNTY

POTOWMARCK RIVER

Raphannock River

St Marys

Falmouth

Pt Tobacco

Tappahanck

Fairfield

Lewis

Rosewel

Roppenhall

WILLIAMSBURG

YORK-TOWN

Burwell
Bray
Burwell

Hog I.

JAMES RIVER

Warrasqueak

Smithfield

I. OF WIGHT C.TY

NORFOLK C.TY

Norfolk

PRINCESS ANN C.TY

Lamberts Pt

Willowbys Pt

Sowels Pt

Graney I.

Rascow

Hampton

ELIZABETH C.TY

Feldon

Back Bay

Halfway House

Fort George
Comfort Pt

Cape Henry

Cape Charles

Long Island

Egg I.

York Point

Mockjack Bay

YORK RIVER

YORK COUNTY

JAMES C.TY

Glocester Fort

CHESAPEAK BAY

Somerset

Cedar I.

Chingoteag I.

Taches I.

Malchapungo I.

Curtis I.

Smiths I.

Armée Navale de France aux Ordres du Cte DE GRASSE avant la Victoire remportée sur l'Amiral GRAVES faisant le blocus de la Baye de Chesapeak

CARTE
DE LA PARTIE DE LA VIRGINIE
OU
L'ARMÉE COMBINÉE DE FRANCE &
DES ÉTATS-UNIS DE L'AMÉRIQUE
a fait prisonniere l'Armée Anglaise
commandée par LORD CORNWALLIS le 19 Octbre 1781.
AVEC LE PLAN DE L'ATTAQUE
d'York-town & de Glocester
Levée et dessinée sur les Lieux par Ordre des Officiers Genx
de l'Armée Française & Américaine.

1

Yorktown – the world turned upside down

THE BRITISH higher command at New York spent much of September and early October debating how to rescue Cornwallis while the refitting of the fleet proceeded painfully slowly due to the lack of proper stores and equipment. There could be no relief overland in the timescale available, and as long as the French fleet blocked the entrance to the Chesapeake – as shown in this stylised French map (1) – any amphibious assault would be very risky. A fireship attack was launched from Yorktown on the French squadron by the *Vulcan* (2) on 23 September, causing panic but no substantive damage.

The Franco-American siege operations opened on 30 September, and by 9 October the British lines were under direct bombardment by forty heavy guns and sixteen mortars. The *Charon*, 44, was set on fire and the rest of the British squadron off the town, including the *Fowey*, 24, and *Guadeloupe*, 28, was then scuttled to prevent its destruction. Yorktown was not naturally defensible, and at this stage Cornwallis reported, 'With such Works on disadvantageous Ground against so powerful an attack we cannot hope to make a long Resistance.' On the night of the 14th two of the principal redoubts were carried by American and French assault ('A' and 'B' in 3), and on the 19th the British fleet finally sailed from New York with a relief force. But they were too late, for on

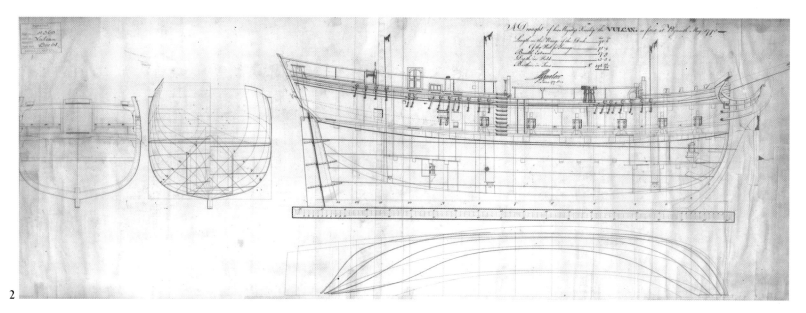

2

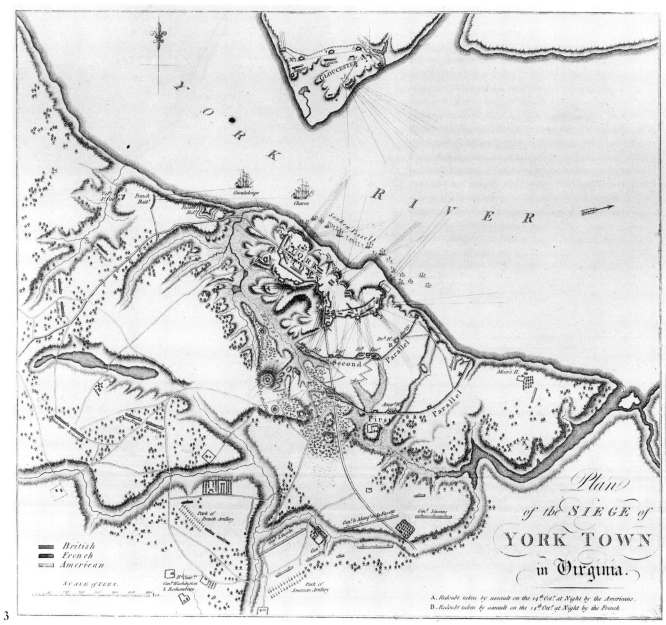

3

4

the very same day Cornwallis surrendered his army of some 7600 men, 2000 of whom were invalids (4 & 5).

Although they still had substantial forces in North America, the capitulation at Yorktown destroyed the British will to fight on, and effectively marked the end of military operations. It was the direct consequence of British naval failure at the battle of 5 September, which has consequently been seen as the key to American independence.

The British army marched out to the tune 'The world turned upside down': significantly for the mother country it was also known as 'The old woman taught wisdom'.

5

1. 'Carte de la Partie de la Virginie ou l'armée combinée de France & des Etats-Unis de l'Amèrique a ait prisonniere l'armée Anglaise commandée par Lord Cornwallis le 19 Octbre. 1781', Esnauts et Rapilly, Paris, 1782. Although accurate in spirit, it cannot be taken literally as much of the topography is wrong, events of many days are truncated, and it was impossible for a fleet to lie across the entrance to the bay because of the Middle Ground shoal.
Beverley R Robinson Collection

2. Lines plan of the fireship Vulcan 'as fitted at Plymouth May 1778'.
Admiralty Collection.
NMM neg 4360-61

3. 'Plan of the Siege of York Town in Virginia', engraved for Stedman's *History of the American War*, London, 1794.
NMM neg X1926

4. 'Reddition de l'armèe Angloises Commandèe par Mylord Comte de Cornwallis . . . le 19 Octobre 1781', published by Monthare, Paris (artist uncredited). Another highly stylised French effort, it purports to show the British army leaving Yorktown and stacking their arms (left middle ground at 'D'); Yorktown is made into a regularly fortified European city ('A'), and the ships of the French fleet in the left foreground all have English-pattern sterns, so the artist's references are very dubious.
NMM neg 221

5. The Surrender of Lord Cornwallis, oil painting by John Trumbull. The British generals—although not Cornwallis, who was ill—are being led by General Benjamin Lincoln between lines of French and American troops.
Library of Congress 21SA7-12774

1

Copper sheathing—the saviour of the Royal Navy

2

THE SHEATHING of ships' hulls with copper was the most important technical innovation made by the naval combatants of the American War of Independence. The technique was developed by the British who, through the improvement in sailing performance it brought, gained a strategic advantage at sea which, in the later stages of the war, did much to offset the numerical disadvantage of the British fleet. In 1780 Rodney attributed much of his success in capturing six Spanish ships of the line off Gibraltar to the copper sheathing of his ships; while in the West Indies de Grasse excused his lack of success against Hood by his own relative lack of manoeuvrability.

The effect of copper sheathing was to reduce weed growth along the hulls of ships. Copper also afforded better protection to hull timbers against the boring of the mollusc *teredo navalis*, which could penetrate the thin wood plank used previously for sheathing. The urgency of finding an alternative to wood plank increased as the worm was brought back from tropical waters and lodged in wood and water in the Medway near Sheerness and, to a lesser extent, at Portsmouth.

Both benefits reduced the frequency of docking for cleaning or repair, a great advantage in wartime, and the first experiments with copper had been made towards the end of the Seven Years War (1). These had revealed the main problem of corrosion by galvanic action of the copper on the iron bolts binding hull timbers. Interest then lapsed until 1775 when there may have been a shortage of plank sheathing. Experiment revealed that galvanic action on iron was reduced when the heads of iron bolts were covered by lead. Various 'compositions' were used to over the iron in a series of experiments over the next two years. Mixed or compound metal—an alloy including copper—was tried instead of iron for nails, braces and pintles. Even using pure copper nails and fittings was tested.

By 1778 a large number of ships were being coppered, almost by way of differing experiment. By the end of that year, one particular method of protecting iron bolts had been tried with particular success: the application of thick paper between the hull and the copper plates. Thereafter that method was refined, ships hulls also being painted with tar, the paper soaked in oil of tar and 'composition', with the inner surface of the copper sheets lacquered with three coats of white lead mixed in linseed oil. The effect was to partially insulate the copper from the iron, delaying corrosion problems till after the American War had ended. From February 1779 selected line of battle ships were coppered, and from May general orders were given for coppering frigates.

There were immediate problems in distributing copper plate, paper and composition to the yards, and in having contractors cast braces and pintles of mixed metal precisely for each ship, no one hull being quite the same shape as another. Nevertheless, with determination, these problems were overcome. During 1780 alone no less than 46 ships of the line were coppered. By January 1782 82 battleships, 14 of 50 guns, 115 frigates, and 102 sloops and cutters had been copper sheathed. Lord Sandwich regarded it as one of the great achievements of his administration as First Lord of the Admiralty. It also owed a great deal to the determination of the Comptroller of the Navy Board, Sir Charles Middleton (2), who fought to overcome each problem, once the decision to adopt copper sheathing was taken.

After the American War the iron bolts of many coppered vessels were discovered to be badly corroded and the safety of the ships was questioned. Nevertheless what was new in 1779 had become orthodoxy by 1783. Experimentation with different types of mixed metal bolts continued until 1786, when a copper-zinc bolt was generally adopted and put into all ships as they were repaired. The improvement had the great benefit of extending the durability of ships' hulls and their sheathing so that less maintenance was needed. By the time of the French Revolutionary and Napoleonic Wars, 74-gun ships of the line (3) were able to go five years before being completely re-coppered. In this respect, ships were able to stay at sea longer, so permitting the dockyards to concentrate on other work that kept more at ships to sea. The innovation consequently enhanced British sea power both in the short term and in the long.

1. The frigate *Alarm*, 32 guns, was the trial ship for copper sheathing in 1761; her log records speeds of 13kts in ideal conditions when newly sheathed. This anonymous engraving depicts the ship conducting a prize into Gibraltar and was published in London on 31 August 1781. *NMM neg 7170*

2. Admiral Charles Middleton, later Lord Barham (1726-1813), anonymous oil painting of the nineteenth century British school. *NMM ref BHC2529*

3. A contemporary model of the 74-gun ship *Bellona*. It is thought that this model was made to Middleton's order and used by him to gain the King's support for the wholesale coppering of the fleet, a measure so expensive that it needed all the influence the Comptroller could muster. *NMM neg C1097*

3

2

St Kitts, 1782

1

ON 11 January 1782 the French fleet under de Grasse (twenty-four ships of the line) anchored in Basse Terre roads, St Christophers—or St Kitts as the island was usually known at the time—having landed troops to besiege the garrison in the fort on Brimstone Hill. Samuel Hood (1), in temporary command of the British fleet in the West Indies, had twenty-two ships of the line at Antigua. He sailed from there late in the afternoon of the 23 January, intending to arrive off the anchorage at daybreak the next morning for a surprise attack. This plan was thwarted by a collision, and the British fleet was not in sight of the French until about 1pm on the 24th.

As de Grasse sailed out to engage, Hood lured him away from the anchorage, because he was considering the possibility of moving into it himself, and mooring in line at the southern end of the bay, along the edge of a

ledge, which then dropped to very deep water. This would make it impossible for an attacker to moor outside the line (2).

Next morning both fleets were to the west of Nevis some eight miles apart. The French had been steering south on the starboard tack, but when the British got under way their opponents came about on the other tack and then came slanting in towards the weaker fleet, which by noon was sailing along the coast of Nevis. The flagship, the huge *Ville de Paris*, was the first to get into range, and opened fire at the British rear. The danger here was that the last few ships in the British line, brushing across the front of the advancing French, would be cut off unless they kept very close together. Hood had taken an enormous risk in this dash across the French line but resisted the temptation to turn back to help; instead he signalled his line to close the anchorage more quickly. The leading ships turning and anchoring one by one in a line were covered by the centre and rear of the British fleet.

The crisis of this stage of the battle was now reached. The slow-sailing third from last in the British line was dropping astern. The French admiral was steering for this gap to cut off the final three British ships. The next three British ships dropped back just in time. An eye-witness saw the bowsprit of the *Ville de Paris* appearing inside the British line, but then disappearing again as she was forced to turn away. The anchored ships were now able to cover the last few British ships as they came down to anchor (3), leading the French line, most of whom were too far astern to fire at them, across the

3

broadsides of their companions. The French ships, as they came up could do little except pass along the line, with the anchored ships getting the better of the exchange. Hood had timed his move superbly. By 5.30 it was all over and the thwarted French were standing away to the southwards.

The anchored line was reorganised to fill gaps and ensure that the lead ship was so carefully positioned that no enemy could reach her in the prevailing wind. From there the line ran to Hood's flagship, *Barfleur* of 98 guns, the most powerful ship he had, and then turned northwards, at an angle, preventing any attempt to turn the line.

Early on 26 January the French were seen to be approaching in line. Their leading ship, aiming for the first in the anchored line, was defeated by a shift in the wind, and was heading for the third when a concentrated fire was opened on her. The French were now experiencing the problem of attacking an unbreakable line. The leader had to approach the line bow-on, completely unable to respond to the full broadsides of all the anchored ships which were in range. Turning brought her own broadside to bear, but carried her to fresh adversaries, whilst the ships that followed her, unable to support her, would, one-by-one, go through the same ordeal (4). The fire on the leading French ship was so intense 'that whole pieces of plank were seen flying from off her side' (5). The French were driven off, managed another, more half-hearted, attack later, but this merely confirmed the earlier lesson.

The French continued to threaten attack (6). However, on 18 February the British garrison surrendered. The next day de Grasse withdrew to Nevis for re-supply, which gave Hood his opportunity. At 11pm the British ships swiftly and silently cut their cables, left decoy lights burning on their anchor buoys, and quietly decamped to Antigua.

1. Admiral Lord Hood (1724-1816), oil painting in the style of Sir Joshua Reynolds. *NMM ref BHC2775*

2. 'Repulse of the French in Frigate Bay, St Kitts, 26 January 1782', oil painting by Thomas Maynard (*fl*1777-1812). *NMM ref BHC0437*

3. 'A View of the English Fleet of 22 Sail of the line under Sir Samuel Hood, Bart forcing by and Possessing themselves of the Anchoring Ground which the French Fleet of 30 Sail of the Line under Count de Grasse had just before Quitted in Basseterre Road, St Christophers, Friday 25 February [sic] 1782', anonymous grey wash drawing, undated. *NMM neg 1729*

4. 'A View of the French Fleet . . . attacking the English Fleet . . . after the French had been dispossessed of their Anchoring Ground in Basseterre Road, St Christophers, Saturday 26 February [sic] 1782', anonymous grey wash drawing, undated. *NMM neg 1728*

5. The Battle of Frigate Bay, 26 January 1782, oil painting by Nicholas Pocock (1740-1821). *NMM ref BHC0436*

6. 'An accurate map of St Christophers and Nevis in the West Indies. By an Officer. With the Position of the English and French fleets February 7th 1782', published by I Fielding, J Sewell, and J Debrett, London, 1 April 1782. *NMM neg D7227*

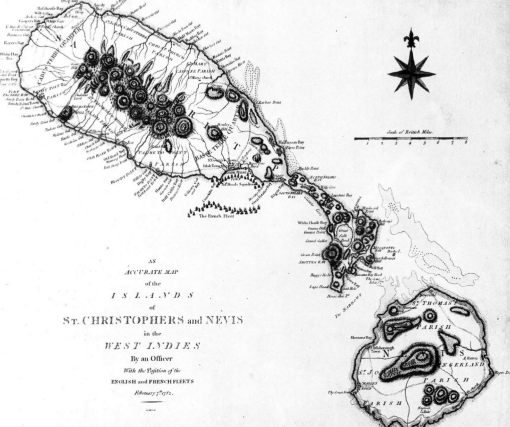

6

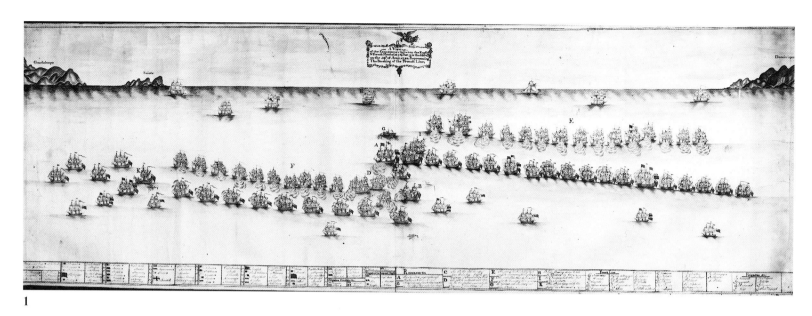

1

Battle of the Saintes, April 1782

ON 25 February 1782 Rodney joined Hood, making the British fleet in the West Indies for the first time numerically superior to De Grasse's force (thirty-six to thirty-five). On 8 March the French sailed from Martinique with a large troop convoy, intended eventually for the invasion of Jamaica, and the British gave chase from St Lucia. The next day the leading eight British ships under Hood, separated from the rest by fluky winds, caught up with the French and were engaged at long range by fifteen French ships. This was near the small group of islets in the channel between Guadeloupe and Dominica called the Saintes which gave their name to the subsequent battle. The French fluffed their opportunity to dispose of Hood's exposed command before the rest of the British fleet came up, and

the initial engagement only resulted in one French ship being damaged enough to be sent into Guadeloupe.

The next two days saw much manouevring by both fleets, the British trying to close and the French (who were to windward) to evade—all to little effect, except that one French ship was damaged in a collision. On the 12th however, dawn showed this ship and a consort to be between the two fleets, and de Grasse came down towards the British to rescue them. In what followed, the wind favoured the British, as they were further off-shore, and had slightly stronger and less fluky airs. They were also in somewhat better order than the French (1).

The two fleets came into action on opposite tacks—passing one another in opposite directions, but with the British coming in at an oblique angle and forcing the

2

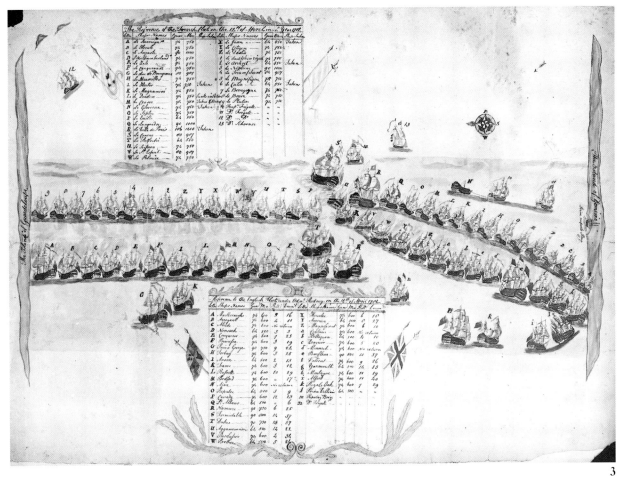

3

4

1. A View of the Engagement between the English & French Fleets (at a ¼ past 9 in the Morning) on the 12th of April 1782: Representing the Breaking of the French Line', anonymous. *NMM neg A6725*

2. Battle of the Saintes, 12 April 1782, oil painting by Thomas Mitchell (1735-1790), signed and dated 1782. *NMM ref BHC0441*

3. 'Position of the English and French fleets between Guadeloupe and Dominica, Windward Islands, 12 Apr 1782', anonymous undated watercolour. *NMM ref PAH5103*

4. Battle of the Saintes, 12 April 1782, oil painting by Thomas Luny (1759-1837), signed and dated 1783. *NMM ref BHC0438*

5. 'Battle of the Saintes, 12th April 1782. The End of the Action', watercolour by Nicholas Pocock (1740-1821). *NMM ref PAH9528*

6. 'Battle of the Saintes, 12th April 1782. The *Barfleur* engaging a French two-decker', watercolour by Nicholas Pocock (1740-1821). *NMM ref PAH9530*

7. 'Surrender of the *Ville de Paris* st the Battle of the Saintes, 12 April 1782', oil painting by Thomas Whitcombe (c1752-1824), signed and dated 1782. *NMM ref BHC0446*

8. 'The French Admiral Count De Grasse, Delivering his Sword to Admiral (now Lord) Rodney (Being a more exact Representation of that Memorable Event than is given in any other Work of this kind) on board the *Ville de Paris* after being Defeated by that Gallant Commander on the Glorious 12th of April 1782 in the West Indies', engraving by Thornton after an original by William Hamilton. *NMM ref PAD5388*

French line to bend round so that their leading ships could stay in contact. About an hour and a quarter after the first shots were fired a change in the wind threw the French line into further disorder (2). This gave Rodney in his flagship *Formidable*, followed by five other ships, an opportunity to steer up and break the French line in the middle (3). The ship ahead of him (*Duke*) did the same, trapping four French ships between two fires from which they suffered badly, whilst the *Bedford*, sixth astern of the flagship, also broke the French line followed by the ships behind her. The French were now split into three disorganised groups (4). The three British groups were in much better order, but Rodney, elderly and in ill-health, was no longer the man to take full advantage

5

6

of this, beyond capturing three of the four battered French ships cut off between *Formidable* and *Duke* (5). Hood in the *Barfleur* (6), with other vessels in support, engaged the French flagship *Ville de Paris* (7) and ensured that both she and de Grasse himself (8) were captured, but when he urged unrelenting pursuit was told: 'Come, we have done very handsomely as it is'. It is difficult not to agree with Hood that more resolution would have produced perhaps four or even five times the four prizes actually taken. At least he had the chance a week later to take two more French line of battle ships in the Mona passage.

The French seem to have suffered considerably more casualties than the British, who had employed that new weapon, the carronade, to considerable effect. The *Ville de Paris* of 110 guns was the largest prize captured during this war, though she was lost in a storm on her way to Britain later the same year. As it was, this battle finally gave the British an unequivocal victory, and helped in creating an atmosphere in which the war could be ended without too much disgrace. This was also the last major battle of the French Royal Navy, and it marked the failure of its challenge to the British. It had performed better than in previous wars, but it had never quite achieved the sort of victory which the British now won at the Saintes, despite its previous advantages in numbers and apparent power.

8

7

1

Aftermath of battle

AS WITH so many sea battles in the age of sail, the victorious fleet was not in a much better state than its vanquished adversary. As a consequence of the French habit of firing high, the British fleet was badly damaged aloft, the *Prince George*, 98, being only one of the ships almost dismasted (1). Rodney himself was exhausted after nearly a week of highly stressful vigilance, and refused to order an immediate pursuit. Hood finally persuaded him to release his own division of ten of the line five days after the battle and on 19 April he came up with some French ships that had been separated from their fleet before the Saintes. The 64-gun *Caton*

and *Jason* were quickly taken by *Valiant*, with the help of the *Belliqueux* (2), and the frigate *Aimable* and sloop *Ceres* were captured at the same time. Hood could not resist reporting that part of the defeated French fleet had slipped through the Mona Passage on the previous day, so instant pursuit could have reaped dividends.

After a rather tardy refit at Port Royal, Jamaica (3), some of Rodney's patched-up ships sailed for home as escorts to the all-important convoys. The first, which left in May, included the *Sandwich*, 90 which conveyed the captured de Grasse to England (4). The Comte fared better than the erstwhile ships of his command: the prizes

2

3

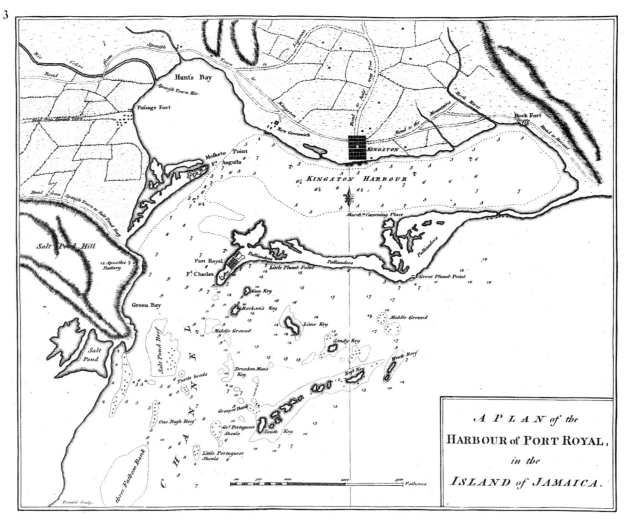

A PLAN of the
HARBOUR of PORT ROYAL,
in the
ISLAND of JAMAICA.

4

sailed in August with a large convoy of 180 sail under Rear-Admiral Graves, which was hit first by a gale and then by a hurricane in the Atlantic. A series by the artist Robert Dodd depicted some of the incidents of its disastrous passage: a lighning strike on the merchantman *Lady Juliana* during the gale (5), and the subsequent towing of the crippled ship (6); followed by the widespread distress of the fleet during the hurricane (7). Of the prize ships, the *Glorieux* and *Ville de Paris* foundered around 18 or 19 September, while the *Hector* was eventually abandoned after surviving both natural and man-made perils in the form of an attack on the under-manned ship by two French frigates, *Aigle* and *Gloire*. The British 74s *Ramillies* (Graves's flagship) and *Centaur* were also lost in the same storm.

Contrary to popular myth, the Saintes did not break French power in the West Indies entirely, and a further year of careful manouevring was required by both sides. There were no further fleet engagements, but the fighting was brought to a close by the capture of the *Solitaire*, 64 off Barbados by the *Ruby*, 64 and her squadron on 6 December 1782 (8). She was the last ship of the line captured during the war.

5

6

7

8

1. 'This view of the *Prince George* disabled by the loss of her foremast . . . in tow of the *Triton* frigate to pass through a line of French ships of war . . . ', coloured aquatint and etching executed and published by Robert Dodd. It represents an incident at the end of the battle when some disabled British ships were threatened by what might have become a French counterattack.
NMM neg A8881

2. The capture of the French 64-gun ships *Caton* and *Jason* by the *Valiant*, 74 in the Mona Passage, 19 April 1782. Engraved by W Skelton after an original by Dominic Serres, published by James Fittler, London, November 1787. Despite the implication of the print, *Valiant* was not alone and Hood's whole squadron was in the offing; the French ships surrendered as the *Belliqueux* came up.
Beverley R Robinson Collection

3. Chart of the harbour of Port Royal, Jamaica, about 1766. It was the only significant British naval dockyard in the West Indies at this time.
NMM neg B5745

4. 'His Majesty's ship the *Sandwich* of 90 Guns Admiral Parker Commander on her Passage home from the West Indies with Compte de Grasse a Prisoner of war on Board', watercolour by Benjamin Toddy, one of a series of primitive portraits by a foot painter who was presumably a disabled seaman.
NMM ref PAG9676

5. One of a series of four views of the West Indies convoy that ran into heavy weather in the Atlantic in September 1782, aquatint and etching by Robert Dodd, published by John Harris, and Robert Sayer and John Bennett, London, 17 February 1783. This first shows the merchant ship *Lady Juliana* losing her main topmast through lightning-strike in the Gulf of Florida.
NMM neg B4621

6. Second in this series by Dodd, showing the *Lady Juliana* being towed by the frigate *Pallas*; the size of the convoy in the background is apparent.
NMM neg B4622

7. Another in the Dodd series: 'A view of the Sea on the morning after the storm with the distressed situation of the *Centaur, Ville de Paris* and the *Glorieux* as seen from the *Lady Juliana*, the *Ville de Paris* passing to windward under close reefed topsails.'
NMM neg B4623

8. The capture of the *Solitaire*, 64 by the *Ruby*, 64, on 6 December 1782. Anonymous black and watercolour pen and ink sketch.
NMM ref PAH9480

Part III   EUROPEAN WATERS 1778–1783

FRENCH STRATEGIC objectives for the European theatre in 1778 were to contain British resources in home waters, so that a detachment could be deployed to take decisive action overseas. The French Marine enjoyed a tremendous advantage as it could use the Brest fleet, safely positioned behind massive defences, to prevent a major dispersal of the British Channel Fleet. The fleet at Toulon could be, and was, used overseas. Vergennes had no interest in invading England: 'Even if I could destroy England, I would abstain from doing so, as from the wildest folly.'[25] France had learnt its lesson in the Seven Years War that threatening any major disruption in the strategic balance of European affairs would lead to a general coalition against her. But the threat of invasion was always latent in the power of the French army, and the readiness of the Brest fleet. In London it could not be ignored. Sandwich had intended to send a fleet to the Mediterranean to watch Toulon, and follow d'Estaing should he break out, but his concern for safety in the Channel had prevented him. Admiral Keppel, Channel Fleet commander, insisted that he needed more than twenty ships prepared for service, even though the intelligence from Brest indicated that the French were far from ready.

Keppel had refused to serve in any capacity which would lead him to shed American blood, a fact which was symptomatic of the political disarray the Revolution had caused in Britain. He was one of the Rockingham clan, and as such a political opponent of the ministry. As his second-in-command he was given a loyal ministerial admiral, Palliser, recently promoted to Vice-Admiral. Palliser, as Comptroller, had ably helped Sandwich build up naval materiél in the early 1770s.

A few days before he received his recall from

Paris in March, Stormont had reported Maurepas's boast to him:

> the great disadvantage the French have hitherto had in every naval war, arose from the beginning it with too small a force–The loss of one or two squadrons undid us, said he–but that will not be the case now.[26]

The activity in French dockyards, and the relatively slow rate of Britain's response, appeared to have created a brief window of opportunity for France. That was a fateful delusion. Keppel sailed in June with only twenty ships of the line, but by the time Admiral the Comte d'Orvilliers sailed from Brest on 10 July with twenty-nine of the line and a 50, Keppel had thirty, and at the end of September, thirty-three. The Admiralty had also been able to send twenty-five others to North America and the Indies.

Technically a state of war did not exist until July. Unlike the opening of the Seven Years War or the recommencement of hostilities after the Peace of Amiens, the British did not seek to anticipate a formal declaration in order to sweep up as many French seamen as possible. The declaration having been made, d'Orvilliers was given orders to cruise in the Channel, but not to seek action.

On 23 July Keppel caught him and after four days manoeuvring was able to bring him to an indecisive and long-range action off Ushant. Langrage fired into the rigging of the British ships disabled them to the point where d'Orvilliers was able to retire into Brest. The moral victory was Britain's, but Palliser came under attack from the opposition, and in anger demanded that Keppel be court martialled.

The court was heavily biased in Keppel's favour, and the result was that Palliser's career was ruined. He demanded a court martial in his own defence, and was largely exonerated, but the damage had been done. The real target,

of course, was Sandwich and the ministry. Keppel continued to be the centre of disaffection, and was ordered to strike his flag. Thereupon Rear-Admiral Harland and several captains resigned. The Howe brothers joined in the political attack, which prevented the King asking Lord Howe to take Sandwich's place at the Admiralty. Fear of facing another political foe also prevented Germain agreeing to Clinton's strident request to resign.

Keppel's conventional tactics at the Battle of Ushant had lost an opportunity to stabilise Britain's strategic situation. The French government was able to persuade the Spanish Foreign Minister, Count Floridablanca, that Britain posed a continuing threat to Spanish interests in the West Indies, and that the war presented an opportunity to reduce her disproportionate naval power. King Carlos III insisted that an offer to mediate a peace settlement be made, which was done in October, but the clear implication was that if London did not accept her obviously biased arbitration, Spain would go to war. Sandwich urged temporising because France and Spain together controlled about eighty ships of the line, to the fifty-five he was able to supply for Channel service, provided he could find the men for them. At the same time, ships had to be found to reinforce Barrington in the West Indies, and to reinforce the East Indies squadron under Rear-Admiral Sir Edward Hughes.

In April 1779 France and Spain signed an offensive alliance against England, the Convention of Aranjuez. Spain was still unwilling to directly support the American colonists, but agreed to make war to recover Gibraltar and Spanish interests in Honduras, and to support French efforts to seize the Newfoundland fishery, recover Senegal and Dominica, and to restore her position in India. On 16 July the Spanish Ambassador presented the British government with a list of grievances which everyone recognised as a declaration of war. Once again thought was given to concentrat-

---

25. A Temple Patterson, *The Other Armada* (London 1960), pp37-9.

26. State Papers 78/306 f351.

ing British forces for local defence, but once again a more courageous policy was adopted.

Spain could not afford to support a protracted war, and pressed the French to undertake joint operations in the Channel. Vergennes still refused to countenance a full-scale invasion of England, but a plan was developed for the occupation of the Isle of Wight on the south coast, from whence the dockyard at Portsmouth could be destroyed, or even occupied. Other port cities could also be subjected to attack, with the intended result that Britain's credit would be destroyed. Without credit, it would be necessary for her to seek peace.

Thirty French ships of the line under d'Orvilliers were to be joined by thirty-six Spanish ships to bring overwhelming force against the Channel Fleet. This had been brought up to a strength of forty ships of the line, and command had been given to the elderly Admiral Sir Charles Hardy because he was the only one who stood outside the political quarrel between ministerial and opposition admirals. To compensate for the fact that he had last been at sea twenty years before, he was given a flag captain of superior talent, Richard Kempenfelt. The latter was to remark that 'There is a fund of good nature in the man, but not one grain of the Commander-in-Chief . . . My God, what have you great people done by such an appointment.'[27]

Not all was well on the Bourbon side either. The French hurried to sea without their full stores five weeks late for the rendezvous with the Spaniards, but Admiral Cordova did not get his fleet to sea for another seven weeks. When finally the combined fleet entered the Channel it outnumbered the British three to two, but there were so many sick and dead, and the ships were so foul with marine growth, that they could not force action. They could not cover an invasion for the number of days that were required knowing that Hardy was away to windward with a fleet in good condition, if relatively small. The danger late in the summer that a southerly gale would drive the scarcely seaworthy fleet onto the English coast was very real.

27. J K Laughton (ed), *Letters and Papers of Charles Middleton, Lord Barham*, Navy Record Society (London 1907), I, pp293, 323.

28. *Barham* I, pp297-8, 311, 329, 333.

To cover himself, Sandwich had obtained a Cabinet order that Hardy should station his fleet to the westward. When finally d'Orvilliers headed westward and sought action, Hardy was able to brush past him and move into the Channel, and even enter Portsmouth for supplies. He had a tremendous technical advantage in the number of his ships which were copper-bottomed to prevent marine growth, and could therefore move more quickly, and more easily keep to windward. Had he been forced to fight to prevent invasion, the Franco-Spanish fleet, slow and encumbered with the need to escort transports, would have been at a disadvantage despite their numbers. The combined fleet had done all that of which it was capable, and was forced to return to its bases.

That was the end of the invasion threat, although Sandwich insisted that Hardy return to his station in the west of the Channel until after the American convoys were home. This impeded the necessary preparations for the 1780 campaign. The Spanish fleet soon left Brest in order to support the siege of Gibraltar, and at the end of the year a strong force of seventeen British ships of the line under Admiral Rodney followed with a convoy of supply ships for the garrison. On its way south it ran into a Spanish supply convoy, which was captured, and south of Cadiz Rodney caught up with a Spanish squadron under Admiral Langara. In a rising gale, he gave chase and engaged the Spanish rear as his ships came up to it. By moonlight seen through gaps torn in the clouds the action continued until six ships of the line had been captured, one other blowing up. Two were driven ashore before they could be secured, but Rodney captured another two a few days later. By then he had sent most of the squadron home under Rear-Admiral the Honourable Robert Digby. He then made his own departure for the West Indies with four of the line. It was the captured Spanish ships, immediately purchased into the navy, which allowed a squadron to be rushed out to New York under Rear-Admiral Sir Thomas Graves.

Hardy's capacity as Commander-in-Chief, Channel, was so limited that morale and discipline suffered greatly. As he was preparing to resume command in May 1780, he died, but the only politically neutral admiral Sandwich could find to replace him was Admiral Sir Francis Geary, who was seventy. Kempenfelt

considered him brave and generous, but 'wholly debilitated in his faculties, his memory and judgment lost, wavering and indeterminate in everything.'[28] When his health gave out, and Vice-Admiral Barrington refused to succeed him, George Darby, who had only raised his

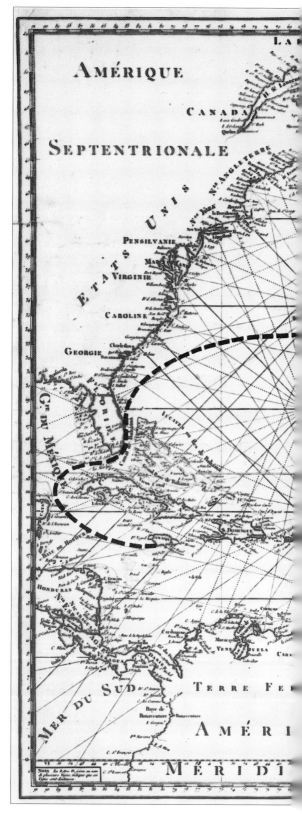

flag as a Rear-Admiral in 1778 and been made Vice-Admiral in 1779, was put in command.

In April 1780 confidential diplomatic efforts to detach Spain from the French alliance, possibly at the price of surrendering Gibraltar, moved into a slightly more formal mode when

The North Atlantic theatre of war, as shown in a French navy official chart of 1786. The confluence of the main trade routes to and from America and the Indies (both East and West) in the Channel approaches, and the major landfalls of Cape Finisterre in northwest Spain and Ushant in northwest France, explain how major battles in European waters were often closely linked to campaigns in the other theatres. Outward-bound trade usually went south along the coast of Europe to Madeira or the Canaries before swinging south (for the East Indies) or southwest for the Caribbean; homeward traffic tended to go further north, northeast from the British Leeward Islands, but around Cuba and through the Bahamas Passage and along the southern coast of America for shipping originating from Jamaica, which thus avoided the long beat up to windward.   NMM neg B9065

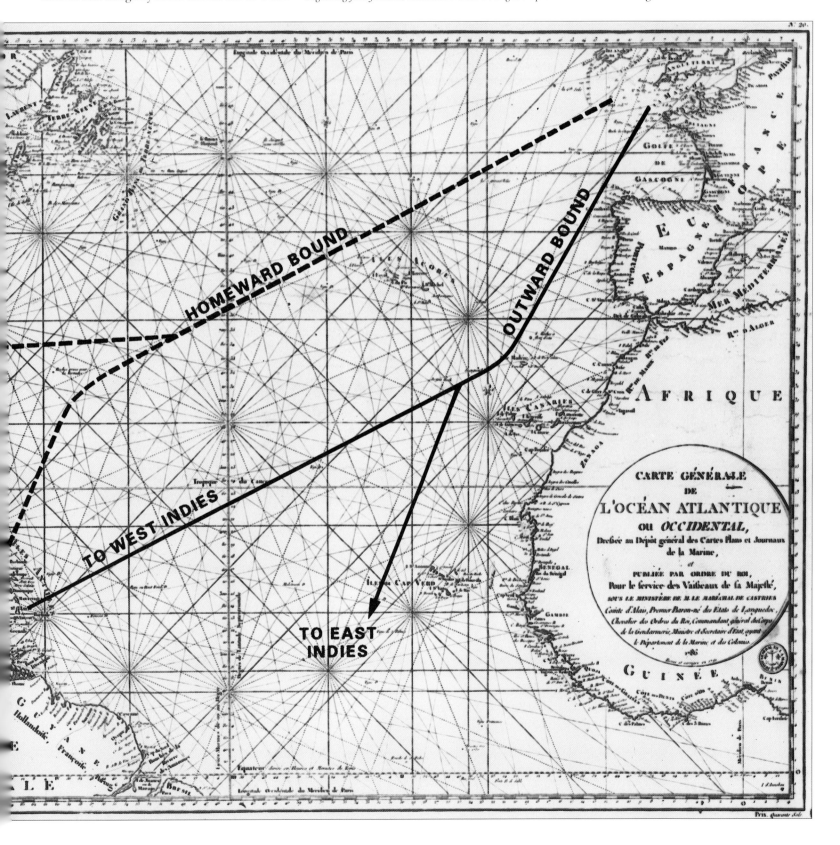

Richard Cumberland was sent to Lisbon to negotiate with Floridablanca, who persuaded him to come to Madrid. Nothing came of this negotiation, except to awaken in Vergennes a degree of apprehension which was reinforced by his realisation that after two years of war French finances were nearly exhausted. The news from America, where two units of the Continental Army had mutinied, was not encouraging. This was known in London. However, the more immediate concern had to be with the efforts of Tsarina Catherine to form a League of Armed Neutrality to prevent Britain using her naval forces to stop the flow of naval stores from Baltic States to French and Spanish dockyards. In November the Dutch States-General voted to join. Dutch shipping carried a large part of the neutral trade on which the Bourbon navies depended, and rather than see it protected by the combined naval forces of Russia, Sweden, Denmark and the Netherlands, the British Cabinet felt obliged to declare war on the Netherlands because of her support for the rebels, and prior to her formally joining the league. Thus, rather than isolating France, the British found themselves faced with a widening war. An offer of Minorca to Catherine, as the price of an Anglo-Russian alliance, was rejected.

There was no slack in British operational strategy, and no room for error. A late cruise by the Channel Fleet in 1780, hoping to catch de Guichen returning from America, failed in its purpose because he had orders to steer for Cadiz where the combined fleet was gathered. It also delayed the departure of the relief convoy to Gibraltar. Orders for it were issued on 1 January 1781, but Darby could not sail with the victuallers from Cork until late in March. This prevented a spring cruise off Brest which might have intercepted de Grasse with his reinforcements for the West Indies, and might therefore have prevented the disaster for the British army at Yorktown. The dispatch of reinforcements for Rodney in the West Indies had to wait until Darby returned from Gibraltar. In order to get them away, and to send forces to the East Indies, risks had to be taken in home waters.

It was possible to starve home forces because it was becoming apparent that, although the Spanish navy had excellent ships and the French navy was in very good form, collectively the combined fleets were inept. In this belief, Vice-Admiral Sir Hyde Parker sailed on 5 June with seven ships to enforce the blockade of naval stores, and to prevent the Dutch fleet interrupting British trade. A formal, but hard-fought, battle followed with Admiral Zoutman, who commanded eight ships. Parker got the best of it, and was able to enforce the trade control, but returned home indignant that he had had to work with ships in poor repair. He refused a knighthood, and resigned.

It was in the Mediterranean that the price had to be paid for deploying such a large proportion of British naval forces to the American, East and West Indian theatres. De Guichen was able to take the Brest fleet south to Cadiz without interruption, and on 23 July the combined fleet sailed to cover the passage of a troop convoy bound for Minorca, where a Spanish army was landed on 18 August. The defending garrison became severely debilitated from scurvy, and surrendered in February 1782.

On its return to the Atlantic the combined fleet again approached the mouth of the Channel in numbers which Darby, with only twenty-seven ships of the line to its forty-five or forty-seven, could not face in close action. On 6 September Sandwich obtained a Cabinet Order for Darby to manoeuvre to cover the inbound convoys, using his superior speed to harry the enemy. Admiral Cordova, however, had already insisted that the fleet return to its respective bases.

In the months following the news of Yorktown, the French began to reinforce the squadron in the East Indies which had been sent out under Admiral Suffren in the belief that a victory there would bring peace, and to reinforce de Grasse in the West Indies. In December de Guichen sailed with a strong squadron to support this movement, but he was met by Kempenfelt, now promoted to Rear-Admiral, who, with an inferior force, managed to capture fourteen ships from the troop convoy. A few days later a storm damaged de Guichen's squadron so severely that it had to return to Brest. Only two ships of the line got safely away to the West Indies.

In London it was decided that in 1782 home forces would have to be reduced still further so that local superiority could be obtained in the East and West Indies. To do so, forces in the Channel were reduced to a squadron of coppered two-deckers with the sole responsibility of making it impossible for the French to mount an invasion. The convoys would be sailed with a reduced escort of 44-gun frigates early in the season before the French would be at sea, and would return by a northerly route around Scotland. To safeguard their approach, all the old three-deckers, which lacked the speed to be used by the Channel Squadron, were deployed to the North Sea. It was calculated, correctly, that the French would not perceive what was being done in time to deploy forces to support the Dutch.

The fall of the North administration on 27 March, followed by Rockingham's death in July, put the strategic direction of British naval forces in the hands of those who were more familiar with opposition criticism. The Earl of Shelburne, as Prime Minister, had little capacity to bring himself or his large cabinet to a decision. Keppel lacked the experience Sandwich had acquired during five years of war of the problems of disposing scarce resources. Ideas about the movement of soldiers around the world were not supported by any awareness of the technical problems of transport.

The biggest problems facing Keppel in European waters were the need to bring safely home a convoy of naval stores from the Baltic, and the need to relieve Gibraltar, where it was known that the Spaniards were about to launch their major assault with the assistance of ten specially-built floating batteries with shot-proof sides. This was launched on 13 September, but the Spanish deployment was weak and at the end of the day all the batteries had been destroyed by the defending forces. The new administration was able to employ Britain's foremost sailor, Lord Howe, to command the relief force. Thirty-four British ships fresh from dockyard hands escorted the convoy and Cordova, with thirty-five ships in poor condition, twice found it necessary to refuse action.

That was the last major action of the war. On 30 November the preliminary articles of peace were signed between the British peace commissioners and the Americans, and in January 1783 the preliminaries of peace were concluded between Britain, France and Spain.

2

The battle of Ushant 1778

THIS WAS the first and only major fleet encounter in European waters of this war, and for the Royal Navy, compared with the relatively easy victories of the Seven Years War, it was a very great disappointment. In the interim the French Navy had been re-equipped, re-organised and better trained, and never again in the age of sail would it be at a higher level of efficiency in relation to its old rival. The British fleet, at the same time, was split, just as was the country, by political feuds and major disagreements about how to deal with the American rebels.

Before war had officially broken out the French had

1

The Engagement off Ushant 27th of July 1778 between the British Fleet Commanded by Adm. Keppel, and the French Fleet under Count D'Orvilliers: Drawn by an Officer on board the Victory.

1	2	3	4	5	6	7
The FORMIDABLE 90	ROBUST 74 &c.	VIGILANT 64 &c.	P. GEORGE 90	FOUDROYANT 80	VICTORY 100	BIENFAISANT 64 &c.
Engaging La Couronne 80	La Glorieux 74 &c.	S.t Michel 64 &c.	Le Vengeur 64	L'Actionnaire 64	La Bretagne 110	La Ville de Paris 92 &c.

Published 20th April 1779 by J. Bew, Paternoster Row.

3

1. Admiral Augustus Keppel (1725-1786), oil painting by Sir Joshua Reynolds (1723-1792). *NMM ref BHC2820*

2. 'Combat de la Frégate Français *la Belle Poule* attaquée par la Frégate Anglais *Arethuse* le 17 Juin 1778. A *La Belle Poule* B *L'Arethuse*. Voyez la Gazette de France no 51', etching published by Gouaz, no date. *Chatham Collection*

3. 'The Engagement off Ushant 27th of July 1778 between the British Fleet commanded by Admiral Keppel and the French Fleet under Count D'Orvilliers: Drawn by an officer on board the *Victory*', engraved by J Collier and published by J Bew, London, 1 April 1779. *NMM ref PAD5336*

4. 'The Sea Engagement fought July 27th 1778 between the English Fleet . . . between Ushant and Scilly Islands', etching produced and published by Robert Sayer and John Bennett, London, 16 September 1778. *NMM neg C851*

5. Hugh Palliser (1723-1796) as a post captain, oil painting by George Dance (1741-1825). *NMM ref BHC2928*

6. German engraving of the acquittal of Admiral Keppel at Portsmouth on 11 February 1779, published by J M Will. The scene is a complete fabrication, the court martial being held on board ship – in this case the *Britannia* – as was the Navy's usual custom, but the print bears witness to the Europe-wide interest in the event. *NMM ref PAD5922*

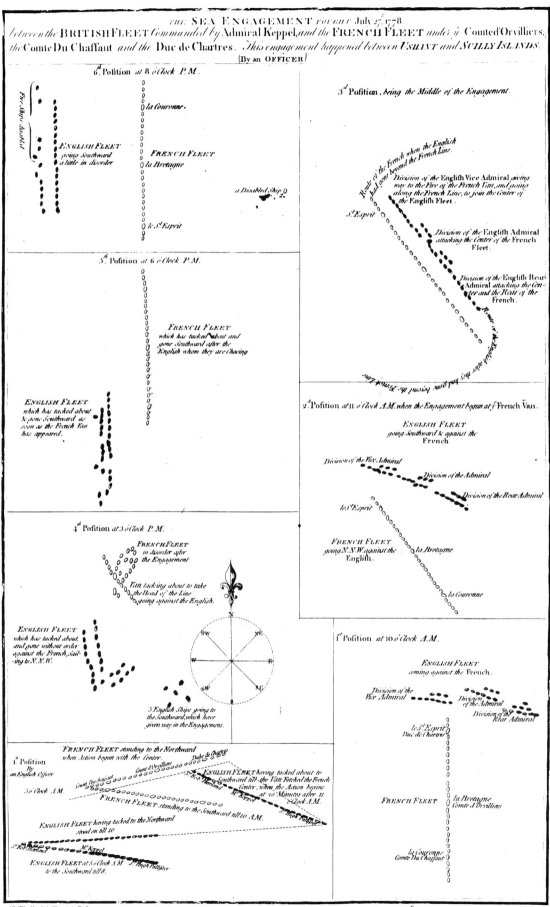

already shown their mettle when, on 17 June, Keppel (1), commanding the British fleet in the Channel, had sent one of his frigates, the *Arethusa*, to stop the French *Belle Poule*, which was paying too close attention to the motions of his fleet. Her captain absolutely refused to obey, and a fierce battle developed. British and French accounts differ, but certainly the French ship held her own until she had to abandon the action when the British fleet came up (2).

In early July Keppel with thirty of the line and the French admiral d'Orvilliers with twenty-nine (plus three small two-deckers unfit for the line) had put to sea. The latter was handicapped by instructions which limited him to offering battle in only the most favourable circumstances. On the 23rd the fleets sighed each other about 100 miles west of Ushant. Keppel was between the French and their base at Brest, but the latter had the weather gage, which enabled them to avoid action until the 27th. On this day shifts in the wind enabled the British to close their opponents. Both sides were by now in a certain amount of disarray. The first encounter was somewhat chaotic and obscured by clouds of gunsmoke (3). The French, in rather better order, withdrew in something approaching a line, and the British were left more widely scattered with a vulnerable group of four or five ships with disabled rigging to leeward. The French appeared to threaten these, though they never actually attacked, as Keppel formed a line to repel them, though the ships of Rear-Admiral Palliser's rear division were some way away. The French declined further battle, and Keppel felt he was being prevented from attacking by Palliser's failure to join him in time. The battle itself (4) had been little more than a skirmish with the result that was to become familiar during this war of the British gunfire causing more French casualties but the French inflicting more damage to the British ships, mostly by firing at the rigging. In many ways the honours were even, not a conclusion the British were used to at this time.

The result was a major political row and a massive self-inflicted wound to the officer corps of the Royal Navy, centred round the feud between Keppel (encouraged by the parliamentary opposition), and Palliser, a strong government supporter (5), two very different types of man and officer who seem to have been personally as well as politically antipathetic. Keppel demanded a court martial on himself and was triumphantly acquitted (6), but was not employed again until nearly the end of the war, as were other competent but anti-government officers. Palliser narrowly escaped with his life from mob violence. Referring to the feuding families in Romeo and Juliet, the factions were dubbed *Montagues* (the family name of the Earl of Sandwich, the First Lord) and *Capulets* (a pun on 'Keppelites').

Acurate Vorstellung des Saales in Gouverneur-Hause in Portsmouth, worin das Kriegs-recht über den Englischen Admiral Keppel gehalten worden und den 11 Febr.1779. ein Ende genommen.

Der Kriegsrath hat die wider Admiral Keppeln erhobene Klage erwogen, Zeugen und Vertheidigung angehört, alles ernstlich u.reiflich überlegt, u.ist nun einmüthig der Meynung, das Admirals Pallisers Anklage boshaft und ungegründet sey, daß der hochgebohrne Admiral August Keppel, statt eine Gelegenheit, dem Staat wesentlich zu dienen, außer Acht zu lazen, sich vielmehr als ein braver und erfahrner Officier betragen habe, und daß also der Kriegsrath gedachten August Keppel, auf das ehrenvollste freyspreche.

Der Admiral Präsident 22 Die Viceadmirale 33 Die Rearadmirale ✳✳✳✳✳✳✳ Die Kapitains .8 Die Schreiber & Platz des Zeugen .7 Der Oberauditeur (Judge Avocat) 8 Keppel 9 seine Freunde .9 Der Admiralitätsmarschall, der Keppeln bewachen muß Palliser u.seine Freunde 11 Plätze für den hohen Adel 12 Plätze für Land und Seeofficiere 13.13. Die Herolde (Masters at-Arms) mit blossen Degen 24 Plätze für die zuhörende Seekapitains. 15. Plätze für Zuhörer von allerley Stande. 16. Weg ins Neben-zimer, wohin sich der Kriegsrath zum Votiren entfernt.

1

Naval administration

THE ROYAL Navy at the time of the American War of Independence was administered by the Board of Admiralty in Whitehall, London (1). The Board's responsibilities at that time comprised not only the ships, officers and men of the Sea Service, as it was called, but the industrial organisation that maintained the navy at sea—the dock and victualling yards—and the medical service that included purpose-built hospitals. These support services were managed by boards subordinate to the Admiralty: the Navy Board, the Victualling Board, and the Sick and Hurt Board. Earlier in the century and after 1794 there was also a Transport Board to manage the transport of the army, its food supplies and equipment, but during the American War all these functions came to be managed by the Navy Board.

2

4

Separate, both physically and administratively, was the Treasurer of the Navy and his Paymaster, who paid the navy's bills, and at whose office (2) seamen could collect wages unpaid by the clerks to the Paymaster, based in all the port towns. Also separate was the Board of Ordnance which supplied guns and powder to the army as well as the navy, and managed yards close to the dockyards at Woolwich, Chatham, Portsmouth and Plymouth.

These departments of the navy did not function independently of the rest of government. Foreign and colonial policy was the responsibility of the Cabinet, which therefore decided strategy, where British fleets should be deployed, and how they should behave towards both allies and enemies. The Cabinet's decisions on these subjects were conveyed to the Admiralty, and sometimes directly to the commanders of the fleets at sea, by orders from the Secretaries of State. Of these, during the American War, there were three: the Secretary of State for the Northern Department—notionally the area of northern Europe; for the Southern Department—southern Europe, Africa and India; and for the North American and West Indian Colonies, the office filled from 1775 by Lord George Germain. Thus Cabinet orders for the transport of troops, for example, went to the Navy Board through the departments of two Cabinet politicians before they could be executed, a circuitous route which was a source of considerable frustration to anxious and energetic administrators, because documents could sit on desks in separate offices for two or three days before being copied and transmitted to the executing board.

In such a bureaucracy, efficient office secretaries and board chairmen were essential. At the Admiralty (3), the Board was chaired between 1771 and 1782 by John Montagu, 4th Earl of Sandwich (4). His reputation for conscientious attention to business has recently been re-established. But he was not helped by a board of six other members of whom only one was a naval officer, with most of the others politicians placed there in return for providing parliamentary support to the King's ministers and expected to do little more than sign their names to letters and orders which, at every stage in the chain of command, were always signed in triplicate. However, at the Admiralty, business was arranged and managed by Sir Philip Stephens, a Secretary from 1759 to 1793. The boards subordinate to the Admiralty were also chaired by conscientious and efficient men, the Navy Board between 1778 and 1790 by the assertive Charles Middleton who would himself later become First Lord of the Admiralty at the time of Trafalgar.

Apart from the transmission of orders, the Board of Admiralty's main function was the management of the officer corps (5). The size of the navy gave it considerable patronage, and it has been assumed in the past that political considerations determined the issue of commissions appointing officers to ships. Yet such considerations were of secondary importance compared to the expertise and experience demanded of sea officers. Ineveitably, officers did have connections that were political, and after 1775 the sentiments aroused by a war against colonists had a political complexion. Moreover, the officers themselves disagreed between themselves, not least about their conduct in action: hence the Keppel-Palliser conflict following the battle of Ushant in July 1778. Nevertheless, by and large, politics did not prevent the system of appointments creating an effective officer corps.

Less effective was the system of manning ships. The complete fleet, which grew to absorb over 110,000 men, could not be manned immediately following the declaration of war. The commander-in-chief at the outports—the Nore, Spithead and in Plymouth Sound—organised impressment of seamen in ports and from in-coming merchantmen to supplement recruitment managed by the Navy Board through 'rendezvous' in all the main towns of the country. But, through these means, men trickled into the navy slowly. Consequently ships prepared for sea were always waiting for more men than there were available.

This bespoke the capability of the dockyards in preparing ships for sea during the early months of mobilisation. The yards were equally productive in refitting ships, rebuilding or repairing them as they became rotten and crank. The efficency of the yards was always condemned by sea officers. But their facilities and manpower were limited, and only Portsmouth, Plymouth and Sheerness yards were close to fleet anchorages. The inland yards at Deptford, Woolwich and Chatham were all between twenty and fifty miles from the sea. Each yard, moreover, depended for its operations on orders issued by the Navy Board, sitting at Crutched Friars, Tower Hill, in London. From there, the board made most of its major contracts for naval stores, which were distributed by contractors and storeships both to the six main yards in England and to smaller yards abroad, for example, Antigua, Jamaica, Gibraltar and Halifax.

The Victualling Board, sitting near the Navy Board, managed the victualling yards, breweries and bakeries at Deptford, Chatham, Portsmouth and Plymouth. Like the work of the dockyards, the victualling supplies of the navy were also much criticised. Yet calculations of the quantities of provisions condemned by survey of three or more ships' masters show that, with the exception of stockfish, far less than one per cent of any commodity was declared unfit for consumption. The quality

3

of the victuals, indeed, ensured that seamen in the Royal Navy were generally better fed than people of the same class on land.

When they became ill or injured, they were also better looked after. The Sick and Hurt Board arranged the examination, entry and equipment of the naval surgeons appointed to most frigates and ships of the line. It managed the hospitals, the main ones at Haslar, near Portsmouth, and at Stonehouse, Plymouth, with other smaller ones close to fleet anchorages around the British coasts and on foreign stations. This provision for the sick, along with innovations in diet, ensured that the death rate from sickness in seamen gradually declined in the second half of the eighteenth century and that Britain's most scarce naval resource was preserved for further service.

---

1. 'A Perspective View of the Admiralty Office, the New Building for the Horse Guards, Whitehall &c', etching, published by (?)F West, London. *NMM ref PAD1372*

2. 'Old Admiralty Pay Office in Broad Street', watercolour by George Sydney Shepherd, undated. *NMM ref PAF5950*

3. 'Board Room of the Admiralty', coloured aquatint produced by J Black after an original by Thomas Rowlandson and A C Pugin, published by R Ackermann, London, 1 January 1808. The wind direction indicator, connected to the weather vane on the roof, can be seen on the far wall, with rolls of charts to the left. *NMM ref PAD1358*

4. 'John Montagu, Earl of Sandwich . . . First Lord Commissioner of the Admiralty . . .' engraved and published by Valentine Greene after an original by Johann Zoffany, London, 30 August 1774. *NMM ref PAG7218*

5. Captain William Carlyon, captain's uniform dress 1774-1787, grey wash drawing by W Wellings, 1782. *NMM ref PAF6284*

5

1

'The Other Armada'

2

IN EVERY war for more than a century France had dreamed of invading the British Isles, where her more powerful military forces could dictate peace on her terms. However ingenious these many and various plans, they had all been contingent upon decoying, circumventing or otherwise eluding the Royal Navy, which was usually superior in numbers if not in skill. However, the American war had drawn large elements of the navy across the Atlantic, and if the Spanish fleet could be added to that of France then a significant Bourbon predominance in the English Channel would be assured. In fact, in the secret negotiations between France and Spain,

Prise d'un Longre *Anglais par les Canots et Chaloupe des Frégates Francaise et Espagnole* l'Athalante *et la* Sta. Catharina *le 15. Août 1779.*

A. *l'Athalante.*   *Voyez la Gazette de France N.º 69.*   C. *Canots et Chaloupe.*

B. *la Sta Catharina.*   D. *Longre Anglois.*

3

the latter had been the leading advocate of an attack on Britain as the prime strategy of the allied forces.

A full-scale invasion was beyond the resources of the Bourbon powers, but the joint plan called for the occupation of the Isle of Wight, prior to landings at Gosport and the bombardment and destruction of the main British dockyard and fleet base at Portsmouth. Over 20,000 French troops were assembled at Le Havre (1) and St Malo, and when the plans were expanded to include the siege and occupation of Portsmouth, the numbers grew to over 30,000 — more than all the regulars then available in England. Before this could be launched, a Franco-Spanish fleet would enter the Channel in overwhelming numbers, and Spain refused to declare war until the French fleet was at sea, which was finally achieved in June, but there followed nearly two months' delay before the Spanish contingent joined up. By this time, the middle of August, disease had broken out in the French fleet, which was also running short of water and stores.

The Royal Navy also had its problems. Because of the political divisions following the Keppel-Palliser affair, the only senior officer who could be persuaded to take up the commander-in-chief's position was the lack-lustre Sir Charles Hardy (2), whose previous employment was as governor of Greenwich Hospital. The British fleet was too late to blockade the French squadron in Brest, and when the enormous Franco-Spanish armada of sixty-six ships of the line finally entered the Channel, Hardy with barely forty could only fall back before it. In

this he had the government's blessing, but many in the fleet regarded this as an ignominious retreat, and it was reported that the seamen of the *Royal George* blindfolded the figurehead (of George II) so 'the old king' would not see to what depths his navy had been reduced.

Dogged by adverse weather, poor training, sickness and shortages, the armada was actually its own worst enemy. It achieved so little that it was reduced to celebrating the capture of a lugger (3) on 15 August by the boats of two of the fleet's frigates. Two days later some of Hardy's reinforcements blundered into a French division off Plymouth, but all escaped except the 64-gun *Ardent*. The ship was ill-prepared for battle and was skillfully harassed by two French frigates until more powerful vessels arrived (4); the British captain was cashiered for his poor performance.

With only the *Ardent* to show for its cruise — it even missed the main returning convoys — the Franco-Spanish fleet was forced back to port by its own inadequacies in early September. Such was its state, that it took five days to get through the Goulet and into Brest. It was planned to sortie again after refit, but the resources were simply unavailable, and in effect the invasion threat was over.

The Annual Register for 1780 summed it up: 'Never had perhaps so great a a naval force been assembled on the seas. Never any by which less was done.' It sounded smug, but it was probably relief: for Britain it had been the most dangerous moment for two centuries.

1. Marshalling troops at Le Havre, one of a portfolio of etchings of French ports by Claude Joseph Vernet (1714-1789). Although this print is undated, the original oil paintings were mostly carried out in the 1760s.
NMM ref PAH9396

2. Admiral Sir Charles Hardy (?1716-1780), oil painting by George Romney (1734-1802).
NMM ref BHC2744

3. 'Prise d'un Lougre Anglais par les Canots et Chaloupe des Frégates Française et Espagnole l'Athalante et la Sta Catharina le 15 Août 1779', French engraving. 'A' is the French frigate, 'B' the Spanish frigate, 'C' the boats, and 'D' the lugger. This cannot be a naval vessel, since the only loss besides the *Ardent* from this campaign was a hired cutter called the *Active*.
NMM ref PAD5345

4. 'Prise de l'*Ardent* Vaisseau Anglois de 64 canons par les Frégates Françaises la Junon et la Gentille le 17 Août 1779', French engraving. 'A' is *la Junon*, 'B' is *la Gentille*, and 'C' is the *Ardent*.
NMM ref PAD5346

4

Prise de l'Ardent Vaisseau Anglois de 64 canons par les Frégates Françaises la Junon et la Gentille le 17 Aout 1779.
A . *la Junon* .
B . *la Gentille* .
Voyez la Gazette de France N.º 69.
C . *l'Ardent* .
3

1

2

The Spanish Navy

THE NAVY which Spain brought into the conflict tipped the scales of seapower against Britain. The third largest in the world, the Spanish battlefleet of fifty-nine ships is calculated to have displaced a total of 143,000 tons in 1780, which when added to that of France gave the Bourbon alliance some 337,000 tons compared with around 234,000 tons for the Royal Navy. This advantage of about 44 per cent was to dominate the strategy of the naval struggle for the rest of the war, since the British could never rely on the control of the sea that assured victory in the other wars of the eighteenth century.

Pride of the Spanish fleet was the 120-gun *Santisíma Trinidad*, built at Havana in 1769. Probably the largest ship in the world at the time, the ship was reconstructed in 1796 with eight extra 8pdrs added in the waist, making her a nominal four-decker - this was the ship that exerted so much awe in the British fleets at St Vincent and Trafalgar, although by this time she was surpassed in sheer size by the largest French three-deckers like the *Commerce de Marseilles*. Even as built the *Trinidad* was over-gunned, and rolled badly, but in 1779 Spain launched the first of a successful class of 112-gun ships (1), the *Purisíma Concepcion*, and there were also three 94-gun ships which were the equivalent of British Second Rates.

The remainder of the battlefleet comprised seven large two-deckers of 76-80 guns, thirty-four of 70-74 guns (2), eleven small two-deckers of around 60 guns and two obsolescent 50-gun ships. Cruising ships were made up of one 40-gun frigate, twenty-one 34s (3), and twelve smaller *corbetas* (4). Besides ocean-going vessels, Spain also kept limited numbers of specialist Mediterranean craft like xebecs, feluccas and even a few remaining galleys. Perhaps most useful of these latter types, however, were the gunboats (5), small craft not much larger than a ship's launch which could be rowed or sailed and were armed with one or two large-calibre forward-firing guns; such were their successes around Gibraltar during the siege that the British were forced to build similar vessels.

3

Spanish ships were renowned for their size and the quality of their construction—particularly those built of tropical hardwoods at the great arsenal of Havana in Cuba—which made them long-lived. Whereas British warships were often criticised for being overgunned, a striking feature of Spanish ships was their relatively light armament to tonnage ratio: most two-deckers carried only 26pdrs on their lower decks, while some of the largest Spanish frigates captured by the Royal Navy mounted 8pdrs in their main batteries. The usual armament (pdrs) was as follows:

Guns	Lower deck	Middle deck	Upper deck	Quarterdeck/ Forecastle
120	36	26	18	8
112	36	26	12	8
94	36	18	8	-
80	36	-	18	8
70/78	26	-	18	8
58/68	26	-	12	8 or 6
50	18	-	8	6

Most frigates carried 12pdr or 8pdr main batteries, with 6pdrs or less on the quarterdecks.

Although Spanish construction impressed the British, the design of the ships, and especially in terms of hull form, was not so highly regarded. The large two-decked 80-gun ship was introduced into the Royal Navy in 1780 with the capture of the Spanish *Fenix* (or *San Alejandro*, Spanish ships often having a formal name and a 'religious' identity), but the renamed *Gibraltar* was always infamous throughout the fleet for her poor sailing qualities. In fact, whereas numerous French hull forms were copied for British warships, there is not a single example of a Spanish design being so employed.

In battle the Spanish navy had a reputation for hard fighting, but its successes were few, for although the ships were well built there were serious problems in manning, training and supplying the fleet. Although Spain possessed well-developed arsenals at La Carraca near Cadiz, at Ferrol in the north, and overseas at Havana and Manila, financial resources were never sufficient to keep them well stocked with the necessary stores. Furthermore, since Spain had a relatively small merchant marine, there was no substantial pool of experienced seamen for the navy to draw on. These factors made mobilisation very slow, and hampered efforts to replace men and material lost in battle. Their French allies were very critical of the quality of Spanish ordnance, poor reserves of stores, and in 1779 of an officer corps containing too many inexperienced juniors promoted to make up numbers. Spanish officers were given

4

little opportunity for sea-time, which meant poor training in seamanship, fleet manoeuvres, and gunnery.

1. Spanish 112-gun ship at anchor. One of a series of ten plates, coloured engravings by Rodriguez and Casco after originals by Augustin Berlinguero first published *c*1790.
NMM ref PAD7332.

2. Spanish ship of the line (two-decker) firing a salute. Berlinguero as (1).
NMM ref PAD7333.

3. Spanish frigate of 36 guns (according to the caption, but 12pdr ships of thirteen ports were usually rated as 34s), hove to, in order to hoist her launch on board. Engraving published by G Antonelli, after Baugean.
NMM ref PAD7196.

4. Spanish corbeta (corvette or post ship) of 24 guns with backed topsails, boats coming alongside. Berlinguero as (1).
NMM ref PAD7336.

5. Spanish *lancha cañonera* (gunboat) with large calibre gun forward; craft of this type were very active during the siege of Gibraltar. Berlinguero as (1).
NMM ref PAD7340.

5

Gibraltar besieged, summer 1779

A MAJOR WAR aim for the Spanish was the recovery of Gibraltar, which had been held by Britain since the War of Spanish Succession at the beginning of the century. Jutting out into the straights to which it gave its name, Gibraltar controlled the entrance to the Mediterranean; it was strategically vital to the Royal Navy since it allowed squadrons based there to move quickly to either the Bay of Biscay or the Mediterranean and potentially blocked any junction between the main French fleets at Brest and Toulon.

It was a natural fortress rising steeply from the sea and approachable by land only across a narrow isthmus to the north, which was easy to defend (1). On the west side was the harbour, which could be attacked from the sea—indeed, Spanish gunboats operating under oars in the frequent morning and evening calms made it difficult for sailing ships entering the bay (2)—but gun batteries and rocks made venturing too close a very dangerous pastime.

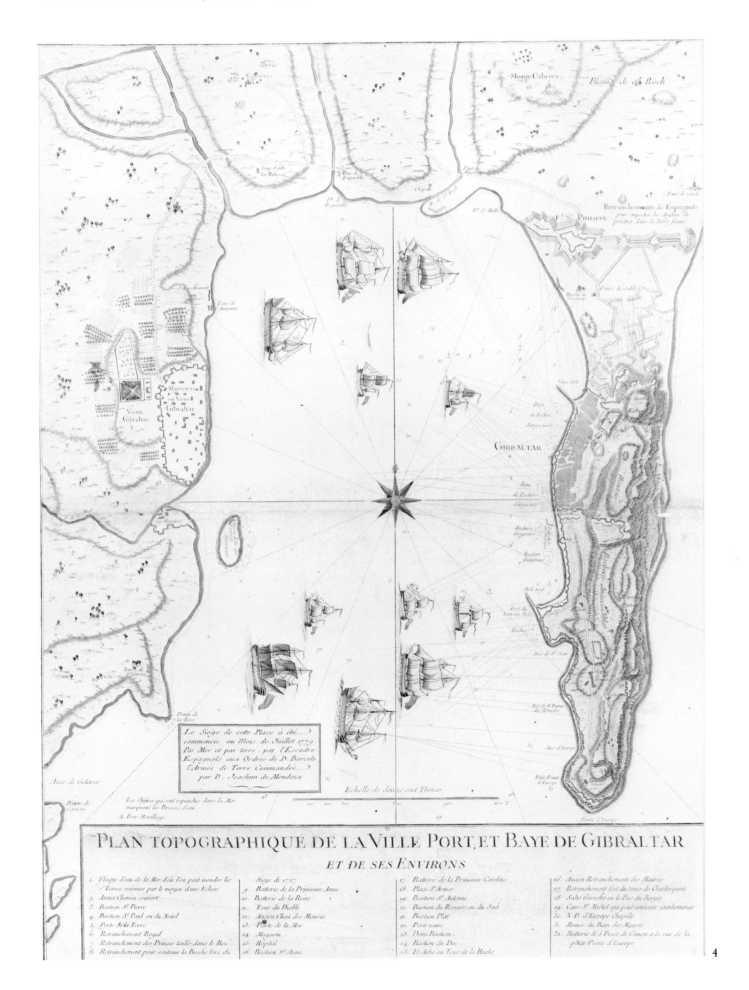

PLAN TOPOGRAPHIQUE DE LA VILLE PORT, ET BAYE DE GIBRALTAR

ET DE SES ENVIRONS

1. Flaque d'eau de la Mer d'ou l'on peut inonder les Terres voisines par le moyen d'une Ecluse	*Siege de 1727*	17. Batterie de la Princesse Caroline	26. Ancien Retranchement des Maures
2. Avant Chemin couvert	9. Batterie de la Princesse Anne	18. Place d'Armes	27. Retranchement fait du tems de Charlesquint
3. Bastion St. Pierre	10. Batterie de la Reine	19. Bastion St. Antoine	28. Salto Guerobo ou le Pas du Berger
4. Bastion St. Paul ou du Nord	11. Tour du Diable	20. Bastion du Rosario ou du Sud	29. Cave St. Michel qui peut contenir 100 hommes
5. Porte John Terre	12. Ancien Chau des Maures	21. Bastion Plat	30. N. D. d'Europe Chapelle
6. Retranchement Royal	13. Porte de la Mer	22. Porte neuve	31. Rance du Bain des Maures
7. Retranchement des Princes taillé dans le Roc	14. Magasin	23. Demi Bastion	32. Batterie de 5 Pieces de Canon a la vue de la
8. Retranchement pour soutenir la Breche tiré du	15. Hopital	24. Bastion du Duc	petite Pointe d'Europe
	16. Bastion St. Anne	25. El Acho ou Tour de la Hache	

4

The British were fortunate in their choice of Governor for the garrison. George Augustus Eliott (1717-1790) was a military engineer by training, and a man of austere and spartan personal tastes who nevertheless thought constantly of the welfare of his men (3). He was an inventive and indomitable soldier who never let the usual 'siege mentality' make him resigned or defeatist—indeed, he took the fight to the enemy whenever possible, and encouraged a number of ingenious devices like the depression gun carriage that made the defence more effective.

The Spanish had tried to recover the Rock (as it was known to the British) by direct assault in 1704-5 and 1727 without success, so this time they opted for an attempt to starve out the garrison. The blockade was initiated in June and the pressure was only gradually stepped up. Eventually, as this French map (4) shows, formal siege lines were constructed, but at first a small Spanish squadron operating from Algesiras opposite took the main part. The British squadron on station consisted only of the old 60-gun *Panther*, commanded by the none-too-active Rear-Admiral Duff, three frigates and a sloop, and was too weak to take offensive action. As supplies began to run low towards the end of the year, the Spaniards imposed a more and more rigid blockade, but

the garrison's morale was lifted in November when a cutter called the *Buck* decoyed the Spanish across to the North African shore, and then cheekily cut across their bows to make a safe arrival in Gibraltar (5). However, if they were expecting a delivery of fresh food they were to be sorely disappointed: the cutter was short of victuals and had put in to pick up supplies.

1. 'A North View of Gibraltar', etching produced by Roberts, London, 16 August 1785.
NMM neg A9565

2. 'A West View of Gibraltar', etching produced by Roberts, London, 16 August 1785.
NMM neg A9563

3. 'General George Augustus Elliott, Lord Heathfield 1717-1790', engraved by T Bengo after an original by G Fred Koehler, published by H Murray and Thomas Holloway, London, 25 July 1794.
NMM ref PAD2983

4. 'Plan topographique de la Ville Port et Baye de Gibraltar et des ses Environs', French hand coloured engraving by Guillaume Dheulland 'Graveur de la Marine', undated but probably c1782.
Beverley R Robinson Collection

5. 'A View of the Bay of Gibraltar, and Ceuta on the opposite coast of Africa, and the famous exploit of the Buck cutter Privateer . . . fighting her way through the Spanish and French blockading fleet . . . 1780', black and watercolour pen and ink by I Robb, dated April 1810.
NMM neg A5948

5

1

The war on trade

FOR CENTURIES the classic tactic for the defence of trade was to gather all ships sailing the same route into convoys and provide the protection of armed vessels. By the late eighteenth century this was a well practised routine for the British merchant service and Royal Navy alike, the strength of the escort depending on the size of the perceived threat. This could go wrong, however, if the convoy were attacked by a force too powerful for the escort—a frequent occurrence in this war, where a strategy of blockade could not be applied to keep the enemy battlefleets bottled up. An example of the effects of marauding battleships was recorded in Captain Robert Richmond's log of the brig *Fame*, whose convoy from Torbay to Quebec was attacked by a French two-decker on 7 June 1780, and forced to scatter (1).

Needless to say, the biggest and the best warships rarely found themselves on convoy duty, which usually fell to older, smaller and less efficient vessels, many of them 'armed ships' purchased from the merchant ser-

vice and barely equal to an attack by privateers. When regular warships were the aggressors, they were as likely to fall victim as the merchant ships they escorted. On 21 July 1781 the 12pdr-armed French frigates *Astrée*, 36 and *Hermione*, 32 attacked an apparently well defended convoy off Cape Breton, the escort comprising the 24-gun *Charleston* (ex-American *Boston*) armed with 9pdrs, the sloop *Vulture*, 16 and three armed ships, *Allegiance*, *Vernon* and *Jack*. Only the last was taken, the rest of the escort and its convoy escaping, but the French regarded it as a victory worthy of this fine print after an original by Rossel (2). As so often with contemporary prints, it flatters the intended audience by underestimating the force of the French ships while exaggerating the opposition.

Many British convoy escorts and small cruisers started life as privateers, and some changed hands more than once. HM brig *Observer*, originally the Massachusetts-built privateer *Amsterdam*, fought a smart little action off Halifax on the night of 29 May 1782 against the American ship rigged privateer *Jack*, probably the vessel

captured by the French frigates the previous July and herself an American privateer before British service. The details of many of these small craft, often pressed into service with the minimum of formalities, are often vague, but according to the usually meticulous Robert Dodd, the brig carried twelve 6pdrs and 60 men and the ship sixteen 9pdrs and 65 men; the three-hour action ended with the *Jack* suffering 15 dead and 9 wounded, and the *Observer* 3 and 8 respectively (3).

Paradoxically, because the Royal Navy had lost command of the sea, which gave more freedom for enemy commerce, this war provided better opportunities for British privateers. Although the Government was slow to authorise general reprisals against the Colonies (which would have been tantamount to recognising them as independent states), they bowed to the inevitable in 1777 and eventually 7352 privateering commissions and Letters of Marque were issued before the end of the war, 2285 against the Colonies. A total of 2670 British and loyalist vessels were engaged in privateering, most of them of fairly small size. Folkestone, for example, which was the centre of Channel privateering, favoured the cutter (4), which was fast and more weatherly than any square rig. This was the largest British fleet in any war between 1689 and 1815 and also the most successful, reaching its zenith in 1781, the first year of war against all four of Britain's maritime adversaries.

The Netherlands provided a particularly rich target, with an estimated 16,000 merchant ships in all trades. But they were also home to a number of successful pri-

4

5

6

vateers of their own, the audacious exploits of Pierre Le Turc of Flushing against British coastal convoys being a popular subject for Dutch printmakers (5).

British privateers carried the majority of the burden of the war against enemy shipping: judging by prizes condemned in London, they accounted for 56 per cent, the rest falling to the navy. On the other hand, head money claimed for their part in the capture of enemy warships or privateers—3.8 per cent by amount—suggests that British privateers were of scant value in the defence of trade. There were individual incidents, but these were celebrated in a way that reinforces their rarity. An example might be the action of the Bristol-registered *Caesar* of 300 tons and 20 guns, which fought off a French frigate in defence of a Jamaica convoy on 27 June 1782. Captain Valentine was voted a valuable piece of plate by grateful Bristol merchants, and the action was commemorated in paint by Nicholas Pocock (6).

One of the most successful centres of British privateering was the Channel Islands, which specialised in

small craft, many armed with the kind of single large-calibre gun on a pivot mounting usually associated with American privateers of the War of 1812. The islands suffered two French attempts at capture by surprise, the first in 1779 which was defeated by a detachment from the Channel Fleet. The second, in 1781, was a better organised affair which captured St Helier, but was routed by a counter-attack by the garrison of Elizabeth Castle (7).

7

2

John Paul Jones's cruise, 1779

1

UNLIKE MANY of the ex-merchant service officers in the Continental Navy, John Paul Jones (1) was a natural fighter and an inspired naval leader. He had been the first lieutenant of the *Alfred* during the attack on New Providence in 1776, and as commander of the sloop *Providence* had proved a resourceful raider. At the end of 1777 he crossed the Atlantic in the new Continental ship sloop *Ranger*, 18 and received the first ever salute to the flag of the United States from a French squadron in Quiberon Bay on 14 February 1778. His raid in the Irish Sea included the capture of the 16-gun *Drake*, a purchased merchantmen but nevertheless a Royal Navy sloop, a raid on Whitehaven, and more controversially the lifting of the Earl of Selkirk's silver.

He was promised a larger command, but he had to wait until the summer of 1779. France was keen to attack the all-important British Baltic trade which included essential naval stores, but they had never had frigates to spare for the task, so a Franco-American squadron was put together. It comprised the American frigate *Alliance*, 36, the French frigate *Pallas*, 32, a French corvette and brig, and a couple of privateers, under the overall command of Jones as commodore in the ex-East Indiaman *Duc de Duras*, which he renamed in honour of Benjamin

Franklin's *Poor Richard's Almanac*, then popular in French translation as *Les Maximes de Bonhomme Richard*.

The scheme was a six-week cruise against Baltic trade before entering the Texel to bring home a French timber convoy—in many ways it was a privateering venture with any profits to be split 50/50 between America and France. Sailing from Lorient in August, Jones had trouble with squadron discipline from the first, particularly with Landais, the French captain of *Alliance*, but he still achieved a degree of success in a cruise around the British Isles, creating panic if not actually doing as much damage as he wanted. His planned attack on Leith (2), the port of Edinburgh, had to be called off, but on 23 September he hit a potential jackpot when he ran into a large Baltic convoy (3) off Flamborough Head escorted by the *Serapis*, 44 (Captain Richard Pearson—4) and *Countess of Scarborough*, armed ship of 20 guns. Jones went straight for the escort, ignoring the convoy which got under the protection of Scarborough Castle.

What followed was one of the greatest single-ship actions of all time. It was witnessed by crowds from the Yorkshire clifftops, and with its spectacular moonlight setting became a favourite with marine artists. One of the most accurate is by Robert Dodd (5), which shows it as the squadron action it actually was—although Jones

4

had no control over the self-willed Landais. The British ship was more powerful than the *Bonhomme Richard* and was on the point of winning more than once during an engagement that lasted 3½ hours, but by sheer force of personality Jones kept his crew fighting. Legends abound about the battle: he is supposed to have knocked down his gunner who was about to strike the ensign in surrender, which was picked up by British propaganda and exaggerated into shooting his lieutenant (6)—in the more lurid versions the officer is even elevated to his brother. At one point Pearson asked him, 'Have you struck? Do you call for Quarters?', to which it seems he replied, 'No. I'll sink, but I'm damned if I'll strike'; however, the fallible memory of Richard Dale later made his response, 'I have not yet begun to fight', which has a finer resonance and as such has been accepted.

The hard facts are that *Serapis* not *Bonhomme Richard* surrendered, and the following day the latter sank from the results of battle damage. Casualties were high on both sides: 54 killed and 75 wounded for the British, and around 49 dead and 67 wounded on the *Richard*.

The British view was that since none of the convoy was taken, the *Serapis* had done her duty, and Pearson was both knighted and given command of the new *Arethusa*, the finest frigate in the Royal Navy. In contrast,

3

5

Jones's treatment was shabby in the extreme, and he never again commanded an American squadron at sea, dying in relative poverty and obscurity. It is only in retrospect that he was recognised as the father of the US Navy, and his remains removed to the Naval Academy in Annapolis.

1. Graphite drawing of John Paul Jones by Henry Rogers, dated 1800.
NMM ref PAD8518

2. The port of Leith with a smack sailing into the harbour, grey pen and ink and wash, produced 1809 by D Giovanni after an original by J T Serres.
NMM ref PAF5866

3. 'North Country Shipping in a calm off Flamborough Head', coloured aquatint and etching, produced and published by Robert Dodd, London, 30 March 1797.
NMM neg 4054

4. Sir Richard Pearson (1731-1806), oil painting by Charles Grignion (1754-1804).
NMM ref BHC2942

5. 'Defence of Captain Pearson in His Majesty's Ship *Serapis* and the *Countess of Scarborough* Arm'd Ship Captain Piercy, against Paul Jones's squadron, 23 Sept 1779', engraved by John Peltro after an original by Robert Dodd, published by John Harris, London, 1 December 1781.
NMM neg 9790

6. 'Paul Jones shooting his Lieutenant for Endeavouring to Lower the American Flag', aquatint and etching published by J Pitts, London, 6 January 1800.
NMM ref PAH6266

6

1

The Moonlight Battle, 1780

IN EARLY 1780 came the first signs that the tide at sea might be beginning to turn in Britain's favour. Admiral Rodney, the newly designated commander in the Leeward Islands, was sent out with reinforcements for that station, but was to go via Gibraltar, now under siege by the Spaniards, escorting a massive combined convoy of the West Indian, Portuguese and Mediterranean trade. Rodney was also given a large detachment from the home fleet—so he started with twenty-two ships of the line and fourteen frigates and smaller vessels as well as the merchantmen. This huge assemblage of ships left Plymouth on 29 December 1779. On 8 January 1780, having just passed the latitude of Finisterre, a Spanish convoy was sighted and in a few hours all twenty-two ships had been hunted down and captured. They included the *Guipuscoana* of 54 guns, three frigates and twelve provision ships. The latter were immediately appropriated for Gibraltar.

On the 16th the Spanish Gibraltar blockading squadron came into view just south of Cape St Vincent; Rodney had been expected this, and he took full advantage. It consisted of eleven ships of the line and two frigates and was clearly no match for Rodney's force. The British commander signalled a 'general chase', and the newly-coppered British ships relentlessly pursued their fleeing enemies towards the Spanish coast. The hunt began in the early afternoon, and the first shots were fired about 4pm. Less than an hour later a Spanish 70-gun ship, the *Santo Domingo*, blew up with all on board (1).

2

3

1. The Moonlight Battle: the battle off Cape St Vincent, 16 January 1780, oil painting by Thomas Luny (1759-1837). *NMM ref BHC0428*

2. The Moonlight Battle: the battle off Cape St Vincent, 16 January 1780, Dominic Serres the Elder (1722-1793). The difficulty of opening lower deck ports on the leeward side in heavy weather is emphasised by the two-decker in the foreground, which has only run out guns from the after ports where the sheer of the deck gave them more freeboard. *NMM ref BHC0430*

3. Rodney bringing the Spanish prizes into Gibraltar after his victory on 16 January 1780, oil painting by Dominic Serres the Elder (1722-1793). *NMM ref BHC3815*

4. 'A View of Gibraltar, with Sir George Brydges Rodney coming to its Relief & bringing with him five Men of War . . . Captured off St Vincent . . .', engraved by Robert Pollard after an original by Dominic Serres, published by Robert Wilkinson and Robert Pollard, London, 1 June 1782. *Beverley R Robinson Collection*

The first surrender happened at 6pm, by which time it was night. The chase went on, which is why it was called the 'Moonlight Battle'. The last shots were fired and the leading Spaniard surrendered about 2am the next morning. It had been a rough night: 'The weather . . . was at times very tempestuous with a great sea,' as Rodney's report stated (2), and now the leading ships, including his own flagship, were close in to the shallows off the Spanish coast. Two of the six Spanish ships of the line captured grounded and were lost, but by the next morning all the others, British and Spanish, had escaped the danger into deeper water. The disparity of forces meant that this action could only have one result, but, never-

theless, Rodney's reaction was rapid, certain and bold, and the chasing of the Spaniards into the shoals argued good nerves and determination in his captains. The battle is a classic chase action.

The arrival of Rodney at Gibraltar with his prizes was a doubly triumphal occasion (3), breaking the siege and celebrating the biggest naval victory of the war to date (4). Nor was British fortune exhausted, for after Rodney had departed for the West Indies, the returning home fleet ships captured the French 64-gun *Prothée* and three storeships bound for Pondicherry, an action which had favourable consequences for the British campaign in India.

4

Single-ship actions

AS A test of the prowess of navies, the engagement between individual ships of comparable type has always exerted a particular fascination. Actions between single ships of the line were rare since by their nature they were usually deployed in squadrons if not whole fleets, so single-ship actions are mainly the province of detached cruisers, the most powerful at this time being frigates of 28 to 38 guns, although the British also employed small two-deckers of 44 guns.

Occasionally victory would be achieved against the odds, but in this war the trend was for the more powerful ship to prevail, and where firepower was more or less equal for the better trained to win. Looking solely at frigates lost in action, the statistics are as follows: British ships of 28-44 guns lost—14 (12 to the French, 2 to the Americans); French frigates of 26-40 guns lost—21; American ships of 28-42 guns lost—10; Spanish frigates lost—6; Dutch frigates lost—3. Beyond this it is difficult to generalise, but a selection of such actions point up some features of this type of warfare.

The unlucky Fox

Although the American *Hancock* also served under three flags, no frigate changed hands as often as the 28-gun *Fox*. When new, she was taken by the American *Hancock*, 32 and *Boston*, 24 (7 June 1777), only to be recaptured a month later when *Hancock* herself was taken. As depicted in this painting (1), she was then captured by the French *Junon*, 32 off Brest on 10 September 1778. The French frigate was a 12pdr-armed ship of greatly superior firepower, and inflicted nearly 50 casualties before the British ship surrendered.

'A Spaniard chased is a Spaniard taken'

This unflattering epigram is not British in origin, but French. However, as far as frigates are concerned it seems to have been largely true. Spain built a number of very large frigates of around 950 tons but they were not outstanding under sail and were regarded as under-armed - they usually carried 12pdrs, but there are known examples of 9pdr main batteries. Four of similar design were captured during this war, one being the *Santa Monica* (2) taken off the Azores on 14 September 1779 by *Pearl*, 32.

1. *Fox* taken by *Junon*, 10 September 1778, French engraving by F Dequevauviller after an original by A L Rossel de Cercy (1736-1804), published by Desras, Paris, 1788. *NMM neg 6674*

2. *Pearl* and *Santa Monica*, 14 September 1779, oil painting by Thomas Whitcombe (c1752-1824). *NMM ref BHC0700*

3. Action between HMS *Quebec* and *Surveillante*, 6 October 1779, oil painting by Robert Dodd (1748-1815), signed and dated 1781. *NMM ref BHC0426*

4. 'A View of the French Frigate L'Amazone . . . Striking her Colours . . . to his Majesty's Frigate the Sta Margaretta', brown aquatint and etching produced and published by Robert Dodd, London, 4 February 1784. *NMM neg C638*

5. *Mediator* and French and American vessels, 12 December 1782, oil painting by Thomas Luny (1759-1837). *NMM ref BHC0455*

6. Action between the *Magicienne* and *Sybille*, 2 January 1783, oil painting by Robert Dodd (1748-1815), signed and dated 1784. *NMM ref BHC0457*

7. 'Combat entre les frégates françaises la Nymphe et l'Amphitrite contre le vaisseau Anglais l'Argo, 16 Fevrier 1783', steel engraving by Chavane after an original by Gilbert and Sandoz, published by Diagraphe et Pantographe Gavard, Paris, no date. *NMM ref PAF4671*

Fight to the death

Most frigate actions concluded with casualties to the losing ship rarely above 20 per cent of the crew, but there were a few fought out with particular stubbornness—the *Serapis* lost nearly 50 per cent killed and wounded, for example, and even the victorious *Bonhomme Richard* lost a third of her crew. One action which flattered the susceptibilities of both sides was the battle between the British *Quebec*, 32 and French *Surveillante* of the same nominal force. They should have been exactly matched, but the *Quebec* had maindeck 9pdrs because 12pdrs were not available when she was refitted, and as usual the French crew was larger. Nevertheless, a two-hour battle ensued, with each ship losing her masts and casualties rising rapidly. Eventually the British ship caught fire, and the French ship, with her captain, du Couëdic, mortally wounded, ceased fire and chivalrously took part in rescuing what survivors they could reach. Captain Farmer of the *Quebec* refused to abandon ship and directed the firefighting, until at sunset the ship blew up; Farmer was last seen sitting calmly on the fluke of a remaining anchor.

Only 68 of her crew of 195 survived, but even in the French ship there were 45 per cent casualties, and it was only with difficulty that *Surveillante* was towed back to Brest. The engagement was very popular with artists and printsellers on both sides of the Channel, but this version (3) by Robert Dodd is one of the most convincing in terms of detail as well as one of the most dramatic.

A failed gamble

Although this war did not produce frigate captains who became household names in the later manner of Lord Cochrane or Stephen Decatur, many achieved a similar degree of confidence in their abilities and an equally aggressive spirit. One such was Elliot Salter who in July 1782 commanded the *Santa Margarita*, one of the big 12pdr 36s like the *Santa Monica* captured from the Spaniards. When he ran into a French fleet off the American coast, he was chased by the *Amazone*, 36 but as soon as he had run them out of sight he turned on the French frigate and after a sharp engagement of a little over an hour dismasted and captured his opponent (4). The armament of the British ship had been augmented with carronades and at the short-range the action was fought the 'butcher's bill' was terrible: one half of the French crew was killed or wounded.

With a French fleet so near, the action was a calculated risk and although supreme efforts were made to get sail on the dismasted prize, which was also taken under tow, in the following morning the sails of the pursuing

squadron came up quickly over the horizon. Salter had to retrieve his prize crew, and had no time to destroy the *Amazone*; indeed, he was fortunate to be able to escape.

One powerful ship beats a number of weaker ones

One principle of small-scale naval combat regularly demonstrated is that one large ship usually has the advantage over a number of smaller vessels, even if the combined firepower of her opponent looks superior on paper. This was shown by the capture of the British sloops *Trepassey* and *Atalanta* by the American frigate *Alliance*, and in multiple by the attack of the French frigates *Astrée* and *Hermione* on a convoy with five small escorts in July 1781. A vivid example was the exploit of the British *Mediator*, 44 against five French and American vessels on 12 December 1782 (5). The squadron was made up of armed storeships and warships *en flûte*, but while in theory they could have banded together for defence, the *Mediator* managed to capture three of them in succession.

Against the odds

Although the more powerful vessel normally won a single-ship encounter, resistance against powerful odds was at times rewarded. Off San Domingo in October 1782, for example, the French frigate *Sybille*, in company with the 74-gun *Scipion*, was attacked by the three-decker *London* and the 74-gun *Torbay*; daring and skillful handling of the frigate temporarily crippled the *London*, allowing the French battleship to escape, although she was eventually chased ashore. In the following January, *Sybille* was involved in a battle with the more powerful *Magicienne* in defence of her convoy, and again escaped after dismasting her opponent (6). However, a week later she herself was dismasted in a storm, and her luck finally ran out when she was spotted off the Chesapeake by the 28-gun *Hussar*. Ironically, *Sybille* would have been too strong for the British ship, but she had been forced to jettison most of her guns and had to resort to a surprise attempt to board, which failed. Since this had been carried out while flying signals of distress, this was regarded as beyond the acceptable limits of a *ruse de guerre*, and Captain Kergariou, whose behaviour up to then had been highly commendable, had his sword ceremonially broken and found himself in close confinement.

Why frigates replaced 44s

For the first half of the century the standard heavy cruiser had been the small two-decker of 40 or 44 guns, but these had been largely replaced by the new frigate-built

6

single-deckers from the 1750s. However, as pointed out in an earlier section, the British rediscovered some value in the type for the particular conditions of the colonial war and large numbers of them were built around this time. Their greatest shortcoming was the lack of freeboard to their lower deck ports, which in heavy weather kept the ports of the 18pdr battery closed and reduced them to the 9pdr or short 12pdr guns on the upper deck. A perfect demonstration of this occurred on 16 February 1783 when the *Argo*, 44 was forced to strike to the French frigates *Nymphe* and *Amphitrite* for just this reason (7).

7

1

2

VEDUTA ESATTA DI MAONE.

*Presa dal Essercito Spagniolo sotto il
Comando del E.mo S.r Duca di Crillon,
il 19 Agosto del 1781.*

1 Citta di Maone.
2 Conv.to del Carm.no
3 Borgo nuovo.
4 la Madonna di Grazia.
5 Batt.e di Can.i n.o 16.
6 Castello di S.Filippo.

8 Forte di S.Carlo.
9 altra Batt.e di 20.Can.i
10 Forte di Malbrugh.
11 Forte di S.Filippetto.
12 diverse Batt.e dell' Ess.e Spa.l
13 Torre de Segni.

15 Isola di Pinte.
16 Arsenale, e Ferrie. del Re.
17 S.Antonio.
18 Punta di Iunquet.
19 Cala Cranc.
20 Truppe avan.te delli Spa.i
21 Mare del Ess.e Spa.e
22 Cala della Mezquita dove s sbar.to l' ess.to Spa.l

23 Rafaello Colon.
24 il Gendaret.
25 Conv.to di S.Fran.co
26 S.Giovanni.
27 Trincea e Accam.to de Spa.i
28 Diversi Corpi di Trup.e Spa.i

Scala de Miglie.

Spanish successes

THE SPANISH contribution to the American struggle is often ignored. In truth, the Spanish monarchy had no interest in encouraging colonies to rebel, and Spain's war aims were entirely parochial, but the addition of the Spanish fleet gave the Bourbons the superiority at sea that eventually ensured the independence of the United States. However, the performance of that navy often seems disappointing: its dilatory preparations destroyed the chances of invading England in 1779; there were major defeats at sea in 1780; the Spaniards captured only four small warships during the whole war; and Gibraltar resisted every assault.

Nevertheless, there were significant victories. In the New World the British were driven out of Florida and posts around the Caribbean coast of South America were reduced. In Europe, despite the failures of 1779, a large fleet was fitted out for the following year and under Don Luis de Córdoba achieved the greatest Spanish naval success of the war when it intercepted the

West Indies convoy in August, capturing 55 ships out of 63. For the British it was the worst commercial disaster in living memory and the outcry was huge. Despite the implication of this Spanish view (1), the escorting warships all escaped and the commander, John Moutray, was made a scapegoat, 'punished according to the magnitude of the object, rather than in proportion to his demerit', as a contemporary historian expressed it.

Although Gibraltar still eluded them, in the summer of 1781 the Spanish transferred their attention to Minorca, also occupied by the British because of another superb naval anchorage, in this case at Port Mahon (2). The French lent 8000 men and 100 guns under the command of the Duc de Crillon who landed in August and quickly overran the whole island, with the exception of the citadel of the port, Fort St Philip (3). The tiny garrison put up an heroic fight, but the navy could not spare ships for a relief convoy, and in February 1782 the 600 sick and starving survivors finally capitulated.

1. The capture of a British convoy by the Spanish fleet under Don Luis de Córdoba, 9 August 1780: only 8 of 63 ships escaped. Spanish coloured lithograph by Leopol and Aygnals de Izio after an original by Vallejo. *NMM neg B9261*

2. Pictorial map of the Spanish attack on Port Mahon, August 1781. Etching by Serafino Giovannini. *NMM ref PAD5377*

3. 'Plan of the Town and Harbour of Mahon, St Phillips Castle, and its Fortifications. For Mr Tindal's continuation of Mr Rapin's *History of England* (with key)', engraving and etching by Basire. *NMM neg B2548*

3

PLAN of the *TOWN* and *HARBOUR* of MAHON, S.ᵗ PHILIP'S CASTLE, and its *FORTIFICATIONS*.

1

The Dutch Navy

SINCE THE height of its glory in the seventeenth century, the navy of the Netherlands had declined into a second-rank force in keeping with the reduced commercial importance of the country itself. In 1780 the fleet in total displaced some 70,000 tons, compared with 196,000 for Spain, 271,000 for France and 372,000 tons for Britain. Furthermore, the navy could not boast a real battlefleet, having barely three ships fit to lie in the line of battle against a first class opponent. The fleet list at that time comprised one 74-gun ship, two 72s, four 68s, five 60/64s, fourteen 52 to 56-gun ships,

six two-decked 44s, one 40-gun frigate, fifteen 36s and eighteen smaller cruisers of 20 to 24 guns. Only the 74 carried 36pdr lower deck batteries, the other two-deckers generally mounting 24pdrs, although the smallest and oldest could only support 18pdrs.

The characteristic Dutch ship, therefore, was a smaller two-decker of 64 guns (1) or less, but even compared to similar rates in other navies Dutch ships were of minimal dimensions. It is often said that Dutch ships were restricted by the narrow and shallow waters of the Netherlands coast, which certainly had some influence, but the Dutch had built a few three-deckers in the late seventeenth century, so this was not an overriding consideration. In truth, the Netherlands navies—there were still five almost autonomous provincial admiralties so the plural is justified—had concentrated on the development of a trade protection force, since the country's carrying trade was still the third largest in Europe after that of Britain and France. For most of the eighteenth century, the Netherlands were in alliance with Britain and so the Dutch could rely on the support of the British battlefleet, devoting their own strained resources to ships powerful enough to deter minor maritime states but small enough to be built in sufficient numbers for convoy duties and protecting overseas interests. Ships of 54 guns like the *Beschermer* (captured in 1799 but built during the American War) had no exact equivalent in major navies, and when captured by the Royal Navy these ships found little active employment (2).

2

3

1. Engraving by Baugean of a Dutch 64-gun ship at anchor with topgallant masts housed and yards struck; Plate 50 from *Collection de Toutes des Especes de Batiments . . .* (fifth edition, 1826) It may represent one of the building programme of the 1780s. *NMM ref PAD7414*

2. Bow showing figure and trailboard decoration of the 54-gun *Beschermer*, a ship captured in the Texel in 1799 but built in 1781. Grey pen and wash drawing by Jan Rood, c1780. *NMM ref PAG9651*

3. A Dutch 44-gun two-decker, armed with 18pdrs and 12pdrs. *NMM neg A9312*

4. Sheer and profile draught of the Dutch frigate *Mars*, 32 guns, captured at the fall of St Eustatius in 1781, shows the usual tall Dutch topside caused by working her cables on the lower deck. Admiralty Collection. *NMM neg 2344*

Even within the Netherlands there was a widespread belief that ship design had fallen behind that of other nations, and there was some controversy earlier in the century when English and Scottish shipwrights had been taken on in senior positions by the Amsterdam Admiralty. An 'English Style' was popular for some decades, but the essential conservatism of Dutch shipbuilding is to be seen in the continued construction of obsolescent types, like two-decked 44s (3) and 24s (similar in layout to those given up in Britain after 1745). Even when the Netherlands adopted the frigate form (where the between-deck height was usually minimised, and the lower deck positioned at waterline level), Dutch cruisers (4) continued to prefer a full height and prominent scuttles on the lower deck, producing a taller and less weatherly profile.

Treaty obligations should have ensured the Netherlands' active assistance against Britain's European enemies, but the Dutch prevaricated until their support of the Armed Neutrality forced a declaration of war by their erstwhile allies. Thereafter the Netherlands embarked on an ambitious programme to construct the battlefleet that their new policy made necessary, but it came too late to influence the current war. Britain was clearly unimpressed by the reduced power of the Dutch navy, but in one respect the Royal Navy was to find nothing changed from its seventeenth-century clashes—the sanguinary nature of the fighting. In the one significant clash between the navies, at Dogger Bank in 1781, as many men were killed and wounded as other fleet engagements of the American War where more than twice the numbers of ships were involved.

4

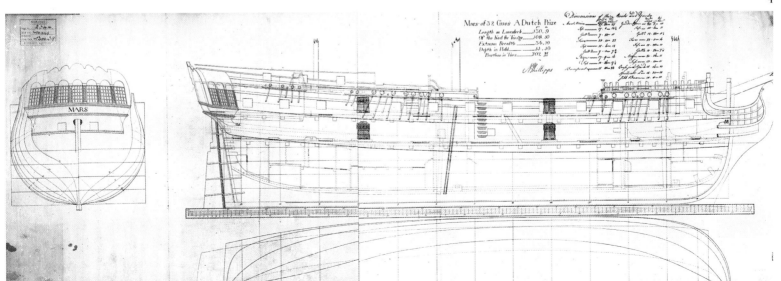

Dogger Bank, August 1781

THE ADDITION of the Netherlands to Britain's list of enemies meant that another squadron had to be scraped together from ever-thinning resources. The Dutch navy was neither large nor were its ships individually very powerful, so the opposing fleet was a scratch collection of very old, and, in the non-technical sense, second-rate vessels, often of reduced armament to preserve their worn-out hulls. The command was given to Vice-Admiral Hyde Parker, recently returned from a rather acrimonious period of service under Rodney in the West Indies, and a man who felt he had something to prove after suffering criticism and censure in his previous post.

On 5 August 1781 Parker's squadron, while convoying a large merchant fleet from the Baltic, spotted a Dutch squadron, under Rear-Admiral Zoutman, with an outward bound convoy in the North Sea. Both prepared for battle, forming a line of seven ships, each with a line of frigates and a cutter on the disengaged side. Sending the convoy on its way, the British squadron of *Berwick*, 74, *Dolphin*, 44, *Buffalo*, 60, *Fortitude*, 74 (flagship), *Princess Amelia*, 80, *Preston*, 50 and *Bienfaisant*, 64 came down rapidly in line abreast on the Dutch (1, 2)—the *Erfprins*, 54, *Admiraal Generaal*, 74, *Argo*, 44, *Batavier*, 54, *Admiraal de Ruyter*, 68 (flagship), *Admiraal Piet Hein*, 54 and *Holland*, 68—calmly hove to, with their convoy under their lee (3). The end-on approach was risky but the Dutch held their fire until Parker's ships rounded-to within half musket shot of

3

their line (4, 5). The battle then became a furious can-nonade, with minimal manoeuvring, that lasted nearly four hours, before the British wore their line and the fighting was over (6).

The battle was tactically inconclusive, but sanguinary: 104 dead and 339 wounded on the British side and 142 and 403 respectively on the Dutch, equivalent to the casualties in battles where three times the numbers were involved. Both squadrons were badly shattered, and the *Holland* sank the following day, but neither could resume combat. The Dutch, with their convoy, returned to the Texel, which allowed the British to claim victory, but since the British had larger and more powerful ships the

Dutch also treated the battle as a success and many senior officers were promoted as a result. It was as popu-lar a theme with printmakers in the Netherlands as it was in England.

Having made it clear that he would accept no honour relating to the battle as a protest against the state of the ships he had been given, Parker was made Commander-in-Chief on the East Indies station, but never arrived, his flagship, the *Cato*, disappearing with all hands on the outward voyage.

As the historian Laird Clowes summarised it, the action was 'a most satisfactory exhibition of valour, and a most unsatisfactory battle; magnificent, but not war.'

4

5

1. Dutch view of their fleet in line of battle, under the command of Commodore J A Zoutman, at the Battle of Dogger Bank, 5 August 1781, engraving and etching by R Muys after an original by Engel Hoogerheyden, published by F W Greebe, Amsterdam, and E Hoogerheyden, Middelburg, 1784.
NMM neg 5625

2. The Battle of the Dogger Bank, 5 August 1781, oil painting by Richard Paton (1717-1791).
NMM ref BHC0433

3. 'A Representation of the obstinate Engagement between the British Squadron . . . and the Dutch Squadron . . . on the Dogger Bank, 5th August 1781', engraved and published by William Byrne after an original by Thomas Luny, London, 1 October 1782.
NMM neg X1928

4. 'Engagement between the English and Dutch Fleets on Dogger Bank,

August 5th 1781', anonymous grey wash drawing. Seen from the British line, with the frigates in the foreground, the numbers of the Dutch fleet appear inflated because of the convoy beyond.
NMM ref PAF4652

5. The Battle of the Dogger Bank, 5 August 1781, oil painting by Thomas Luny (1759-1837), signed and dated 1781.
NMM ref BHC0434

6. Dutch view of an incident towards the end of the Battle of the Dogger Bank, when the British appeared to attempt the capture of the damaged *Batavia* lying defenceless to windward with *Amphitrite* and *Waakzaamheid* going to her assistance; *Batavia* then hauled down the signals of distress and rehoisted her colours, which the British regarded as a trick and luffed way from the stricken Dutch ship. Engraving and etching by R Muys after an original by Engel Hoogerheyden, published by F W Greebe, Amsterdam, and E Hoogerheyden, Middelburg, 1784.
NMM neg 5626

6

Gibraltar: the second relief and after, 1781-1782

FOLLOWING RODNEY'S relief of the Rock in January 1780, Spanish activity had been sporadic rather than continuous. A fireship attack at the beginning of June caused no damage, but the gunboats earned new respect later that month when they attacked the guardship, *Panther,* and eventually became such a danger that a boom had to be constructed around the anchorage. Trials also began of a new design of mortar boat (1) derived from the rowing gunboats, and Spanish galleys were sent against the colony's fishing boats, which further reduced food stocks. By the turn of the year reinforcement and resupply was again a major priority.

The morning of 12 April broke with a thick but low-lying fog, through which could be seen a forest of mast-heads, and as the sun burnt off the fog a convoy emerged under escort of the Channel Fleet—twenty-eight ships of the line commanded by Vice-Admiral Darby (2), flying his flag in the First Rate *Britannia.* As the garrison turned out to cheer in the ships (3), the Spanish choose this moment to open fire for the first time with a siege battery they had been assiduously preparing for several months. Very little damage was done to the convoy, but thereafter the bombardment became a constant feature of daily life —apart from the siesta hours, which were religiously observed by the Spaniards.

Besides Gibraltar, Spain was also also keen to recover Minorca, whose fine harbour at Port Mahon was another Royal Navy base. Darby therefore detached a small squadron to Minorca, whose escort, the frigates *Flora,* 36 and *Crescent,* 28, ran into a new enemy on the return voyage when they encountered the Dutch frigates *Castor* and *Briel,* both 36s (4) on 23 May. The *Flora* was one of the new 18pdr ships, and had carronades as well, but the 12pdr Dutch ship put up a creditable fight before being forced to surrender; the 9pdr-armed *Crescent,* however, struck to the *Briel* before being rescued by the victorious *Flora.*

1. 'Lancia Bombardiera Spagnola alla Vela' (Spanish mortar boat under sail), watercolour from an anonymous portfolio of Mediterranean ship types with Italian captions, dated about 1780.
NMM ref PAF8289

2. Vice-Admiral George Darby (c1720-1790), oil painting by George Romney (1734-1802).
NMM ref BHC2643

3. 'A View of the straits of Gibraltar with the coast of Barbary from Cape Spartel to Ceuta Point', showing arrival of Darby's convoy, etching engraved by Roberts after an original by Vego, published London, 16 August 1785.
NMM ref PAF4665

4. 'Action between the Dutch Castor and Briel and the English Flora and Crescent, 30 May 1781', Dutch etching by Mattias de Sallieth after an original by Jan Kobell, no date.
NMM neg B2549

5. Battle between the *Nonsuch* and the *Actif*, 14 May 1781.
NMM neg A7410

6. 'References to the print of the Sortie made by the garrison of Gibraltar in the morning of the 27th of Novr 1781', coloured etching, produced and published by A C de Poggi, London, 25 May 1792.
NMM ref PAG8895

7. 'An Ordnance Store Ship of 18 Guns . . . Fighting her way between a Spanish Frigate of 36 Guns, a Xebec of 18 Guns, & 4 Gun boats, in sight of the Garrison, Feb 20 1782', hand coloured aquatint and engraving produced and published by F Jukes after an original by Nicholas Pocock, London, December 1789.
Beverley R Robinson Collection, Annapolis

8. 'Engagement between His Majesty's Ship *Success* . . . and the *Santa Catalina*, a large Spanish frigate . . . off Cape Spartel, on the 16th March 1782. Plate 3rd. Captn Pole . . . being becalmed . . . setting her (*Santa Catalina*) on fire and making sail with the Prisoners to the number of 286 on board', coloured aquatint and etching by P Mercier and Richard Harraden after an original by J Wilson, published by Carver and Gilder, London, 1 March 1786.
NMM ref PAH7823

9. 'Draught of a Gun Boat', dated Navy Office, 9 October 1782.
Admiralty Collection.
NMM neg 4069

5

One of Darby's lookout ships, the 64-gun *Nonsuch* was also involved in a fight with the larger French 74, *Actif*, in the Bay of Biscay that month, but the French ship did not press its advantage (5).

Pressure on Gibraltar let up in the summer, when the Spaniards transferred their attention to an invasion of Minorca, but by October an assault on the Rock itself seemed imminent. True to his principles, Eliott decided

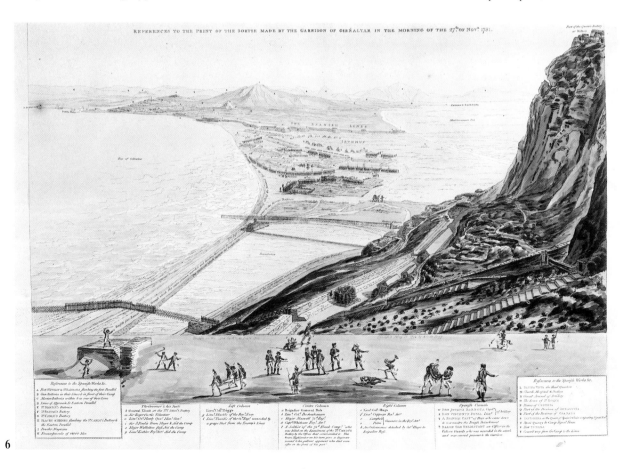

6

7

on a pre-emptive strike and on the night of 26/27 November 2200 men of the 6000 active defenders made a sortie against the Spanish lines in the middle of the isthmus (6). Surprise was complete, and ten 13in mortars and eighteen 26pdr guns were spiked, works destroyed and magazines blown up. The troops then withdrew with minimal casualties.

Food shortage was again a problem by the beginning of 1782, but it was elective, a particular need being fresh fruit and wine for medicinal purposes. Since spying was rife on both sides, Eliott had to organise a secret mission whereby a storeship called the *Mercury* was apparently sent back to England but actually went to Lisbon for the much needed supplies. Her return should have been a secret but she still had to fight her way past a Spanish frigate, xebec and gunboats as she sailed into the bay on 20 February, cheered wildly by the watching garrison (7). For his bravery, the ship's master, Heighington, was granted a commission in the Royal Navy.

In some ways more important arrivals in the following weeks were two ordnance transports, *St Ann* and *Vernon*, carrying twelve rowing gunboats, which had been dismantled and shipped to the Rock to oppose the similar Spanish craft that were such a nuisance. They had not arrived without a fight either, as the Spanish had sent the frigate *Santa Catalina* to intercept the *Vernon*, but she had been captured by the transport's escort, the frigate *Success*, 32 (8). The importance of the mission was underlined by the burning of the valuable prize when threatening sails hove in view.

The reconstructed gunboats (9) began to take to the water from 17 April. Under the command of Sir Roger Curtis they were to play a major part in defeating the grand assault later in the year.

8

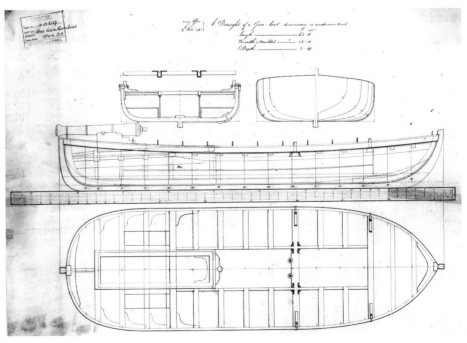

9

Lord Howe takes over the Channel Fleet, 1782

1

WITH THE change of government following the debacle at Yorktown, Britain's finest admiral, Lord Howe, again consented to serve at sea, and on 20 April 1782 hoisted his flag over the *Victory* of 100 guns as commander of the Channel Fleet. With the French, Spanish and Dutch to contend with, his fleet was greatly outnumbered, but it was better supplied, manned and trained than its opponents, and Howe was fortunate in his subordinates, particularly Rear-Admiral Richard Kempenfelt and Vice-Admiral Barrington. Kempenfelt (1) had provided the brains behind such geriatric commanders as Hardy and Geary in the dangerous days of the Franco-Spanish Grand Fleet, and in December 1781 won a brilliant action, cutting out a large part of convoy of reinforcements for the West Indies under the nose de Guichen's more powerful fleet. Barrington, the hero of St Lucia, repeated Kempenfelt's achievement against an East Indies convoy in April, when besides thirteen transports the 74-gun *Pégase* (2) was taken after a three-hour fight by the *Foudroyant*, commanded by John Jervis, later the famous Earl of St Vincent.

Howe spent much of the summer outwitting a large combined fleet under the Spanish admiral Don Luis de Cordóba in order to see home safely large convoys. In this he was aided by his ships being coppered and their underwater hulls clean, making them faster than their enemies. However, the main task of the summer was to be another relief of Gibraltar, which was believed to be in imminent danger of assault. It would be difficult to

avoid the combined fleet, so clean hulls were again at a premium. Docking was time-consuming, so ships were partially careened by heeling them over, to expose some of the underwater section for cleaning. On 29 August, this procedure was being applied to Kempenfelt's flagship, the 100-gun *Royal George*, at Spithead when she heeled too far, capsized and took down the admiral and some 900 people (3,4). It was a major disaster which inspired artists, poets and eventually conspiracy theorists, the official verdict being that the hull of the ship was rotten and simply fell out under the additional stress of careening, although it is possible that the ship simply overset due to inattention during what was a routine, if tricky, undertaking.

Since three-deckers gave the British fleet advantage beyond their nominal firepower, the loss of the second largest ship in the navy was a massive blow to Howe's planned operation.

---

1. Rear-Admiral Richard Kempenfelt (1718-1782), oil painting by Tilly Kettle (1735-1786).
NMM ref BHC 2818

2. Sheer draught of the *Pégase*, taken off after capture, dated Portsmouth, 27 June 1782. Admiralty Collection.
NMM neg X685

3. 'Sinking of HMS Royal George at Spithead at 9 o'clock AM Augt 29th 1782, from an original Drawing in the possession of Henry Slight, Esqr by whom this print is Published', coloured lithograph by W Mitchell, published London, 1839.
NMM ref PAF7938

4. 'Loss of the Royal George',watercolour by Thomas Buttersworth (1768-1842), dated 1800.
NMM neg PAH9500

2

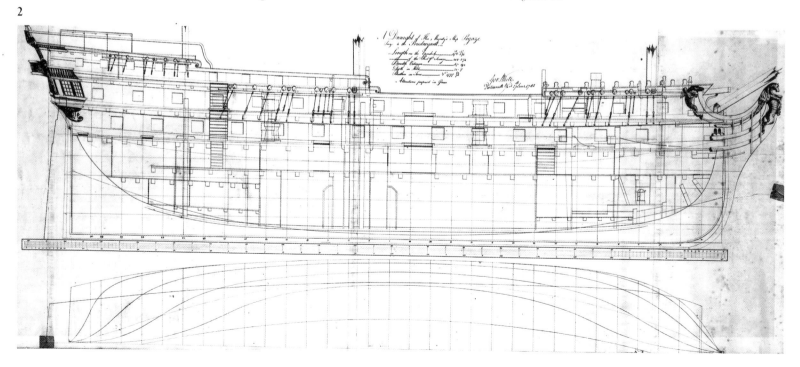

3

4

The carronade: a British secret weapon

1

THERE WERE two important technical innovations of the American War period that helped offset the numerical advantage of the many enemies facing the British Navy. The first was copper sheathing which kept underwater hulls cleaner for longer, making ships faster and allowing them to stay out of dock for longer, thus increasing the number available at any one time. The other was a powerful new addition to their armament, the carronade, named after the Carron foundry in Scotland that developed it. It was short-barrelled, lightweight gun that could be mounted in places like the poops of battleships where for reasons of stability long guns were prohibited.

Their range was very short, but they were initially seen as auxiliary weapons, and the first experiments emphasise the damage they could do to rigging and tophamper early in an action. Compared with the usual British tactic of firing into the hull, this seems rather defensive—the full significance of Bourbon superiority at sea was worrying the administration at this time—but ships' captains found other uses for the new weapon.

John Macbride (1), who was to become a leading advocate of carronades, spoke eloquently of the value of his poop 12pdrs in suppressing small-arms fire (a French speciality) during *Bienfaisant*'s action with the *Artois*.

Carronades began to be fitted from 1779, initially in relatively small calibres, and from the end of the year they were established on the quarterdecks of all frigates. One of the first actions in which they had a significant impact was the *Flora*'s battle with the *Nymphe*, where one 18pdr carronade manned only by the bosun and a boy created havoc. Some idea of the effect of carronades on the unsuspecting can be seen from the relative losses form this hour-long action: 26 killed on the *Flora* but 139 on the *Nymphe* (2).

Although its fundamental principles remained unchanged, details of the carronade developed rapidly during the war, much of it at the instigation of individual captains. This was particularly true of their mountings, which were radically different from the four-wheel 'truck' carriage used for long guns since the sixteenth century. Macbride, now commanding the *Artois*, had a

2

3

particularly successful engagement with two Dutch privateers in 1781 (3), and drawings of his pattern of mounting were circulated to all dockyards as a model (4).

By the end of the war 68pdrs were in service, and carronades were replacing long guns as well as augmenting them. Thereafter, the nominal rating of a British warship ceased to be an accurate indicator of the number of guns carried.

4

1. Captain John Macbride (1730-1800), engraving and etching by James Fittler after an original by James Northcote, printed by T Shore Jnr, March 1792.
NMM ref PAH5448

2. The capture of the French frigate *Nymphe*, 32 by the *Flora*, 36, engraved by Robert Pollard from a painting by Robert Dodd, published by John Harris, London, 2 July 1781. Note that the caption quoting the force of the ships omits the British ship's six 18pdr carronades.
NMM neg B9258

3. 'The Artois capturing two Dutch privateers, 3 December 1781', oil painting by Robert Dodd (1748-1815).
NMM ref BHC0435

4. 'A Drawing shewing the the mode of fixing the Carronades on board His Majesty's Ship Artois . . .', 12 December 1781.
PRO

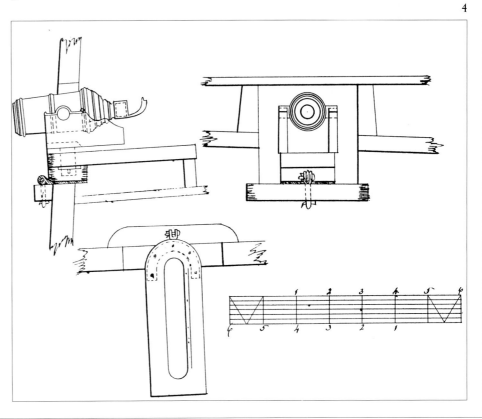

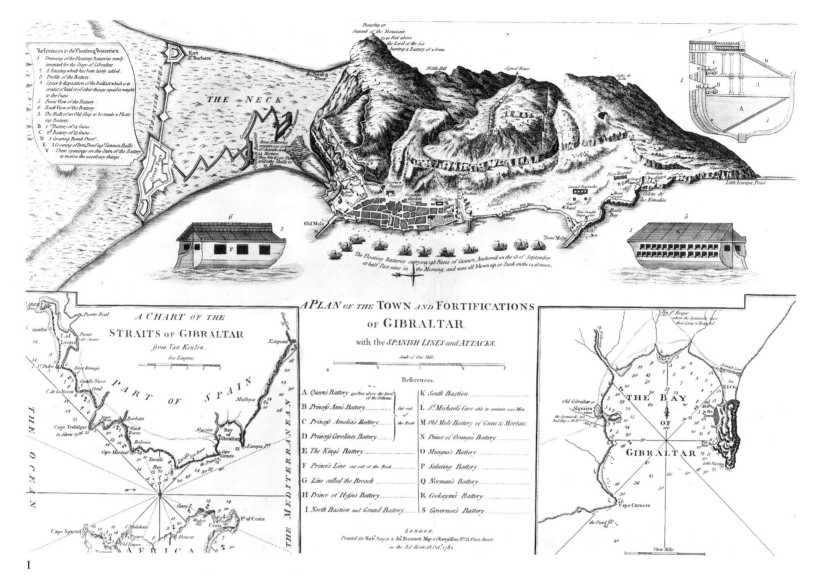

The grand assault on Gibraltar, September 1782

SINCE JULY 1779, when the Rock was first besieged, all conventional methods of assault had failed miserably, but as the war in America wound down during 1782 the Spanish and French redoubled their efforts to capture the fortress (1). A degree of desperation can be seen in some of the fanciful, if not downright crazy, proposals entertained by the allies—a mounted charge from the sea by cavalrymen on horses of cork, the building of a giant cofferdam around the fortress which could then be flooded, and even the construction of an artificial mound higher the Rock itself, were all suggested in varying degrees of seriousness.

However, in the spring of 1782 it was decided to prepare a number of special battering ships for a planned grand assault later in the year. Designed by a prominent French military engineer, Michaud d'Arçon, they were conventional ships cut down and 'armoured' with additional layers of timber, lined with splinter-proof sand, cork and cables woven together, and a bomb-proof pent-roof over, and since red-hot shot was a prime defensive measure, they were equipped with large water cisterns and an elaborate system of pipework to keep exposed timbers wet and quench any hot shot lodging in the structure. They were armed and protected on one side only—the intended engaged side—and there were ten vessels in all, ranging from 1400 tons, 21 guns and 760 men to 600 tons, 6 guns and 250 men. The rig was much cut down, and their appearance according to one eye-witness was like 'an oblong floating hay-rick'.

By courtesy of allied deserters and their own intelligence sources, the British defenders were well informed about the preparations, and strengthened their defences accordingly. The long-anticipated assault finally opened on 13 September, with the battering ships being slowly manoeuvred into position opposite the King's Battery in the lower town (2), but they never reached their planned position (3). Once they were anchored bow and stern with their iron chain cables, a tremendous cannonade broke out, the 142 guns of the blockships being joined by 186 Spanish guns and mortars on the isthmus, with counter-battery fire from over 100 guns on the British side. Over 25,000 allied troops stood by for a land assault, and there were rumoured to be around 80,000 sightseers on the heights opposite the Rock (4).

Firing went on all day, producing a spectacle almost without precedent as the wreaths of smoke were only broken by gun flashes and the fiery trails of shells and carcasses. It became an immensely popular subject with artists, possibly the most dramatic series being those engraved by James Fittler after originals by Richard Paton (5, 6, 8). The Paton series depicts the main events of the assault, beginning with the battering ships in close action with the King's Battery and the ruined lower town (5). Gradually the blockships were beaten out of the line and by evening all had ceased firing, but as day turned into night the red-hot 'roast potatoes' as they were known to the British gunner, began to take effect, and the flagship of the blockships, *Pastora*, began to burn. The British sent in the gunboats and the Spanish abandoned the assault and ordered all the battering ships to be set on fire to prevent capture (6).

The siege of Gibraltar produced many eyewitness accounts, both written and graphic, but the most authoritative must be that of Lieutenant G F Koehler, RA, who was aide de camp to General Eliott and inventor of the 'depression carriage' that was used to such devastating effect from the higher batteries. The engraving by T Malton (7) is based on one of Koehler's sketches and shows the moment when the first blockship finally blew up. The British gunboats, under Sir Roger Curtis, ceased offensive action and by the middle of the night were

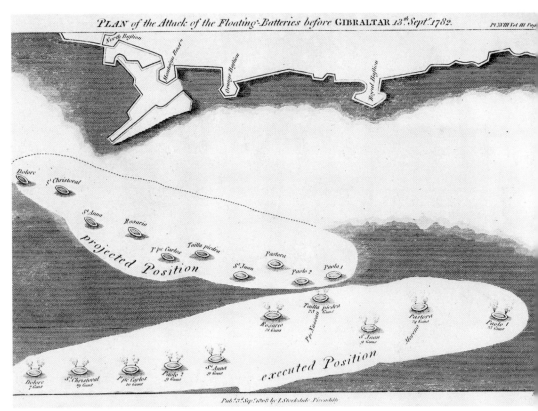

PLAN *of the Attack of the Floating-Batteries before* GIBRALTAR *13th Sept. 1782.*

3

busy rescuing as many Spanish survivors as possible. It was a harrowing task, as Curtis himself reported:

> The scene at this time before me was dreadful to a high degree. Numbers of men crying from amidst the flames, some upon pieces of wood in the water, others appearing in the ships where the fire had as yet made but little progress, all expressing by speech and gesture the deepest distress and all imploring assistance, formed a spectacle of horror not easily to be described.

Perhaps it is better left to Paton and Fittler (8).

4

1. 'A Plan of the Town and Fortifications of Gibraltar with the Spanish Lines and Attacks (shown enlarged details of floating battery): A Chart of the Straits of Gibraltar. The Bay of Gibraltar', coloured etching published by Robert Sayer and John Bennett, 28 October 1782.
NMM ref PAH7799

2. 'Approach of the Floating Batteries before Gibraltar on the Morning of the 13th of Septr 1782', brown aquatint engraved by Francis Jukes and C Tomkins after an original by J Cleveley, published by C Tomkins, 9 February 1782.
NMM ref PAF4661

3. 'Plan of the Attack of the Floating Batteries before Gibraltar 13th Sept 1782', engraving by Neele, published by I Stockdale, London, 3 September 1808.
NMM ref PAD5405

4. 'A View of the Grand Attack upon Gibraltar September 13th 1782', etching by Roberts after an original by Lieutenant Sanby, published 16 August 1785.
NMM ref PAF4663

5

6

5. The defence of the King's Bastion, Gibraltar on the afternoon of 13 September 1782. Engraving by James Fittler after a painting by Richard Paton, published by James and Josiah Boydell, 4 March 1787.
Beverley R Robinson Collection, Annapolis

6. The firing of the Spanish battering ships during the night of 13/14 September 1782. Engraving by James Fittler after a painting by Richard Paton, published by James and Josiah Boydell, 1 June 1786.
Beverley R Robinson Collection, Annapolis

7. 'A View of the North Part of Gibraltar, with the Attack by Land and Sea, on the 13th of Sept 1783 [sic, should read 1782]. Engraving by T Malton, after an original by Lieutenant G F Koehler, RA, Aide de Camp to General Eliott, published by W Faden, 4 August 1785.
Beverley R Robinson Collection, Annapolis

8. British gunboats and small craft from Gibraltar rescuing Spanish survivors from the blazing blockships during the night of 13/14 September 1782. Engraving by James Fittler after a painting by Richard Paton, published by James and Josiah Boydell, 1 November 1784.
Beverley R Robinson Collection, Annapolis

7

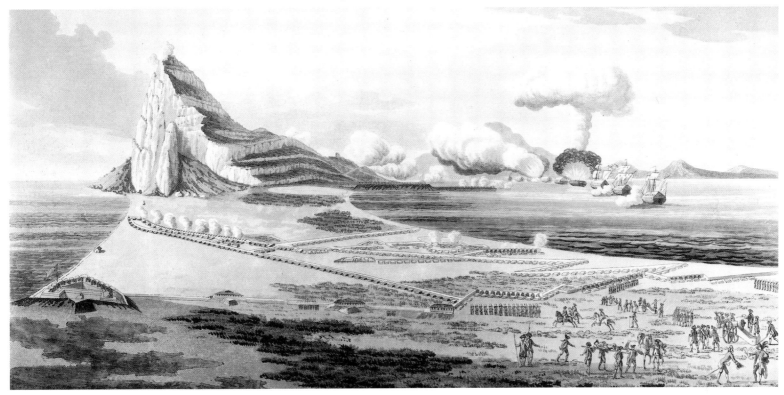

8

1

Howe's relief of Gibraltar, October 1782

DESPITE THE loss of the *Royal George*, the Channel Fleet sailed from Spithead on 11 September. It comprised thirty-four ships of the line, a dozen cruisers and about 140 merchantmen, and made necessarily slow progress down channel, but survived a serious gale without a single vessel losing touch. After Finisterre the various convoys were detached, and Howe pressed on with the remaining thirty-one supply ships for Gibraltar. The Spanish blockading fleet had also been dispersed by the storm, and one ship, the *San Miguel*, had been forced under the batteries of Gibraltar and had to surrender, but the remaining forty-eight ships of the line still posed an enormous threat.

On 11 October the British force was spotted from the Rock, the fleet in three divisions with *Victory* leading, shepherding the merchantmen before them. Despite Howe's detailed briefing, all but four of them missed the entrance and the fleet had to follow the rest into the Mediterranean some fifty miles before they could be collected up. In the Paton painting (1), the fleet, with *Victory* in the centre, is being driven past Gibraltar, but the four ships that made port can be seen in the distance beneath the Rock itself; the Spanish fleet occupies the left horizon.

Two days later the Spanish fleet made a sortie, but despite their superiority did not close for action, and

3

2

were themselves driven to the eastward (2). When the wind came round easterly on the 15th they were in no position to interfere and Howe was able to shepherd the transports into Gibraltar, a task completed by the 18th. The Spanish offered battle on the following day, too late to prevent the resupply; Howe was not inclined to fight in the Straits, but needed to prevent the pursuit of his inferior fleet which might result in stragglers being picked off, so brought to off Cape Spartel. The ensuing battle was partial, with similar casualties on both sides, but the Spanish did not renew the action, and Howe's fleet arrived at Spithead intact, having succeeded brilliantly in a difficult task against substantial odds.

Gibraltar was saved, and such was the strength of feel-ing in Britain as a result of its epic defence that the diplomats had to exclude it from the bargaining table at the peace conference, in spite of the most intense Spanish pressure.

1. The relief of Gibraltar by Earl Howe, 11 October 1782, oil painting by Richard Paton (1717-1791).
NMM ref BHC0453

2. 'An East View of Gibraltar', etching produced by Roberts, London, 16 August 1785.
NMM neg A9564

3. A panorama of Howe's relief of Gibraltar, 11 October 1782, hand coloured engraving by R Pollard after an original by Dominic Serres the Elder (1722-1793), published by J S Copley, London, 22 May 1810.
NMM neg 1040

Part IV

THE EAST INDIES 1778-1783

WHEN THE French had entered the war on the side of the Americans, the British and French navies in the East Indies had each possessed only one ship of the line. After a brief skirmish with Admiral Vernon, the French had withdrawn to their post at Isle de France (Mauritius). Command of maritime communications was as important in the Indian theatre as it was in America and the British were able to seize control of the French posts at Mahé and Pondicherry. In the winter of 1778-79 Rear-Admiral Sir Edward Hughes had sailed to the Indian Ocean with three ships of the line, believing that the French were reinforcing their forces there. It was not until the declaration of war against the Netherlands at the end of 1780, however, that the East Indies became an important theatre of war. It then became an object of the first importance to ensure that the French did not recover their position in Asia through the leverage provided by the Dutch posts at the Cape of Good Hope, in Ceylon (Sri Lanka) and in Indonesia.

The British East India Company had an inveterate enemy in Hyder Ali, the ruler of Mysore, and were also beset by the Mahrattas. The French were able to make good use of this local support. In September 1780 British forces in India lost 4000 men in action with Hyder Ali's vast army. In January 1781 Admiral d'Orves brought the French East Indies squadron of six two-deckers north from Isle de France to co-operate with Hyder, using the recaptured Pondicherry as a base from which to blockade Sir Eyre Coote's forces at Madras. However, d'Orves had orders to return to Isle de France in April, and departed when, unknown to the French, Madras was reduced to two days' rations. Coote then launched his offensive, and at the battle of Porto Novo routed Hyder Ali's army against odds of ten to one. To deny the French use of the only good har-

bour in the Bay of Bengal, Trincomalee, Admiral Hughes captured it from the Dutch.

Vergennes decided to dispatch in March 1781 a squadron of five ships of the line under Admiral Bailli de Suffren, with 11,000 soldiers under the Marquis de Bussi. This was soon known about in London, where it was decided to send an expedition to capture Cape Town, which was an important key to naval operations in the Indian Ocean, and dominated the French post at Mauritius. The movement to Gibraltar of the Channel Fleet early in 1781 was used to cover the departure of Commodore Johnstone with two ships of the line and three 50s carrying General Medows with three battalions of infantry. The squadron under de Grasse which ultimately struck the decisive blow at the Chesapeake, and Suffren's, sailed from Brest nine days later, and Suffren attacked Johnstone's force as it lay at anchor in the Cape Verde Islands. He was beaten off, and pursued for a while, but got to Cape Town three week ahead of the British and helped the Dutch governor to fortify it against attack.

At the Cape the British heard about Hyder Ali's campaign. Medows insisted on continuing on to India with his full force, but Johnstone, who was more interested in taking prizes, took his warships back towards home waters. Other ships had to be sent from Britain with another regiment, but the convoy could not sail until Darby returned from Gibraltar. In the early months of 1782 Sir Richard Bickerton sailed for India with five ships of the line. This was to prove a decisive movement in the Eastern theatre because reinforcements intended for the French East Indies squadron were intercepted in European waters, first by Kempenfelt in December 1781, and then by Barrington on 20 April 1782, when twelve of a small troop convoy of eighteen transports, a *flute* and a 64-gun ship of the line were captured.

When Suffren, who succeeded to the command when d'Orves died, reached the Carnatic in early 1782, he had twelve ships of the line to Hughes's nine. Hughes, after initially sheltering under the guns of Madras, engaged him at sea. The action was a draw because Suffren's captains failed to carry out his tactical plan of an attack on the British rear. After Hughes received the first two of his reinforcements there was another inconclusive engagement with Suffren, but Suffren made the better use of the occasion by capturing Trincomalee while Hughes was awaiting Bickerton's arrival. Hughes was obliged to retreat to Bombay which was the closest dockyard where he could make repairs.

The arrival of Bickerton with his squadron gave Hughes a decisive numerical advantage. Suffren tried to persuade the Dutch at Sumatra to attach their squadron to his, but they were afraid of a British raid and refused. The French also had to deal with an outbreak of plague, which so infected one of the ships that it had to be burnt. Nevertheless, Suffren was one of the most capable commanders of the age and succeeded in putting the French army ashore at Cuddalore to co-operate with Hyder Ali.

Coote had died, and his successor, General James Stuart, was faced with a desperate situation. He managed to make a lodgement in the enemy lines, but Suffren then reappeared and beat off the British fleet which was short of men. Hughes retired to Madras leaving the French in control of the coast. Two thousand more French soldiers were landed, but Colonel Fullarton responded to the appeal for help and marched from the southern Carnatic to support Stuart. On the very eve of the battle, however, news was received that peace had been concluded in Europe five months before.

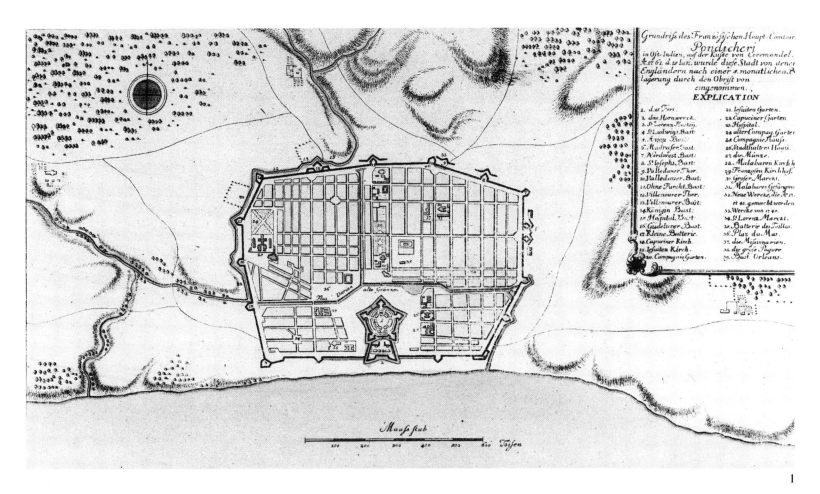

1

Suffren and Hughes

AS SOON as the news of the French declaration of war reached India the British besieged Pondicherry (1), the main French base in the sub-continent. After a skirmish between the small naval forces present, the French squadron left for Mauritius (then known as the Ile de France) and on 17 October 1778 Pondicherry surrendered.

In 1779 six of the line arrived in India under the command of Rear-Admiral Sir Edward Hughes (2), a competent but uninspired officer (he was known as 'old hot-and-hot' because of his liking for piping-hot food, and plenty of it, as is evident from the size of his belly). For the next couple of years the main events were in the land wars between the British and the Mahrattas and, in further south in India, with Hyder Ali of Mysore.

However, in 1781 the French sent out a new naval force under the Bailli (he had been a knight of Malta) Pierre André de Suffren, an extraordinary commander who was single-handedly nearly to reverse the tide of British victory in this part of the world. Suffren, like Hughes, was a devotee of the pleasures of the table, and much the same shape (3), but was both a much deeper thinker and a more aggressive and forceful man. Almost

alone amongst French admirals of the era he was not inhibited by caution. If anything he was too thrusting, and certainly was a bully. He could also be absolutely charming: there is a memorable description of him by an Anglo-Irish prisoner who had a great deal of kindness from him and ended by respecting him deeply; which describes him as looking like a slovenly pork-butcher, who used to shove his bare feet out of his cabin windows to keep them cool, but who was clearly a very intelligent commander with an extraordinary force of character.

The British had sent out an expedition under Commodore Johnstone to take the Cape of Good Hope from the Dutch, and Suffren had the additional aim of interfering with this and landing troops at the Cape. He had his opportunity at Porto Praya in the Cape Verde Islands. He found Johnstone's squadron moored in harbour with no precautions taken against surprise attack. He seized the opportunity and immediately led his five ships of the line amongst the unprepared British. Unfortunately his own captains were not prepared either; his next astern had not cleared for action when she moored amongst the enemy! The third ship was about to anchor when her captain was killed, she collid-

2

4

3

ed with a merchantmen in the subsequent confusion and drifted out of action, and the two other ships never effectively came into action (4). The British recovered well and gave Suffren's two ships in close action an increasingly rough time. His own gunners could not match the accuracy or rate of fire of their opponents, and he was forced to retreat with his second ship losing all her masts as he did so. Despite this and the fact he had suffered less damage and casualties than the French, Johnstone completely flunked his half-hearted pursuit (5). Suffren not only escaped but went on to land his troops at the Cape, which therefore remained in Dutch hands. Johnstone made no attempt to carry on with the expedition and made an ignominious return to Britain, having proved himself probably the most ineffective British naval commander of the entire war.

1. Pondicherry in 1761. German engraving produced 1764, but the fortress had changed little by 1780.
NMM ref PAD1851

2. Admiral Sir Edward Hughes (?1720-1794), oil painting by Sir Joshua Reynolds (1723-1792).
NMM ref BHC2792

3. Pierre-Andrè de Suffren de St Tropez (1726-1788), coloured aquatint by Marie de Cernel, Maire after an original by F Gerard, published by Blin, Paris, 1789.
NMM ref PAD2965

4. ' Combat Naval de la Praya 16 Avril 1781', steel engraving by Gilbert and Sandoz, engraved by Chavane and published by Diagraphe et Pantographe Gavard, Paris.
NMM ref PAD5366

5. ' Johnstone pursuing Suffren at Porto Praya, 16 April 1781', black and wash, grey pen and ink original by Admiral Hamilton.
NMM ref PAG9672

5

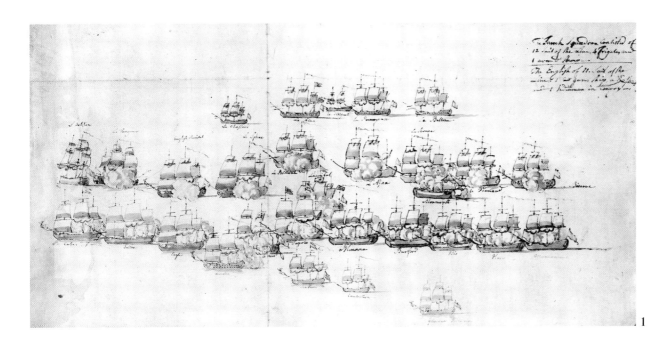

1

Battles in the Eastern Seas

UFFREN ARRIVED at Mauritius in October 1781. With the ships already there (and the subsequent death of the admiral commanding them) he arrived off the Indian coast in February 1782 with twelve ships of the line (including 50-gun ships and converted Indiamen) under his command. On 17 February he fought the first of an extraordinary series of battles with Hughes off Pondicherry, now captured by Hyder Ali. In

this, the Battle of Sadras, Hughes was at a numerical disadvantage with only nine ships. However the general effectiveness of his captains was on a much higher level than that of most of Suffren's, few of whom either understood or approved of what he was trying to do. In this case Suffren, a bold and innovative tactical thinker was trying to concentrate all of his ships on the rear of Hughes' line of battle. Hughes remarked that: 'the

2

3

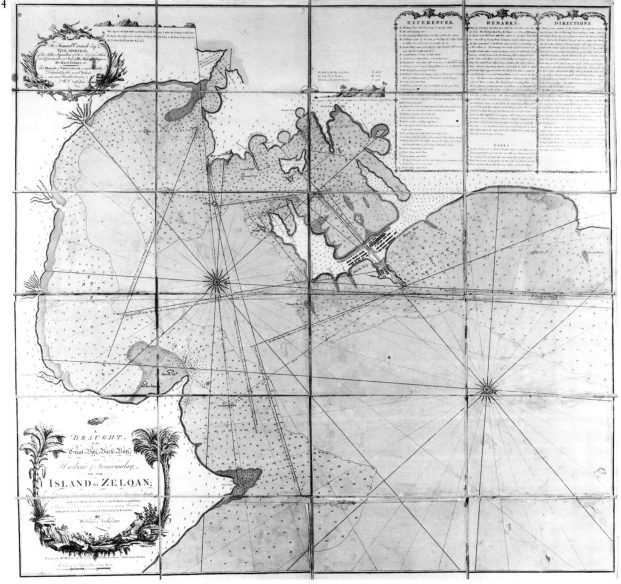

4

1. 'Trincomalee 12th April 1782. The
French Squadron consisted of 12 sail of
the line, 4 frigates and 1 armed – The
English of 11 sail of the line, 1 20-gun
ship, a – and 1 Indiaman in Convoy
(with key)', black and watercolour
pen and ink original by Dominic
Serres.
NMM neg 9803

2. 'His Majesty's Ship Monmouth . . .
Action in the East Indies . . . the Hero
of 74 guns, and two other French
ships, in the general engagement of
the 12th of April 1782, Trincomalee',
engraving and etching by John Peltro
after an original by Dominic Serres,
published by Robert Wilkinson,
London, 20 October 1786.
NMM neg 863

3. The Battle of Negapatam, 6 July
1782, oil painting by Dominic Serres
(1722-1793).
NMM ref BHC0448

4. 'A Draught of the Great Bay, Back
Bay and Harbour of Trincomalay on
the Island of Zeloan' by William
Nicholson, published by William
Herbert, London, 1765.
NMM neg A1711

5. 'Combat naval on vue de
Gondalour [Cuddalore] 20 Juin 1783',
steel engraving by E Chavane after an
original by J M A de Jugelet, published
by Diagraphe et Pantographe Gavard,
Paris, no date.
NMM ref PAD5420

enemy brought eight of their best ships to the attack of five of ours', but the other French ships failed to support Suffren, and the gunnery of the engaged ships let them down. Casualties and honours were about even.

The next engagement, Providien, was fought when Hughes was trying to reinforce Trincomalee (taken from the Dutch and used by him as a base) on 12 April 1782. Hughes had been reinforced and now had eleven of the line. Suffren, with twelve ships, led his line slanting down towards the British. The ships in the middle of his line, around his flagship engaged the British at short range, but his van and rear failed to close (1). There was a very fierce and bloody conflict in the middle of the line, but with no clear result, the British *Superb* and *Monmouth* being particular sufferers (2). The same number (137) of men were killed on both sides, though the fact that the British had, unusually, more wounded than their opponents indicated that French gunnery was improving with practice.

On 5 July the two fleets met again off Negapatam, which the British had taken from the Dutch. This time there were eleven ships a side, and it was the British who came steering down towards their opponents. The two lines then exchanged broadsides (3), but were then thrown into confusion by a shift of wind, causing ships of either side to turn either way. A melee followed, but the two sides finally separated with the French having had much the worst of the exchange as far as casualties were concerned, losing more than twice the number of their opponents.

Suffren then took Trincomalee on 31 August (4), but Hughes arrived on 3 September and the two doughty antagonists fought the battle of Trincomalee, with twelve British ships against fourteen French. Hughes was retreating slowly and in good order to leeward, Suffren with a rag-bag of ships and some unreliable captains was handicapped in his attempt to bear down on the British line. His ships were thrown into some disorder, and most failed to support their admiral whose flagship and couple of other vessels were almost surrounded by enemies. Despite this, casualties were fairly equal.

Next year Hughes came to the support of the British army's attack on Cuddalore and Suffren to its rescue. The ensuing battle of 20 June 1783, fought off, and named after, the town, was Suffren's triumph (5). With fifteen ships he attacked eighteen British. Casualties were again nearly equal, but Suffren drove off Hughes, and the British had to abandon their siege. Nine days later news arrived that peace had been signed in Europe.

5

POSTSCRIPT

FOR THE military action which was taken to repress the American rebellion to be acceptable to Thomas Aquinas' idea of the 'Just War', there would have had to be good grounds for expecting that British arms could prevail without causing disproportionate injury. Events proved that they could not, and the injury inflicted on American society by the violence committed by both sides produced long-term effects. British failures were in the strategic direction of the land campaign, the co-ordination of land and sea operations, and the concentration of effort against the rebels when the more dangerous enemy were the French. These weaknesses were made more critical by the political disunity in Britain. The Royal Navy was affected by the political turmoil, but nonetheless carried out its task with a remarkable degree of efficiency. The odds against it once Spain had entered the war, however, made it difficult to recover from any error of timing or direction. The intervention of French land and sea forces in the American theatre was decisive.

The outcome of the war was the establishment of the American Republic, and the reduction of Britain's preponderant maritime power. For France these were positive results, and Vergennes' refusal to help the Americans annex Canada to their country delayed the time when American economic power would threaten the place of France in the world. On the other hand, the crushing economic burden on France left by the war was a catalyst for the French Revolution. The old order in France was overthrown. After a period of horror unparalleled for a century, it was replaced by Napoleon's empire which threatened the liberty of all Europe. Britain, although shorn of her American colonies, was nevertheless able to provide the naval and economic muscle needed to defeat Napoleon. The lesson learnt about imperial relations ensured that Britain retained the support of overseas territories until after the Second World War.

The so-called 'Red-Lined Map' was used by Richard Oswald, an agent for the Americans in the peace negotiations, and marks the boundaries of the newly independent United States. Oswald signed the preliminary articles of peace in November 1782, and this copy of the map appears to have been made for George III.
British Library K Top CXVIII 49.b

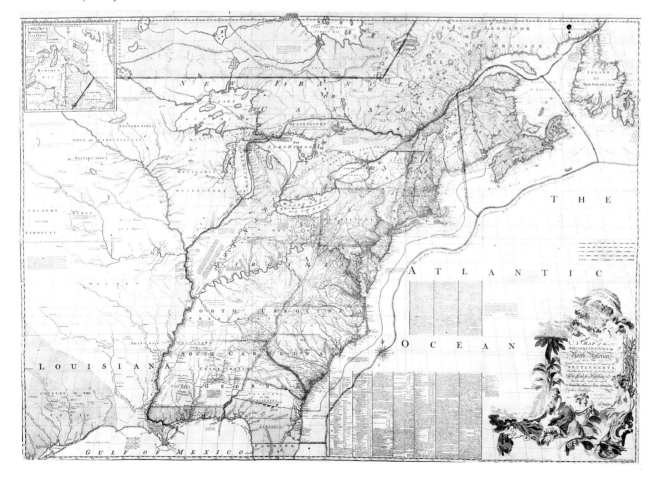

Sources

General – prints and paintings

E H H Archibald, *Dictionary of Sea Painters* (Woodbridge 1980)

M V and Dorothy Brewington, *Marine Paintings and Drawings in the Peabody Museum* (Salem, Massachusetts, second edition 1981)

National Maritime Museum, *Concise Catalogue of Oil Paintings in the National Maritime Museum* (Woodbridge 1988)

Kenneth Nebenzahl, *A Bibliography of Printed Battle Plans of the American Revolution 1775-1795* (Chicago and London 1975)

———, *Atlas of the American Revolution* (Chicago 1974)

Harry Parker (ed), *Naval Battles from the Collection of Prints formed and owned by Commander Sir Charles Leopold Cust* (London 1911)

P C F Smith, *More Marine Paintings and Drawings in the Peabody Museum* (Salem, Massachusetts 1979)

Sigrid Trumpy (ed), *Naval Prints from the Beverley R Robinson Collection, Vol I: 1514-1791* (Annapolis, Maryland 1991)

Introductions

Piers Mackesy, *The War for America 1775-1783* (London 1964)

David Syrett, *Shipping and the American War, 1775-83* (London 1970)

———, *The Royal Navy in American Waters, 1775-1783* (Aldershot 1989)

Nicholas Tracy, *Navies, Deterrence and American Independence* (Vancouver 1988)

Brian Tunstall (ed Nicholas Tracy), *Naval Warfare in the Age of Sail* (London 1990)

Colonial seafaring

I R Christie, *Crisis of Empire. Great Britain and the American Colonies, 1754-1783* (London 1966)

G B Nash, *The Urban Crucible. The Northern Seaports and the origins of the American Revolution* (Cambridge, Massachusetts 1986)

E J Perkins, *The Economy of Colonial America* (New York 1980)

J F Shepherd and G M Walton, *Shipping, Maritime Trade and the Economic Development of Colonial North America* (Cambridge, Massachusetts 1972)

E Wright, *The Search for Liberty. From Origins to Independence* (Oxford 1995)

The Royal Dockyards

J Coad, *The Royal Dockyards, 1690-1850. Architecture and Engineering Works of the Sailing Navy* (Aldershot 1989)

R J B Knight (ed), *Portsmouth Dockyard Papers 1774-1783: The American War, a Calendar*, Portsmouth Record Series (Portsmouth 1987)

R A Morriss, *The Royal Dockyards during the Revolutionary and Napoleonic Wars* (Leicester 1983)

Boston and Bunker Hill, June 1775

The British Library, *The American War of Independence, 1775-1783* (London 1975)

William P Cumming and Hugh Rankin, *The Fate of the Nation* (London and New York 1975)

National Maritime Museum, *1776: The British Story of the American Revolution* (London 1976)

Charles Stedman, *The History of the Origin, Progress, and Termination of the American War*, 2 vols (London 1794)

The campaign against Canada, May 1775-May 1776

The British Library, *American War*

William P Cumming and Hugh Rankin, *Fate of the Nation*

Justin Winsor (ed), *A Narrative and Critical History of America*, Vol 6 (London 1888)

A marine artist's sketchbook

E H H Archibald, *Dictionary of Sea Painters* (Woodbridge 1980)

The Battle of Valcour Island, 11-13 October 1776

William J Morgan (ed), *Naval Documents*, Vols 6 and 7 (Washington, DC 1972 and 1976)

Lake warfare vessels

Howard I Chapelle, *The History of the American Sailing Navy* (New York 1949)

David Lyon, *The Sailing Navy List* (London 1993)

William J Morgan (ed), *Naval Documents of the American Revolution*, Vols 6 and 7 (Washington, DC 1972 and 1976)

The first naval moves, fall 1775-spring 1776

William Bell Clark and William J Morgan (eds), *Naval Documents of the American Revolution*, Vols 1 and 2 (Washington, DC 1964 and 1966)

David Syrett, *The Royal Navy in American Waters 1775-1783* (Aldershot 1989)

George III and his navy

J Brooke, *King George III* (St Albans 1974)

B Dobree (ed), *The Letters of King George III* (London 1968)

Sir John Fortescue (ed), *The Correspondence of King George III from 1760 to December 1783*, 6 vols, (London 1928)

Information from John Graves, National Maritime Museum

Parker and Clinton at Charleston, June 1776

William P Cumming and Hugh Rankin, *Fate of the Nation*

William J Morgan (ed), *Naval Documents*, Vol 6 (Washington, DC 1972)

David Syrett, *The Royal Navy*

Gunpowder – the sinews of war

H C Tomlinson, *Guns and Government* (London 1979)

J West, *Gunpowder, Government and War in the Mid-Eighteenth Century* (Woodbridge 1991)

Assault on New York: first phase, June-August 1776

Sir William James, *The British Navy in Adversity: A Study of the War of American Independence* (London 1926)

William J Morgan (ed), *Naval Documents*, Vol 6 (Washington, DC 1972)

David Syrett, *The Royal Navy*

Colonial warfare vessels

Robert Gardiner (ed), *The Line of Battle*, Conway's History of the Ship (London 1992)

David Syrett, *The Royal Navy*

Assault on New York: second phase, September-November 1776

Sir William James, *The British Navy in Adversity*

William J Morgan (ed), *Naval Documents*, Vol 7 (Washington, DC 1976)

Alex Roland, *Underwater Warfare in the Age of Sail* (Bloomington, Indiana 1978)

David Syrett, *The Royal Navy*

Rhode Island: a textbook amphibious operation

William J Morgan (ed), *Naval Documents*, Vol 7 (Washington, DC 1976)

David Syrett, 'The Methodology of British Amphibious operations during the Seven Years and American Wars', *The Mariner's Mirror* 58/3 (August 1972)

The Continental Navy

Gardner W Allen, *A Naval History of the American Revolution*, 2 vols (Cambridge, Massachusetts 1913)

K Jack Bauer & Stephen S Roberts, *Register of Ships of the US Navy 1775-1990* (Westport, Connecticut 1991)

Jean Boudriot, *The History of the French Frigate 1650-1850* (Rotherfield 1993)

Howard I Chapelle, *The History of the American Sailing Navy*

Robert Gardiner, *The First Frigates* (London 1992)

Guérre de course

Gardner W Allen, *A Naval History of the American Revolution*, 2 vols (Cambridge, Massachusetts 1913)

William Bell Clark, *George Washington's Navy* (Baton Rouge, Louisiana 1960)

Patrick Crowhurst, *The Defence of British Trade 1689-1815* (Folkestone 1977)

Ralph Davis, *The Rise of the English Shipping Industry* (London 1963)

D J Starkey, *British Privateering Enterprise in the Eighteenth Century* (Exeter 1990)

A forgotten incident in the trade war

Gardner W Allen, *A Naval History of the American Revolution*

William J Morgan (ed), *Naval Documents*, Vol 7

The occupation of Philadelphia, summer 1777

David J Hepper, *British Warship Losses in the Age of Sail* (Rotherfield 1994)

Sir William James, *The British Navy in Adversity*

David Syrett, *The Royal Navy*

The road to Saratoga, May-October 1777

Gardner W Allen, *A Naval History of the American Revolution*

William P Cumming and Hugh Rankin, *The Fate of the Nation*

The French Navy

Jean Boudriot, *The 74 Gun Ship*, Vol III (Rotherfield 1987)

Jonathan R Dull, *The French Navy and American Independence* (Princeton, New Jersey 1975)

Robert Gardiner, *The First Frigates*

Jan Glete, *Nations and Navies* Vol I (Stockholm 1993)

D'Estaing in America: the French view

Sir William James, *The British Navy in Adversity*

David Syrett, *The Royal Navy*

West Indies 1778 – St Lucia

William Laird Clowes, *The Royal Navy: A History*, Vol III (London 1898)

Piers Mackesy, *The War for America 1775-1783*

Ships of the battlefleet

Sir William Laird Clowes, *The Royal Navy: A History*, Vols III & IV (London 1898 and 1899)

Robert Gardiner, *The Heavy Frigate, Vol I: 1778-1800* (London 1994)

Brian Lavery, *The Ship of the Line: The Development of the Battlefleet 1650-1815*, 2 vols (London 1983 and 1984)

David Lyon, *The Sailing Navy List*

West Indies 1779 – Grenada

William Laird Clowes, *The Royal Navy: A History*, Vol III (London 1898)

Piers Mackesy, *The War for America 1775-1783*

Florida and Central America 1779-1780

William Laird Clowes, *The Royal Navy: A History*, Vol III (London 1898)

Piers Mackesy, *The War for America 1775-1783*

Tom Pocock, *The Young Nelson in the Americas* (London 1980)

Penobscot fiasco, August 1779

Sir William James, *The British Navy in Adversity*

David Syrett, *The Royal Navy*

Supplying the British army in America

D Syrett, *Shipping and the American War*

Siege of Savannah, October 1779

William P Cumming and Hugh Rankin, *Fate of the Nation*

Sir William James, *The British Navy in Adversity*

David Syrett, *The Royal Navy*

Capture of Charleston, 1780

William P Cumming and Hugh Rankin, *Fate of the Nation*

Sir William James, *The British Navy in Adversity*

David Syrett, *The Royal Navy*

West Indies, 1780

Sir William James, *The British Navy in Adversity*

West Indies, 1781 – St Eustatius

Sir William James, *The British Navy in Adversity*

David Spinney, *Rodney* (London 1969)

The struggle for the Chesapeake, 1781

Sir William James, *The British Navy in Adversity*

H A Larrabee, *Decision at the Chesapeake* (New York 1964)

Yorktown – the world turned upside down

William P Cumming and Hugh Rankin, *Fate of the Nation*

David J Hepper, *British Warship Losses*

Copper sheathing – the saviour of the Royal Navy

R J B Knight, 'The introduction of Copper Sheathing into the Royal Navy, 1779-1786', *The Mariner's Mirror* 59 (1973), pp299-309

St Kitts, 1782

Sir William James, *The British Navy in Adversity*

Brian Tunstall (ed Nicholas Tracy), *Naval Warfare in the Age of Sail*

Battle of the Saintes, April 1782

Sir William James, *The British Navy in Adversity*

Brian Tunstall (ed Nicholas Tracy), *Naval Warfare in the Age of Sail*

Aftermath of battle

David J Hepper, *British Warship Losses*

Sir William James, *The British Navy in Adversity*

The Battle of Ushant 1778

Brian Tunstall (ed Nicholas Tracy), *Naval Warfare in the Age of Sail*

Naval administration

D Baugh, *British Naval Administration in the Age of Walpole* (Princeton, New Jersey 1965)

N A M Rodger, *The Admiralty* (Lavenham 1979)
——— , *The Insatiable Earl. A Life of John Montagu, Fourth Earl of Sandwich, 1718-1792* (London 1993)

'The Other Armada'

A Temple Patterson, *The Other Armada: The Franco-Spanish Attempt to Invade Britain in 1779* (Manchester 1960)

The Spanish Navy

Jan Glete, *Nations and Navies*, Vol I
Christian de Saint Hubert, 'Ships of the Line of the Spanish Navy 1714-1825', Part III, *Warship 39* (1986)

Gibraltar besieged

T H McGuffie, *The Siege of Gibraltar, 1779-1783* (London 1965)
John Drinkwater, *A History of the Late Siege of Gibraltar* (London 1785)

The war on trade

Patrick Crowhurst, *The Defence of British Trade*
Ralph Davis, *The Rise of the English Shipping Industry*
Alexander Laing, *American Sail* (New York and London 1961)
D J Starkey, *British Privateering Enterprise in the Eighteenth Century*
Damer Powell, *Bristol Privateers and Ships of War* (Bristol 1930)

John Paul Jones's cruise

Jean Boudriot, *John Paul Jones and the Bonhomme Richard* (Paris and Annapolis, Maryland 1978), Ch 4 by Peter Reaveley

The Moonlight Battle, 1780

Brian Tunstall (ed Nicholas Tracy), *Naval Warfare in the Age of Sail*

Single-ship actions

William Laird Clowes, *The Royal Navy*, Vol IV
Robert Gardiner, *The First Frigates*

Spanish successes

William Laird Clowes, *The Royal Navy*, Vol III
Sir William James, *The British Navy in Adversity*

The Dutch Navy

Jan Glete, *Nations and Navies*, Vol I
J R Bruin, *The Dutch Navy of the Seventeenth and Eighteenth Centuries* (Columbia, South Carolina 1993)

Dogger Bank, August 1781

J R Bruin, *The Dutch Navy of the Seventeenth and Eighteenth Centuries*
Sir William James, *The British Navy in Adversity*
Brian Tunstall (ed Nicholas Tracy), *Naval Warfare in the Age of Sail*

Gibraltar: the second relief and after, 1781-1782

T H McGuffie, *The Siege of Gibraltar, 1779-1783*
John Drinkwater, *A History of the Late Siege of Gibraltar*

Lord Howe takes over the Channel Fleet, 1782

Sir William James, *The British Navy in Adversity*
R F Johnson, *The Royal George* (London 1971)

The carronade: a British secret weapon

Robert Gardiner, *The Heavy Frigate*, Vol I
Brian Lavery, *The Arming and Fitting of English Ships of War 1650-1850* (London 1987)

The grand assault on Gibraltar, September 1782

T H McGuffie, *The Siege of Gibraltar, 1779-1783*
John Drinkwater, *A History of the Late Siege of Gibraltar*

Howe's relief of Gibraltar, October 1782

William Laird Clowes, *The Royal Navy*, Vol III
Sir William James, *The British Navy in Adversity*
T H McGuffie, *The Siege of Gibraltar, 1779-1783*

Suffren and Hughes

William Laird Clowes, *The Royal Navy*, Vol III
Sir H W Richmond, *The Navy in India, 1763-1783* (London 1931)

Battles in the eastern seas

William Laird Clowes, *The Royal Navy*, Vol III
Sir H W Richmond, *The Navy in India*

Notes on Artists, Printmakers and their Techniques

E H H Archibald, *Dictionary of Sea Painters*
E Bénézit, *Dictionnaire critique et documentaire de Peintres, Sculpteurs, Dessinateurs et Graveurs* (Paris 1976)
Ian Mackensie, *British Prints: Dictionary and Price Guide* (Woodbridge, England, 1987)
Lister Raymond, *Prints and Printmaking* (London 1984)
Wendy J Shadwell, *American Printmaking: The First 150 Years* (Washington DC 1969)
Ronald vere Tooley, *Tooley's Dictionary of Mapmakers* (New York and Amsterdam 1979)
Ellis Waterhouse, *The Dictionary of 18th Century Painters in Oils and Crayons* (Woodbridge, England 1980)
Arnold Wilson, *A Dictionary of British Marine Painters* (Leigh-on-Sea, England 1967)

NOTES ON ARTISTS, PRINTMAKERS AND THEIR TECHNIQUES

These brief notes cover most of the artists and printmakers who appear in the volume, as well as the principal printing techniques. They are intended only to put the artists in context with the period and readers wanting further information on their art and lives should turn to the sources; in many cases there is little more to tell.

Abbott, Lemuel *(1760-1803)* English portrait painter, known principally for his portraits of Nelson.

Abernethie American engraver who is known to have travelled to Charleston in 1785.

Andrews, P *(fl mid-late eighteenth century)* English engraver who worked on, amongst others, *Mary Ann Rocque's Plans and Forts of America* (1763) and *American Pilot* (1772)

Aquatint A variety of etching (*qv*) invented in France in the 1760s. It is a tone rather than a line process and is used principally to imitate the appearance of watercolour washes. The process involves the etching of a plate with acid through a porous ground of powdered resin. The acid bites small rings around each resin grain and gradations of tone are achieved by repetition of the biting process and the protection of areas of the plate with varnish.

Baugean, Jean-Jérôme *(1764-1819)* French painter and prolific engraver best known for his collection of shipping prints, *Collection de toutes des Especes de Batiments* which went through numerous editions in the early nineteenth century. Also well known is his depiction of 'The Embarkation of Napoleon onboard *Bellerophon*'.

Bowen, Thomas *(fl late eighteenth century)* English engraver who worked on *British American Plantations* (1749) and *Forster's History of Voyages* (1786). He died in the Clerkenwell workhouse.

Bowyer, Robert *(1758-1834)* English portrait painter and miniaturist. He worked at the court of George III, and his portraits illustrated a *History of England*.

Bromley, William *(1769-1842)* English engraver. He worked for the British Museum but is remembered principally for his portraits of Wellington and Napoleon.

Buell, Abel *(1742-1825)* American engraver, mapmaker and publisher. He drew and published the first map of the newly independent United States in 1784.

Bowles, Carington *(fl late eighteenth century)* London engraver and publisher of decorative and allegorical subjects and topographical views.

Burgis, William *(fl early eighteenth century)* American engraver.

Buttersworth, Thomas *(1768-1842)* English marine painter who served in the Royal Navy from 1795 until he was invalided out in 1800. His vivid watercolours of the battle of St Vincent and the blockade of Cadiz, painted while he was at sea, suggest first-hand experience. After leaving the Navy he devoted himself full-time to his painting and created a very considerable body of work.

Buys, Jacobus *(1724-1801)* Dutch painter and engraver of portraits and history subjects.

Chavane, E English engraver active around the 1850s.

Chavanne, Jean Marie *(1766-1826)* French engraver from Lyon.

Chesham, Francis *(1749-1806)* English draughtsman and engraver.

Cleveley, John the Elder *(c1712-1777)* English marine painter and father of John the Younger *(qv)*, Robert *(qv)* and James, who became a ship's carpenter. He worked in Deptford Dockyard and may have learnt his painting skills from the dockyard painters responsible for external ship decoration. He is best known for his scenes of dockyards and shipbuilding.

Cleveley, John the Younger *(1747-1786)* English marine painter, son of the shipwright and painter John Cleveley the Elder *(qv)*, and twin brother of Robert Cleveley *(qv)*. He was brought up in the Deptford Dockyard and learned his craft from his father and the watercolourist John Sandby. He travelled with Joseph Banks as draughtsman on his exhibition to Iceland in 1772, and again to the Arctic in 1774, and it is for his depictions of the Arctic that he is best known.

Cleveley, Robert *(1749-1809)* English marine painter, son of John Cleveley the Elder *(qv)* and twin brother of John Cleveley *(qv)*. He was Captain's Clerk in the *Asia* and served on the North American and West Indies stations in the 1770s. He is known mainly for his history paintings of the American Revolutionary War.

Cook, Henry R *(fl the first half of the nineteenth century)* English engraver, mainly of portraits.

Copely, John Singleton *(1737-1815)* American painter. He was self-taught as an artist and became the first American painter to gain an international reputation. He worked as a portrait painter in Boston before moving to London in 1774. As well as portraits he painted historical works, notably 'The Death of Major Peirson' which met with considerable success; he succeeded Reynolds *(qv)* as President of the Royal Academy in 1792.

Coulet, Anne Philiberte *(fl mid eighteenth century)* French engraver, born in Paris, of land- and seascapes.

Debrett, John *(fl the late eighteenth and early nineteenth centuries)* English publisher whose works include a *Chart of the Indian Ocean* (1800) and *Serres Little Sea Torch* (1801).

Demarne, Jean-Louis *(1744-1829)* French animal and history painter and engraver who also painted land- and seascapes.

Des Barres, Joseph Frederick Wallet *(1721-1824)* British surveyor of Swiss extraction, particularly famous for his surveys of North America which appeared in *The American Neptune* in 1784. He was trained at Woolwich as a military engineer and then posted to North America in 1756 where he attracted the attention of General Wolfe whom he accompanied on the Quebec campaign. He then spent ten hazardous years surveying the coasts of Nova Scotia before returning to England in 1774 to supervise publication of his work.

Dodd, Robert *(1748-1815)* English marine and landscape painter and successful engraver and publisher, best known for his portrayals of the naval battles of the Revolutionary American and French wars. His is also known for his formal portraits of ships in which three views are included in a single image.

Dripps, Matthew *(fl mid-nineteenth century)* American publisher whose work included *Plan of New York* (1854).

Drypoint Intaglio *(qv)* engraving *(qv)* technique in which the image is scratched into a copper plate with a steel needle which is held like a pen. Ridges—burr—are created around the lines which give drypoint its characteristic fuzzy effect. The burr is delicate and quickly wears away during the printing process so that print runs are short.

Elliot, Captain William *(fl mid-late eighteenth century)* English marine painter who served both in the merchant marine and the Royal Navy. His large battle scenes include the action between the *Serapis* and the *Bonhomme Richard*.

Emeric, F J *(fl late eighteenth century)* French naïve ship portrait painter.

Engraving The process of cutting an image into a block or metal plate, which is used for printing, by using a number of techniques such as aquatint *(qv)*, drypoint *(qv)*, etching *(qv)*, or mezzotint. An engraving is a print made from the engraved plate.

Etching An intaglio *(qv)* process by which the design is made by drawing into a wax ground applied over the metal plate. The plate is then submerged in acid which bites into it where it has been exposed through the wax. An etching is a print made from an etched plate.

Faden, William *(1750-1836)* English cartographer and publisher, and the partner of Thomas Jeffereys *(qv)* whose business he ran in the Charing Cross Road after the latter's death in 1771. He is best known for his *North American Atlas*, published in 1777, *Battles of the American Revolution* and *Petit Neptune Français*, both of 1793.

Fielding, John *(fl late eighteenth century)* English publisher whose works included Andrews' *History of the War* (in America) published in 1785.

Fittler, James *(1758-1835)* English engraver who is best known for his naval works such as 'The Victory of Lord Howe' and 'The Battle of the Nile' .

Gilks, Thomas *(fl mid nineteenth century)* English engraver.

Gold, Joyce *(fl early nineteenth century)* English printer whose works included Rowe's *English Atlas* (1816). Also the publisher of the *Naval Chronicle*.

Gwyn, Edward *(fl late eighteenth century)* An unknown English draughtsman who produced at least one sketchbook of ship portraits which is held by the National Maritime Museum.

Hamilton, William *(1751-1801)* English painter mainly of portraits and history subjects. He also did illustrations for Bowyer's *History of England*.

Harraden, Richard *(1756-1838)* English engraver best known for his scenes of Paris, after Thomas Girtin.

Harris, John *(fl early-mid eighteenth century)* British etcher and line engraver of architectural views, naval subjects and maps.

Holman, Francis *(fl mid-late eighteenth century)* Prolific, if little-known, English marine painter. He depicted a wide variety of maritime subjects including dockyard scenes and ship portraits and a number of history paintings of the American Revolutionary War.

Hunter, James *(fl late eighteenth century)* English officer who drew the illustrations of a *History of the Indies*.

Intaglio printing The method of printing using metal plates which can be worked as aquatints *(qv)*, drypoints *(qv)*, engravings *(qv)*, etchings *(qv)*, or mezzotints. Once the lines have been made on the plate, by whatever method, printing is done by pressing damp paper hard enough against the plate so that the ink is lifted out of the incised lines. This explains why prints done by this method have slightly raised lines, a distinct characteristic of the process.

Jefferys, Thomas *(c1710-1771)* English cartographer and publisher, and one of the most important map publishers of the eighteenth century. His huge output included *The Maritime Ports of France* (1761), and between 1751 and 1768 he produced important maps of America and the West Indies. After bankruptcy, Robert Sayer *(qv)* acquired many of his interests and published much of his work posthumously, notably his *North American Pilot* and *West Indies Atlas* in 1775.

Jugelet, Jean-Marie-Auguste *(1805-1875)* French marine and landscape painter.

Jukes, Francis *(1747-1812)* English painter and etcher of aquatints. As well as his popular 'Views of England' and his sporting prints he was a prolific exponent of marine subjects.

Kettle, Tilly *(1735-1786)* English history painter and successful society portraitist. He travelled to India in 1769 and worked there through the 1770s, one of his best-known sitters being Warren Hastings.

Kobell, Jan *(1756-1833)* Dutch painter and engraver of portraits and marine subjects.

Laurent, Pierre *(1739-1809)* French engraver, born in Marseilles. He exhibited at the Salon and acquired considerable success with his works after, in particular, De Loutherbourg.

Laurie & Whittle *(fl late eighteenth and early nineteenth centuries)* English publishers and engravers who amalgamated with Imray, Norrie & Wilson. Works included *American Atlas* (1794) and *East India Pilot* (1800).

Lithograph A print made by drawing a design on porous limestone with a greasy material. The stone is then wetted and ink applied to it which adheres only to the drawn surfaces. Paper is then pressed to the stone for the final print. Lithography was discovered only at the very end of the eighteenth century but quickly developed into a highly flexible medium.

Lodge, John *(fl mid-late eighteenth century)* English line engraver.

Luffman, J *(fl1776-1820)* English engraver, publisher and goldsmith amongst whose work was an atlas of Antigua published in 1788.

Luny, Thomas *(1759-1837)* One of the leading English marine painters of his generation. A pupil of Francis Holman *(qv)*, he served in the Royal Navy until around 1810 when he retired to Teignmouth. His remarkable output amounted to some 3000 paintings and many of these were engraved.

Malton, Thomas *(the Elder 1726-1801, the Younger 1748-1804)* English engravers. Both father and son depicted mainly topographical scenes.

Marshall, Joseph *(fl late 1770s)* English painter known for his portraits of ship models which were presented to George III by the Earl of Sandwich in order to stimulate the King's interest in the Navy.

Mason, James *(1710-1780)* English engraver known mainly for his landscapes.

Maynard, Thomas *(fl1777-1812)* English portrait painter.

Mercier, Philippe *(1689-1760)* French landscape and portrait painter who travelled extensively in England and whose works were widely copied by engravers.

Millar, James *(fl late eighteenth century)* English painter of portraits and history subjects.

Mitchell, Thomas *(1735-1790)* English marine painter who was by profession a shipwright at Deptford. He is known principally for his depictions of naval battles.

Mitchell, William *(fl early eighteenth century)* Publisher whose work included *Nantucket* (1838).

Montresor, Captain John *(1736-1788)* English military cartographer whose works included *Action at Bunker Hill* (1775) and *Boston & Environs* (1777).

Mosnier, Jean Laurent *(1743-1808)* Successful French portrait painter who emigrated to London on the outbreak of the Revolution in 1789. In 1802 he moved to St Petersburg where he died.

Nicholson, William *(1781-1844)* English portrait painter and engraver.

Northcote, James *(1746-1831)* English portraitist and history painter. He was a pupil of Reynolds *(qv)* and travelled to Italy before settling in London in 1781. A large number of his history paintings were engraved.

Ozanne, Nicholas Marie *(1728-1811)* French draughtsman and painter of marine subjects and brother of Pierre Ozanne *(qv)*. He was made draughtsman to the Navy in 1762 and is remembered chiefly for his accurate recording of maritime and naval events.

Ozanne, Pierre *(1737-1813)* French marine painter and engraver, and the pupil of his brother, the engraver Nicolas Marie Ozanne *(qv)*, whom he succeeded as draughtsman to the Navy in 1811. He is best known for his sixty engravings of ship types, entitled *Vaisseaux et Autres Bâtiments de Mer.*

Paton, Richard *(1717-1791)* English marine painter, self taught, who served in the Royal Navy for a short time before being appointed Assistant Accountant with the Excise Office in 1742. He became one of the leading painters of the naval battles of the eighteenth century, and published many engravings of his work.

Peachy, William *(fl mid-late eighteenth century)* English landscape painter and engraver.

Pocock, Nicholas *(1740-1821)* Foremost English marine painter of his day. He was apprenticed in the shipbuilding yard of Richard Champion in Bristol before being appointed to command the barque *Lloyd*, setting sail to Charleston in 1768. This was the first of a number of voyages for which there are illustrated log books, some of which are at the National Maritime Museum. He was present at the West Indies campaign in 1778 or '79, and completed an oil painting in 1780, receiving helpful criticism from Sir Joshua Reynolds. Thereafter he devoted himself to his art and painted numerous depictions of the struggles with Revolutionary France.

Poggi, Antonio *(fl late eighteenth century)* Italian portrait and history painter who came to England in 1769. His portrait of Lord Heathfield was painted in Gibraltar in 1783.

Pollard, Robert *(1755-1838)* English painter and engraver of land- and seascapes.

Revere, Paul *(1735-1818)* American revolutionary silversmith and engraver who is best remembered for his midnight ride to Lexington in 1775 to warn the colonists of the imminent arrival of the British.

Reynolds, Sir Joshua *(1723-1792)* Foremost English portrait painter whose early reputation was made with his portrait of Keppel with whom he sailed to Italy in 1749. He returned to London in 1753 and established himself as the leading portrait painter of his day. He was made President of the Royal Academy upon its foundation in 1768 and in his 'Discourses' —lectures— he endeavoured to create an intellectual foundation for English art.

Ridley, William *(fl late eighteenth century)* English portrait engraver.

Rigaud, Jean Francis *(1742-1810)* English painter descended from Protestant French emigrants who came to England in 1777. He painted portraits and history subjects.

Rising, John *(1753-1817)* English portrait painter, many of whose works were engraved.

Romney, George *(1734-1802)* English portrait painter who made his early reputation with his depiction of 'The Death of Wolfe' (1763). His reputation today rests mainly on his series of portraits of Emma Hart who later became Emma Hamilton, Nelson's mistress.

Robertson, Archibald *(1765-1835)* Scottish portrait painter who studied at the Royal Academy under Joshua Reynolds *(qv)*. He moved to America in 1791 where he painted Washington and his family and acquired a considerable reputation. He was the author of *Sketches of America*.

Rood, Jan *(fl late eighteenth century)* Dutch draughtsman who specialised in marine subjects.

Rossel de Cercy, Auguste Louis de *(1736-1804)* French naval officer and marine painter who was commissioned by the French Ministry of Marine in 1786 to depict a number of battle scenes of French successes in the American Revolutionary War.

Sallieth, Mattias de *(1749-1791)* Austrian engraver who worked in Vienna, Paris and Rotterdam and who depicted, among other subjects, numerous naval battles.

Sayer, Robert and Bennett, John *(fl mid-late eighteenth century)* London publishers, based in Fleet Street, of sporting subjects, topographical views and maps.

Serres, Dominic the Elder *(1722-1793)* French marine painter, born in Gascony, who, after running away to sea, was captured by a British frigate in 1758 and taken to England. He became a pupil of Charles Brooking and was a founder member of the Royal Academy. Though a Frenchman he became one of the most successful marine painters of the Seven Years War and of the American Revolutionary War.

Sewell, J *(fl late eighteenth century)* English publisher and member of the short-lived Society for the Improvement of Naval Architecture.

Skelton, William *(1763-1848)* English engraver who is best known for his portraits of the Court of George III.

Smith, Samuel *(fl late eighteenth century)* English engraver of history subjects, after De Loutherbourg.

Suntache, Antoine *(fl late eighteenth century)* French engraver and publisher who carried on his business in London in the latter years of the eighteenth century.

Thornton *(fl late eighteenth century)* English line engraver.

Tomkins, Charles *(1757-1823)* English landscape painter and engraver. After 1779 he turned exclusively to engraving at which he had considerable success.

Trumbull, John *(1756-1843)* Foremost American artist of the Revolution. In 1775 he accepted a commission in the Continental Army, but resigned after the Rhode Island Campaign to go to London and study under Benjamin West. In 1786 he began his series of paintings of American history, clearly inspired by West and encouraged by Thomas Jefferson. He played a pivotal role in the founding of the American Academy of Fine Arts in 1802 in New York

Vernet, Claude Joseph *(1714-1789)* French landscape painter who is probably best known for his series of paintings of the ports of France which he painted in the 1750s and '60s and which were engraved at the same time.

Vinkeles, Reinier *(1741-1816)* Dutch engraver of portraits and landscapes.

West, Benjamin *(1738-1820)* American painter who is now regarded as the founding father of the American school. He settled in London in 1763, and though he retained his contacts with his native land, he remained there for the rest of his life. His history paintings, as personified by 'The Death of General Wolfe', became an inspiration for young American painters depicting the history of their young nation.

Whitcombe, Thomas *(born c1752)* English marine painter who, like Pocock *(qv)* and Luny *(qv)*, was celebrated for his huge output of paintings depicting the French Revolutionary Wars. He contributed some fifty plates to the *Naval Achievements of Great Britain* and also painted numerous works for engravings. There is no record of his death.

Wilson, John *(1774-1855)* Scottish marine and landscape painter who began his career as an apprentice to a house decorator. His is best known for his painting of the battle of Trafalgar.

Worthington, William Henry *(fl early to mid nineteenth century)* British line engraver of allegorical and historical subjects.

INDEX

All ships are British unless otherwise indicated in brackets following the name

Abbreviations

Cdre = Commodore	Lt = Lieutenant	R/A = Rear-Admiral	Sp = Spain	
Conn = Connecticut	Mass = Massachusetts	RI = Rhode Island	Va = Virginia	
Fr = France	Neths = Netherlands	Sgt = Sergeant	V/A = Vice-Admiral	
GB = British merchant ship	NY = New York	s/m = submersible		

Actaeon 17, 44, 55
Actif (Fr) 168
Active 42, 44, 55-6
Adams, John 69
Admiraal de Ruyter (Neth) 164
Admiraal Generaal (Neth) 164
Admiraal Piet Hein (Neth) 164
Aeolus (GB) 107
Africa 10, 20, 103, 133, 140, 146, 181-2
Aigle (Fr) 130
Aimable (Fr) 129
Albany 100
Albany (NY) 72
Alert 56, 94
Alfred (USA) 37, 64, 70, 152
Algesiras 146
Allegiance 149
Allen, Ethan 28
Alliance (USA) 152-3, 159
Amazone (Fr) 158
America 9-11, 186
  Army 15-17, 24-9, 42, 44, 46, 49-51, 57-8, 61, 64, 77-9, 79-90, 105, 119, 136
    supplies 46, 50
    loyalists 17, 42, 77-8, 81, 151
  Navy
    establishment of 14, 16, 37, 64-6
    fleet size 12-13, 34-5
    naval operations
      in Europe 67-9, 94, 152-4
      in North America 16, 20, 33-5, 37-8, 42-4, 61-2, 64-9, 70-1, 74-6, 78, 100-1, 107, 149-50, 157, 159
    privateers 14, 20, 66-71, 149-50
    shipbuilding 12-14, 64-5
    ship types 64-5, 93
    trade and trade war 9, 12-16, 19-20, 66-71, 78, 149-50
  shipbuilding 55
  War of 1812 151
America 80
America (USA) 65
Amherst, General Lord 77
Amiens, Peace of 133
Amphitrite (Fr) 159
Amsterdam (USA) 149-50
Andrew Doria (USA) 37, 64
Anglo-Dutch Wars 69
Annapolis (Nova Scotia) 46
Antigua 46, 78, 125, 141
Aranjuez, Convention of 133
Arbuthnot, V/A Marriot 78-81, 107, 114
Arcon, Michaud d' 174
Ardent 143
Arethusa 94, 139, 153
Argo 159
Argo (Neth) 164
Ariel 56, 78, 104-5
Arnold, Brigadier Benedict 15, 28-9, 32-5, 80-1, 114
Artois (ex-Fr) 172-3
Asia 14, 54-5
Astrée (Fr) 149, 159
Atalanta 159
Augusta 20, 54-5, 74
Azores 157

Bahamas 16, 46
  see also individual islands
Baltic Sea 136, 152-3, 164
Baltimore 13
Barbados 78, 89, 108, 130
Barfleur 93-4, 125, 128
Barras, General de 81
Barrington, V/A Samuel 78, 89, 91, 95-6, 100, 116, 133-4, 170, 180
Batavier (Neth) 164
Bedford 80, 127
Belize 98
Belle Poule (Fr) 139
Bellqueux 129
Berwick 40, 109, 164
Beschermer (Neth) 162
Bickerton, Sir Richard 180
Bienfaisant 164, 172
Biscay, Bay of 19-20, 146, 168
Blonde, 36, 100

Bolton 16
Bombay 180
Bonhomme Richard (Fr) 152-3, 158
Boston 12-13, 15-16, 67, 78, 87
  siege of 24-6, 38, 66-7
  Tea Party 9-10
  see also Breed's Hill, Bunker Hill, Charlestown
Boston (USA) 20, 35, 65, 107, 157
Boux, Chevalier 65
Boyne 15, 54
Brandywine, battle of 73
Breed's Hill 24-6
Brest 17, 20, 78-80, 83, 111, 133, 136, 139, 143, 146, 157-8, 180
Bretagne (Fr) 83
Briel (Neth) 167
Brisbane, Captain 65, 86
Bristol 42, 44, 54-5, 109
Britain
  Army 91, 95, 98-9, 107, 111, 125, 136, 146-8, 175, 180, 185
    in North America 9, 15-17, 20, 24-6, 28-9, 32, 38-40, 42, 45-6, 49-51, 57, 61-3, 66-7, 72-81, 84-5, 100, 104-5, 107, 114, 119-21, 168-9
    supplies 9, 17, 20, 102-3, 136
  dockyards and shipbuilding 11, 18-23, 31, 40-1, 94, 102-3, 109, 122-3, 133, 140-1, 144-5, 163, 170, 172-3
    see also individual dockyards and ports
  fleet size 9-11, 15, 17-19, 35-6, 82, 103, 162, 180
  foreign policy and strategy 9-11, 15-20, 77-81, 133, 135-6, 162, 180-6
  naval administration 39-41, 140-1
  naval operations
    in Europe 11, 17-19, 67, 94, 133-9, 142-3, 149-51, 150-1, 153, 155-60, 164-70, 172-3, 178-9
    India and East Indies 133, 136, 170, 180-5
    in North America 13-20, 24-9, 32-8, 42-5, 48-80, 84-7, 100-7, 114-19, 157-9
    in South America 98-9
    in West Indies 78, 80-1, 88-91, 93, 95-7, 108-9, 111-13, 114, 124-32, 136, 164
    recruitment 10, 15, 17-18, 133, 141
    ship types 35-6, 54-6, 83, 92-4, 157, 159, 170
    supplies 12, 47, 140-1, 146
    trade convoys 66-7, 149, 152-4, 155, 159, 161, 164
    trade restrictions and blockades 9, 12-15, 19-20, 78, 81, 100, 136, 149-51
Britannia 92, 94, 167
Brooklyn Heights (NY) 17, 51
Brune 56
Buck 146
Buffalo 164
Bunker Hill 9, 11, 15-16, 24-6, 51
Burgoyne, General John 20, 24-5, 32, 72, 75-6
Burke, Edmund 10
Bushnell, Mr 61
Bussi, Marquis de 180
Bute 36
Byron, V/A John 41, 78, 87, 93, 95-6, 117

Cabot (USA) 37, 64
Cadiz 136, 145
Caesar (GB) 151
Camden, Lord 20
Camilla 56, 100
Campbell, General 99
Canada 9, 17, 20, 32, 49, 103
  American advance into 15-17, 28-9, 32-6, 38, 42, 186
Canceau 37
Cape Beton 149
Cape Fear 17, 42, 114
Cape Finisterre 19
Cape Henry, battle of 114
Cape of Good Hope 180-2
Cape Ortegal 19
Cape Spartel 179
Cape St Vincent, battle of 108, 144, 155-6

Cape Town 180
Cape Verde Islands 180-1
Capture Act (1775) 15
Carcass 51, 58
Carleton 33, 36
Carleton, Sir Guy 28-9, 32, 81
Carlisle, Lord 77
Carlos III, King of Spain 133
carronades 94, 158, 167, 172-3
Carron Company 46
Carysfort 58
Castine (Maine) 78, 100-1
Castor (Neth) 167
Catherine II, Empress of Russia 136
Cato 165
Caton (Fr) 129
Centaur 130
Central America 80, 98
Centurion 50, 55
Cerberus, 56
Ceres (Fr) 129
Ceylon 180
Chaffault, Admiral du 17, 19
Chambly 34-5
Champlain, Lake 28-9, 32-7, 49, 75-6
Chandernagore 15
Charles River (Quebec) 29
Charleston 149
Charleston (S Carolina) 13, 17, 42-5, 51, 55, 79-81, 107
Charlestown (Boston) 24-6, 49
Charlotta 50
Charon 119
Chartres, Duc de 17
Chatham 50, 55
Chatham, Lord 20
Chatham Dockyard 21, 23, 46-7, 140-1
Chesapeake Bay 78, 101
  battle of 20, 80-1, 116-18, 121, 180
Chesapeake River 73, 80, 114-19, 159
Choiseul, Duc de 82
Clinton, General Henry 17, 24, 42, 44, 49-50, 62, 76-81, 85, 107, 114, 133
Colhoun (GB) 70
Collier, Cdre Sir George 78, 100-1
Columbus (USA) 37, 62, 64
Commerce de Marseilles (Fr) 144
Conanicut Island 62, 85
Concord 9, 24
Concorde (Fr) 88
Confederacy (USA) 65
Congress (USA) 33-5, 76
Connecticut 12, 65-6
Connecticut (USA) 34-5
Convert (USA) 34
Conyngham, Gustavus 67-8
Cook, Captain James 41
Cooper River 107
Coote, Sir Eyre 180
copper sheathing 122-3, 170, 172
Córdoba, Admiral Don Luis de 134, 136, 161, 170
Cornwall 94
Cornwall, Maj-Gen Lord 42, 61, 80-1, 114-17, 119, 121
Corsica 10
Countess of Scarborough 153
Couronne (Fr) 83
Crescent 167
Crillon, Duc de 161
Crown Point 28, 32-3
Cuba 79, 99, 144-5
Culloden 80, 94, 114
Cumberland, Richard 136
Curtis, Sir Roger 169, 175

Dale, Richard 153
Darby, V/A George 134-6, 167-8, 180
Dartmouth, Lord 24
Dawson, Captain 87
Defence (USA) 101
Defiance 54
Delaware 12, 65
Delaware River 15-17, 20, 54, 65, 73, 84
Delaware (USA) 73

Demerara (West Indies) 81
Denmark 15, 136
Deptford Dockyard 21, 23, 103, 141
Des Barres, JFW (artist) 42
Destouches, Captain 80, 114
Dettingen, battle of 40
Digby, R/A the Hon 134
Dodd, Robert (artist) 130, 151, 153, 158
Dogger Bank, battle of 163-6
Dolphin 164
Dolphin (USA) 67
Dominica 78, 88-9, 126, 133
Douglas, Captain Charles 36
Drake 152
Drake, R/A 113
Druid 70-1
Duc de Bourgogne (Fr) 83
Duff, R/A 146
Duke 127-8
Dunkirk 10, 15
Dutch East Indies 180

Eagle 50, 55, 61
East India Company 47, 180-2
East Indies 77, 136, 140, 165, 180-5
East River (NY) 51, 57
Edinburgh 153
Egmont, 109
Eliott, General George Augustus 146, 168-9, 175
Elizabeth River 78, 80, 114
Elk River 20, 73
Elphinstone, George Keith 107
Emerald 56, 58
Enterprise (USA) 34
Erfprins (Neth) 164
Esopus (NY) 76
Essequibo 81
Estaing, Admiral Comte d' 77-9, 82, 84-7, 89, 91, 95-6, 104-6, 133
Eveille (Fr) 80, 114
Exeter 19
Experiment 42, 44, 78, 104-5

Faden, William (publisher) 26, 44
Falcon 25, 86
Falklands Islands 10
Falmouth (Maine) 15, 37, 100
Fame 149
Fantasque (Fr) 84
Farmer, Captain 158
Faversham 47
Fenix (Sp) *see Gibraltar*
Ferrol 145
Fittler, James (artist) 175
Flamborough Head 153
Flora 20, 56, 65, 86, 94, 167, 172
Florida 79, 99, 105, 161
Floridablanca, Count 133, 136
Fly (USA) 37
Formidable 94, 127-8
Fort Clinton 76
Fortitude 164
Fort Lee 61
Fort Mercer 20
Fort Mifflin 20
Fort Montgomery 76
Fort Moultrie 44, 107
Fort Nelson 78
Fort Red Hook 51
Fort Royal 97
Fort St Philip (Minorca) 161
Fort Ticonderoga 28, 32-4, 38, 75
Fort Washington 17, 58, 61
Foudroyant (Fr) 19, 44, 170
Fowey 119
Fox, Ebenezer 68
Fox 20, 65, 157
France 44, 67
  Army 19-20, 77-8, 80-1, 87, 89, 91, 104-5, 114, 119, 142-3, 161, 180
  fleet size 18, 133, 144, 157, 162, 180
  foreign policy and strategy 9-11, 15-16, 20, 39, 77, 133-6, 142-3, 180, 185-6
    declaration of war 18, 54, 77, 92, 133, 180

and invasion of Britain 17-18, 133-4, 136, 142-3
  naval operations
    in Europe 133-9, 142-4, 149-52, 157-9, 161, 170, 174-5
    India and East Indies 136, 180-5
    in North America 19, 44, 78, 84-7, 104-5, 107, 114-19, 133, 142, 149, 158-9
    in West Indies 18-20, 77-81, 84, 87-91, 94-6, 108-9, 111-14, 122, 124-30, 136, 151, 170
  privateers 152-3
  shipbuilding 9-11, 18, 20, 65, 82, 133, 145
  ship types 64, 82-3, 93-4, 145
  trade war 15-16, 19-20, 47, 68, 151-3
  see also individual ports and towns
Franklin, Benjamin 20
Franklin (USA) 67
Frederick II, King of Prussia 12
French East India Company 15
French East Indies 180
Fullarton, Colonel 180

Gage, General Thomas 9, 16, 24
Galatea 56, 100
Galvez 99
Gambia, River 10
Gambier, R/A 78
Gaspee 13-14
Gates, General 76
Gates (USA) 34-5
Geary, Admiral Sir Francis 134, 170
George I, King of England 40
George II, King of England 40, 143
George III, King of England 10, 20, 39-41, 81, 133
Georgia 12, 78, 104
Germain, Lord George 12, 77-8, 81, 133, 140
Gibraltar 46, 76, 80, 103, 122, 135, 141
  siege of 133-4, 136, 144, 146-8, 155-6, 161, 167-70, 170, 174-80
Gibraltar 145
Glasgow 16, 25-6, 55-6
Gloire (Fr) 130
Glorieux (Fr) 130
Grafton 40
Grant, Major-General James 91
Grasse, Admiral Comte de 78, 80-1, 83, 91, 111, 113-18, 122, 124-6, 128-30, 136, 180
Graves, R/A Sir Thomas 80-1, 93, 114-17, 130, 134
Graves, V/A Samuel 15-16, 37
Gravesend (NY) 17, 51
Green, General Nathaniel 80
Greenwich 46
Grenada 78, 95-7, 117
Grenville, George 10
Greyhound 51, 56, 100
Guadeloupe 81, 126
Guadeloupe 56, 119
Guerrier (Fr) 84
Guichen, Admiral de 80, 108-9, 136, 170
Guipuscoanoa (Sp) 155
gunpowder, supply of 46-7, 58, 67
Gwyn, E (artist) 65

Haiti 77
Halifax 37
Halifax (Nova Scotia) 15-17, 38, 46, 49, 77, 104, 141, 149-50
Hamond, Sir Andrew Snape 54, 74
Hampden (USA) 78, 101
Hancock (USA) 20, 65, 157
Hanover 39-40
Hardy, Admiral Sir Charles 134, 143, 170
Harland, R/A 133
Harland, R/A 133
Harrison (USA) 67
Haslar Naval Hospital 141
Hawke 16
Hector 109, 130
Hector (Fr) 84, 87
Heighington (master of *Mercury*) 169
Hermione (Fr) 149, 159
Hessian troops 20, 61, 63, 74
Holland (Neth) 164-5

Holland *see* Netherlands
Honduras 10, 98, 133
Hood, Admiral Lord 20, 81, 91, 93, 111,
    114-17, 122, 124-6, 128-9
Hope (USA) 67
Hopkins, Cdre Esek 16, 37-8, 55, 62
Hornet (USA) 37
Hotham, Cdre William 50-1, 76, 78, 89
Howe, Admiral Lord 17, 19-20, 38, 44, 50-1,
    57, 61, 77-8, 84-7, 133, 136, 170, 178-9
Howe, General William 16-17, 19-20, 24-5,
    49-51, 57-8, 72-4, 76-7, 85, 133
Hudson River 17, 20, 49-50, 58, 61, 65, 72,
    76, 78, 80, 104
Hughes, R/A Sir Edward 133, 180-5
Hunter (artist) 75
Hunter (USA) 78, 101
Hussar 159
Hyder Ali 180-1, 183

India 47, 133, 140, 156, 180-5
Indien (Netherlands) *see South Carolina*
Indonesia 180
Inflexible 33, 36
Invincible 94
Ireland 67-8, 136, 152, 181
Iris see Hancock (USA)
Isis 29, 31, 36, 55, 78, 86-7

Jack (USA) 149-50
Jamaica 15, 46, 80-1, 104, 126, 129, 141
Jason (Fr) 129
Jasper, Sgt William 44
Jenkinson, Charles 9
Jersey 68
Jersey (USA) 33-6
Jersey (Channel Islands) 151
Jervis, Admiral John 170
John Island 107
Johnstone, Cdre 180-2
Jones, John Paul 38, 54, 100, 152-4
Juno 36, 56, 86
Junon (Fr) 157

Kempenfelt, Admiral Richard 134, 136,
    170, 180
Keppel, Admiral 81, 133, 136, 139, 141, 143
Kergariou, Captain 159
Kingfisher 55-6, 86
Kipps Bay (NY) 17, 57, 63
Knox, Henry 38
Koehler, Lt GF 175

Lady Juliana (GB) 130
Lafayette, Marquis de 80-1
La Motte-Picquet, Captain 19, 78, 97
Landais, Captain 153
Langara, Admiral 134
Languedoc (Fr) 78, 82-3, 84, 86-7
Lark 56, 86
Latona 94
La Vigie (St Lucia) 89, 91
League of Armed Neutrality 136, 163
Lee (USA) 33-5
Leeward Islands 15, 78, 80, 109, 155
Le Havre 143
Leith 153
Leslie, Maj-Gen 80
Le Terc, Pierre 151
Lexington 9, 15, 24
Lexington (USA) 67-8, 94
Liberty (USA) 34
Lincoln, Maj-Gen Benjamin 80
Lion 40
Lisbon 136
Lively 24-5
Liverpool 56
Lizard 56
London 93-4, 159
Long Island (NY) 17, 42, 49-51, 57, 77-8, 87
Lord Howe 36
L'Orient 20, 153
Louis XVI, King of France 19
Loyal Convert 34-5
Luny, Thomas (artist) 30-1, 70-1
Luttrell, Captain 98
Lynnhaven Bay 116

Macbride, Captain John 172-3
Madras 180
Magicienne 159
Mahé 180
Mahratta Wars 180-1
Maine see Massachusetts
Malton, T (artist) 175
Manhattan 49, 51, 57
Manila 145
    Ransom 10

Manley, Captain J 20, 65
Maria 36
Marlborough, 1st Duke of 40
Mars (USA) 111
Marseillais (Fr) 78, 84, 86-7
Martin 29, 56
Martinique 78, 81, 87-9, 97, 111, 126
    battle of 80, 93, 108-9
Maryland 12, 66
Massachusetts State 17, 28, 65-6, 78, 100
    see also Boston
Mathew, Brigadier Edward 78
Maurepas, JFP de 19, 133
Mauritius 180-1
McNeill, Captain 65
Mediator 159
Medows, General 78, 180
Mercury 169
Merlin 20, 74
Mermaid 84
Middleton, Sir Charles 102, 123, 140
Miguel, Admiral Don Gaston 17
Milford Haven 109
Minerva 88, 94
Minorca 103, 136, 161, 167-8
Mitchell, Thomas (artist) 58
Mobile (Florida) 79
Monmouth 185
Montgomery, Richard 15, 28-9
Montreal 15, 28
Moonlight Battle *see* Cape St Vincent
Moore's Bridge 17, 42
Morris, Captain 44
Moultrie, Colonel 44
Moutray, Captain John 161
Mowat, Henry, 'Mad' 37, 100
Mugford, James 67
Mulgrave, Lord 77
Mysore 180-1

Nantes 20
Nantucket 13
Napoleon I, Emperor of France 186
Nautilus 100
Navy Board 17-18, 20, 23, 102-3, 140-1
Negapatam, battle of 185
Nelson, Captain Horatio 100
Netherlands 11, 69, 181-2, 185
    fleet size 157, 162, 173
    foreign policy and strategy 10, 15, 111,
        136, 163, 180
    naval operations 136, 163-5, 167, 170, 180
    privateers 68, 150-1
    shipbuilding 65, 163
    ship types 162-3
    trade and trade wars 15, 47, 81, 111,
        150-1, 162
Nevis Island 81, 124-5
New Bedford 78
Newcastle, Duke of 12
Newfoundland 10, 15, 133
New Hampshire 12
New Haven (USA) 34-5
New Jersey 12, 20, 65, 72, 74
New London (Conn) 81
Newport (RI) 17, 62-3, 77-8, 80-1, 87, 114,
    117
New Providence (Bahamas) 16, 37-8, 152
New York 13
    British occupation of 16-17, 19, 32, 38,
        42, 44, 49-62, 68, 73, 76-81, 85, 89, 104,
        117, 119, 134
New York State 12
New York (USA) 34-5
New Zealand 41
Nicaragua 80, 98
Niger 56
Noailles, Louis Vicomte de 20
Nonsuch 55, 168
Nore 21, 141
Norfolk (Va) 13, 15, 37, 55
North 100
North, Lord 10-11, 19-20, 81, 136
North Carolina 12, 17, 80, 114
Norwich (Conn) 65
Nova Scotia 15, 81, 100
Nymphe (Fr) 94, 159, 172

Observer 149, 151
Oliver, Captain William 70
Oliver Cromwell (USA) 66
Omoa (Honduras) 98
Orpheus 56, 58, 86
Orves, Admiral d' 180
Orvilliers, Admiral Comte d' 133-4, 139
Otter 55-6, 100
Ozanne, Pierre (artist) 84-7, 105

Page, Lt 26
Pallas (Fr) 152
Palliser, Admiral 133, 139, 141, 143
Panther 146, 167
Paraguay 15
Paris, Admiral 65
Paris, Peace of 9, 15
Parker, Admiral Sir Hyde 58, 80, 96, 105,
    136, 164-5
Parker, Captain Hyde 16
Parker, Admiral Sir Peter 17, 42, 44, 50-1,
    54, 62
Pastora 175
Paton, Richard (artist) 175, 178
Paulus Hook (NY) 58
Pearl 36, 56, 58, 61, 157
Pearson, Captain Richard 153
Pégase (Fr) 170
Pellew, Edward 33
Pells Point 17, 61
Pennsylvania 12, 66, 74
Penobscot River 78, 100-1
Pensacola (Fla) 78-9, 99
Percy, Lord 58
Petersburg (Va) 80
Philadelphia 13
    British occupation of 20, 72-4, 77, 84-5
Philadelphia (USA) 34-5
Phoenix 50-1, 56-8, 109
Piedmont 10, 17
Pigot, Admiral 81
Placentia (Newfoundland) 46
Plymouth 21-2, 23, 46, 140-1, 143, 155
Pocock, Nicholas (artist) 30, 151
Point Levis 28
Pombal, Marquis de 15, 18, 20
Pondicherry 156, 180-1, 183
Port Mahon 161, 167
Porto Novo, battle of 180
Porto Praya (Cape Verde) 181
Portsmouth 21, 23, 40, 46-7, 122, 134, 140-1,
    143
Portugal 15, 18, 20, 136, 155, 169
Preston 15, 55, 78, 86, 164
Prince George 129
Princess Amelia 164
Princess Royal 93-4
Princeton, battle of 72
privateers 66-9, 149-54
    see also under America, Britain, France,
        Netherlands
Protecteur (Fr) 84, 87
Prothée (Fr) 156
Provence (Fr) 84
Providence (RI) 14
Providence (USA) 34-5, 37, 62, 64, 107, 152
Providien, battle of 185
Prussia 12, 39
Purisima Concepcion (Sp) 144

Quebec 15-16, 28-9, 31, 37, 149
Quebec 158

Rainbow 20, 56, 65
Raisonnable 55, 100
Raleigh (USA) 64, 70
Ramillies 130
Randle, Lt C 35
Ranger (USA) 107, 152
Raven 67
Rawdon, Lord 26
Renown 55, 58, 78-9, 87
Reprisal (USA) 67
Repulse 56, 58
Revenge (USA) 34, 67
Revere, Paul 24
Rhode Island 12, 14, 62-3, 77-8, 80, 85, 104
    see also Newport
Richelieu River 28
Richmond (Va) 80
Richmond, Captain Robert 149
Richmond, Duke of 9
Richmond (Va) 114
Robuste (Fr) 19
Rochambeau, Comte de 80
Rochefort 63
Rochford, Earl of 9, 15
Rockingham, Marquis of 81, 133, 136
Rodney, Admiral Sir George 80-1, 91, 93-4,
    108-9, 111, 113-14, 122, 126-9, 134, 136,
    155, 164, 167
Roebuck 56, 58, 79, 107
Romulus 79-80, 107, 114
Rose 50-1, 56, 58
Rossel de Cercy (artist) 149
Rotherham 46
Rotherhithe 47
Royal George 75, 92-3, 94, 143, 170, 178

Royal Savage (USA) 33-4
Ruby 130
Russell, Lt Thomas 67
Russia 10, 136

Sadras, battle of 183
Sagittaire (Fr) 84
Saintes, battle of the 81, 91, 93, 126-32
Salem (Mass) 12
Salter, Elliott 158-9
Saltonstall, Captain Dudley 100
San Domingo 159
Sandwich 93-4, 129
Sandwich, Lord 12, 18, 20, 23, 40-1, 77, 123,
    133-4, 136, 139-40
Sandy Hook 77, 85
San Miguel (Sp) 178
Santa Catalina (Sp) 169
Santa Domingo (Sp) 155
Santa Marguerita (Sp) 158-9
Santa Monica (Sp) 157
Santisima Trinidad (Sp) 144
Saratoga 20, 33, 75-7
Savannah (Georgia) 15, 54, 78-9, 81, 104-5
Schank, Lt 36-7
Scipion (Fr) 159
Scotland 136, 153, 163, 172
Selkirk, Earl of 152
Senegal 133
Senegal 50, 87
Serapis 54, 56, 153, 158
Seven Years War 9-11, 18, 28, 62-3, 82-3, 96,
    122, 133, 137
Sheerness 21, 23
Shelburne, Earl of 136
Shuldham, R/A Molyneux 16
Skenesboro (NY) 34
Solebay 56
Soleil Royal (Fr) 82
Solitaire (Fr) 130
Somerset 15, 25, 54-5
South Africa 180-2
South America 20, 98-9, 161
South Carolina 12, 17, 65, 80, 105, 107, 114
South Carolina (USA) 65
Spain 12, 157-8, 186
    fleet size 18, 144, 162
    foreign policy and strategy 9-11, 15, 17,
        19-20, 78, 80-1, 133-6, 142-6, 161, 179
        and invasion of England 142-3, 161
    naval operations 10
        in Central America 98-9
        in Europe 17, 122, 134, 136, 143, 146-8,
            155-7, 161, 167-9, 170, 174-5, 178-9
        in North America 10, 79, 99, 161
        in South America 10, 161
        in West Indies 10, 109, 161
    shipbuilding 10-11, 82, 144-5, 145, 157
    ship types 93-4, 144-5
Sphynx 44, 56
Spitfire 37
Spitfire (USA) 35
Spithead 41, 141, 170, 178-9
Squirrel 56
St Albans 55
St Alejandro (Sp) *see* Gibraltar
St Ann 169
Staten Island (NY) 17, 48, 63
St Augustine (Florida) 78, 81
Stephens, Sir Philip 140
St Eustatius 81, 111-13
Stirling Castle 108-9
St John's (Newfoundland) 28-9, 33-6, 46
St Kitts 81
    battle of 91, 117, 124-5
St Lawrence River 28-9, 34, 36
St Lucia 77-8, 89-91, 95, 100, 108-9, 113, 116,
    126, 170
Stonehouse Naval Hospital 141
Stony Point (NY) 78
Stormont, Lord 15-17, 19, 133
St Pierre (Quebec) 10
Stuart, General James 180
St Vincent (West Indies) 78, 95
Success 169
Suffren de St Tropez, Admiral
    Pierre-André de 96, 136, 180-5
Sullivan Island (Charleston) 17, 42, 44, 54
Sumatra 180
Superb 185
Surprise 29, 56
Surprise (USA) 67
Surveillante (Fr) 158
Swan 50, 56
Sweden 10, 12, 136
Sybille (Fr) 159
Symmetry (GB) 26, 37
Syren 44

Tahiti 41
Tamar 56
Tappan Zee (NY) 17, 58
Tartar 58, 67
Ternay d'Arsac, Chevalier de 80-1
Terrible 81, 117
Thetis 18
Throg's Neck (NY) 17, 61
Thunder 44, 51, 87
Thunderer 36, 109
Ticonderoga *see* Fort Ticonderoga
Tobago 81, 113
Tonnant (Fr) 84
Torbay 159
Toulon 17, 77, 84, 133, 146
Townsend, Viscount 46
Trafalgar, battle of 144
Trenton, battle of 72
Trepassey 159
Trincomalee 180, 185
    battle of 185
Triton 36
Trumbull, John 26
Trumbull (USA) 34-5
Tryal 50, 58
Tucker's Mill Point 15
Turgot, Anne Robert Jacques 16, 18
Turkey 10
Turks Island 10
Turtle s/m (USA) 61

Unicorn 56
Ushant, battle of 83, 133, 137-9, 141

Vaillant (Fr) 84, 87
Valcour Island, battle of 32-6, 75
Valentine, Captain 151
Valiant 129
Valley Forge 74
Vaughan, General 111
Vergennes, Duc de 9, 18-20, 80-1, 133-4,
    136, 180, 186
Vernon, Admiral 180
Vernon 149, 169
Victor 20
Victory 83, 92, 94, 170, 178
Vigilant 63
Ville de Paris (Fr) 83, 93, 124, 128, 130
Virginia 12, 80, 114
Virginia 100
Vulcan 119
Vulture 149

Walker & Co 46
Waltham Abbey 47
War of the Spanish Succession 146
Warren, Dr 26
Warren (USA) 62, 100
Washington, General George 17, 20, 38, 46,
    50-1, 61-2, 66, 72-4, 77, 80-1, 85, 114, 117
Washington (USA) (frigate) 76
Washington (USA) (gundalow) 33-5
Washington (USA) (schooner) 67
Wasp (USA) 37
Westchester (NY) 61
West Indies 164
    naval operations 78, 80-1, 88-91, 94-7,
        111-13, 161
    shipbuilding 13
    and strategy 10, 15, 18-20, 77-8, 80-1, 87,
        103, 133-4, 136, 140, 155-6
    trade 12, 70, 77
    see also individual islands and battles
West Point 80
Weymouth, Viscount 9, 17, 20
Whipple, Cdre 107
Whitehaven 152
White Plains (NY), battle of 17, 61
Wickes, Captain Lambert 67
Williams, Mr 41
Wilmington (NC) 80
Windward Islands 70
Wolfe, General J 29
Woolwich Dockyard 21, 23, 46-7, 140-1
Wynkoop, Jacobus 34

Yarmouth 55
Yorktown 80-1, 114, 117, 119-21, 136, 170

Zélé (Fr) 84
Zoutman, Admiral 136, 16